PRICING FOR PROFITABILITY

PRICING FOR PROFITABILITY

ACTIVITY-BASED PRICING FOR COMPETITIVE ADVANTAGE

JOHN L. DALY

John Wiley & Sons, Inc.

New York • Chichester • Weinheim • Brisbane • Singapore • Toronto

This book is printed on acid-free paper. ♾

Published by John Wiley & Sons, Inc.

Published simultaneously in Canada.

Library of Congress Cataloging-in-Publication Data:

Daly, John L. (John Lawrence), 1953–
Pricing for profitability : activity-based pricing for competitive advantage / John L. Daly.
p. cm.
Includes index.
ISBN 0-471-41535-9 (cloth; alk. paper)
1. Activity-based costing. 2. Managerial accounting. 3. Cost accounting. 4. Pricing. I. Title.

HF5686.C8 D215 2001
658.8'16—dc21 2001026891

10 9 8 7 6 5 4 3 2 1

To my wife,

Nancy J. Daly

Her contributions helped make this book a reality

CONTENTS

ACKNOWLEDGMENTS

I wish to acknowledge the contributions of the following people:

- **Gary Cokins**, Director of Industry Relations at ABC Technologies, Inc., provided valuable insights into the workings of his company's activity-based costing software.
- **Robert A. Erickson**, Program Director–Costing Systems at the Michigan Manufacturing Technology Council, reviewed a draft of Chapter 8 and provided valuable insights.
- **Gary Grigowski**, Vice President of Team One Plastics, Inc., provided background about plastics manufacturing and computer-aided design technology.
- **Nancy J. Daly**, my wife, whose editing, feedback, and Marketing MBA significantly improved the quality of this book.

PREFACE

Most pricing books have been written by marketing professors. These books concentrate on techniques that enhance revenue, as if maximizing revenue were the same as maximizing profit. However, profit equals revenue minus expenses, and profit can only be maximized when the interrelationships between revenue behavior and cost behavior are clearly understood. No single business discipline can provide this insight and it is my belief that pricing decisions are best made by teams of people from various business disciplines bringing their own viewpoints from marketing, sales, cost accounting, engineering, economics, and business strategy to the pricing process. *Pricing for Profitability* is intended to be used by people from all of these disciplines. This is a sharply different approach from other popular pricing books. As a whole, the book is designed to give everyone involved in the pricing process a comprehensive understanding of how to use pricing to derive a competitive advantage and increase profitability.

Pricing practice has rapidly evolved in the past few decades. Early computer spreadsheets such as VisiCalc gave corporate financial managers the power to perform pricing and profitability analyses that were simply impossible with pencil and paper. Like many corporate controllers, one of the very first uses that I found for these new tools was to develop a model for pricing the products that my small company produced. I used what I called "rational" methods to study costs. When the common-sense techniques of activity-based costing were first described to me, our own techniques were far enough advanced that I could honestly say, "Oh yes, that is the costing method that we use." I wrote my first article on the uses of activity-based costing for pricing in 1993, coining the term *activity-based quoting* for that article. I later concluded that *activity-based pricing* was a better description for these techniques because all companies price their products, whereas only some businesses prepare actual quotes.

Pricing for Profitability is designed to provide tools that will allow companies to consistently earn a real economic profit on the things that they sell. It is about the interrelationships of price and sales volume, and sales volume and cost. Other pricing books treat the relationship between price and cost lightly, as if cost were a minor consideration in pricing strategy. My own consulting experience has shown that too many companies unknowingly price their products at a loss, sometimes a substantial loss, because they have not understood these interrelationships.

The objectives of activity-based pricing are as follows:

- Establish price based on a solid knowledge of customer demand and product cost.
- Never unintentionally price a product at a loss.
- Know how much of price is profit.
- Generate a superior financial return through superior financial knowledge.

This book has been organized so that it can be read at several different levels of detail. There are 12 chapters. Chapter 1 provides an overview of the book and Chapter 12 provides a summary of all of the other chapters. The chapters in between provide an in-depth look at 10 different topics followed by chapter summaries. Chapter 7, "Activity-Based Pricing," gets to the heart of what the book is all about. A glossary of terms may be found in the back of the book. These terms are italicized in the text the first time that they appear.

The field of activity-based pricing is in its infancy. There will undoubtedly be issues that I have not thought of or practices that I did not discover in my research. The techniques that we use today are likely to look primitive by the standards of a decade from now. I invite readers of this book to contact me with their thoughts on this topic, so that future editions of *Pricing for Profitability* truly can be a collaboration of all of the best minds on the topic.

John L. Daly
Chelsea, Michigan
March 2001
Daly@ExecutiveEducationInc.com
Phone: (734) 475-0600

PRICING FOR PROFITABILITY

1

PRICING FOR PROFITABILITY

The objective of activity-based pricing is not to establish pricing based on rote formula, but to provide a set of high-powered tools for the pricing toolbox.

THREE THINGS CAN HAPPEN

The careers of a few college football coaches stand above all of the others. These include Bear Bryant (University of Alabama), Eddie Robinson (Grambling), Knute Rockne (Notre Dame), and Woody Hayes (Ohio State). Hayes played football at Denison University in the days of the single wing offense before football teams conventionally had a position called quarterback. Hayes's successful Ohio State teams in the 1960s and 1970s were famous for their "three yards and a cloud of dust" running games, only occasionally throwing a forward pass. Hayes might rationalize his aversion for passing with a common coach's viewpoint: "There are only three things that can happen, and two of them are bad." An opponent may intercept a passed football or it may fall incomplete for no gain and a loss of down. Only when the quarterback manages to throw the football into the hands of a teammate is the outcome favorable.

In a sense, product pricing is a lot like passing a football. Three things can happen when establishing prices, and two of them are bad:

1. Overprice and lose a sale that would have been profitable at a lower price.
2. Underprice and make an unprofitable sale.

Only the third outcome is favorable:

3. Price appropriately and make the sale as well as a profit

Although this is an oversimplified view of a complex issue, many companies are burdened with pricing methods that consistently give away profitable sales to competitors while undercutting those competitors on money-losing propositions. When these companies make a sale that actually produces a profit, it often seems to be more by accident than intentional design.

Many companies believe falsely that they are competent at pricing. Many presidents of small companies will say, "Pricing is an art. I know that our pricing is good because I do it myself." Pricing is not an art. However, a well-designed pricing model may be beautiful in the same way as a well-designed piece of machinery. Pricing is a science as much as the design of that machinery is a science. Knowledge is power in pricing. Although pricing for profitability allows considerable latitude for creativity in structuring a deal, pricing remains as much a science as marketing, cost accounting, business strategy, engineering, and economics—the disciplines that converge in product pricing. If the person responsible for establishing price says, "Pricing is an art," it is a good indication that he or she is missing much of the basic data necessary to make informed pricing decisions.

There is another easy test to determine if a company has good pricing methods. Does the planned profit on the company's standard pricing worksheets approximate the actual profit for the company as a whole? If the planned profit is consistently the same as the profit that the company actually earns, then the company is managed by godlike creatures that have no need for the assistance of a pricing book. However, if a significant difference exists between quoted profit and actual profit, then there is room for improvement—often substantial improvement. Good pricing methods can improve profitability and actually create a competitive advantage.

THE PROFIT EQUATION

In business school, on the first day of Accounting 101, every student learns the Accounting Equation:

$$\text{Assets} = \text{Liabilities} + \text{Equity}$$

This simple formula is so important that if a student remembers nothing else about accounting, it is that a balance sheet must balance. Another lesson from Accounting 101, perhaps even covered on that same first day, is another simple formula, the Profit Equation:

$$\text{Profit} = \text{Revenues} - \text{Expenses}$$

Many business people seem to forget the Profit Equation in the everyday bustle of managing their business. Sales and marketing people seem to forget the expense part of the equation. From their perspective, selling as much as possible is good. Of course, high sales do not necessarily equate to high profit. In fact, one prescription for bottom-line disaster is to give salespeople control over price and then to compensate them based on how much they sell. Given such an opportunity, salespeople will have a strong motivation to maximize sales at the expense of profit. Even if salespeople do have an incentive to maximize profit, allowing them to have control over pricing may still lead to poor profit performance. A 1997 survey of the plastic molding industry by the accounting firm of Plante & Moran, LLP, found that companies whose presidents spend the majority of their time on selling had the lowest profit performance in the industry. Apparently the rewards to the psyche of making a sale outweigh the financial rewards of making a profit.

Although sales and marketing people seem to forget the expense portion of the Profit Equation, financial people seem to get involved a lot with reducing expenses, spending little time trying to enhance revenue or managing the revenue–expense relationship. Every accountant seems to go into a budget meeting saying, "We've got to cut costs." Cost-cutting efforts by financial managers are often misguided. Financial managers often act as if they thought that profit would be maximized if the company could somehow eliminate all of those pesky expenses. It is as if those accountants have also forgotten the business maxim, "You have to spend money to make money."

Many financial managers have rationalized their emphasis on cost cutting by saying that if the company's net profit margin is 5% of sales, then $1 of cost cutting equals $20 of increased revenue, whereas $1 of increased revenue is worth only 5 cents of profit. In this book we will find that it is often possible to increase revenue by $1 and have that entire dollar go to the bottom line. Armed with knowledge of product pricing methods, profitability can be increased by reducing or outright eliminating pricing mistakes that rob too many companies of profit.

RESPONSIBILITY FOR PRICING

Establishment of pricing policy is a basic responsibility of top management and should be an integral part of corporate strategy. This does not imply that local front-line managers should have no discretion on price. Corporate strategy may allow for local control of pricing as established by corporate guidelines.

Pricing is a multifaceted discipline. Pricing is a mixture of marketing, cost accounting, business strategy, engineering, and economics. Besides these disciplines, pricing requires a good working knowledge of the company's products, processes, customers, and competitors. Rarely does a single person exist who would be well versed in all of these areas. Therefore, pricing is best done as a collaboration of people from various parts of the business.

How the responsibility for establishing price is divided varies from industry to industry and situation to situation. In some industries, such as consumer goods, the marketing department may identify a demand in the market for a particular type of product that could be sold at a particular price. That price becomes the target price. From the target price is inferred a target profit and in turn a target cost. Engineering will then proceed to analyze the feasibility of producing the product within the target costs, assisted by cost accounting. Management examines the product proposal with respect to corporate strategy and uses marketing and economic theory to examine how the market is likely to react to the introduction of the product.

In other industries, the customer may define the desired product and request bids. Someone with the formal title of estimator may gather cost data from the purchasing department for material costs, data from engineering regarding the processes to be used, and competitor information from sales, and accumulate it all into a quotation model with rates provided by cost accounting.

It is surprising how many companies, many of them large and publicly traded, have little or no interaction between people of various disciplines when establishing price. It is not uncommon for estimating people to have a set of cost standards that is different from the cost standards used in engineering that is different still from those used in accounting. Which costs are "real"? Obviously, the estimating and engineering people cannot have good costs without good data from accounting, yet the knowledge possessed by accounting also will be deficient without the operations knowledge of engineering. Each of these groups has inadequate information without the input of the others.

Management in some companies just does not "get it." At a seminar on the east coast about skills for corporate controllers, one attendee wrote on the course evaluation form, "I don't know why we spent time on pricing. After all, we don't have anything to do with pricing, we're accountants!"

PLANNING FOR PROFITABLE SALES

How should price be determined? Economic theory describes a balance of supply and demand where many buyers compete for sales to many customers. Price competition will force inefficient sellers from the market, reducing supply. Then the market establishes equilibrium at a particular price. Economic theory places numerous conditions on the pure application of supply and demand. These include the existence of knowledgeable buyers and sellers, acting in their own enlightened self-interest with a selection consisting of undifferentiated products available at the same place and time. Although the theories of economics are of great help in understanding and predicting market behavior, the real world creates few situations that fit the pure conditions of economic theory exactly.

Planning for profitable sales requires an understanding of the interrelationships of price and cost. After all, to have a profitable sale requires that price be higher than full real costs. Many marketing texts advise that the price should be set to maximize overall revenue. As we will see in Chapter 2, this model is faulty. Taking into account product cost structure and customer reaction to price, profit is maximized in all real-world situations at a higher selling price and a lower sales volume than the selling price that maximizes revenue.

The cost of almost any product is made up of both fixed and variable components. Many companies struggle due to a lack of understanding of their fixed costs. When an accounting firm takes on a new audit client, the first year's work normally includes considerable up-front work to establish "permanent" files to document the client's procedures and methods of internal control. These efforts will not be necessary in subsequent years and are independent of the number of years that audits will be performed for this client. These "launch" costs are fixed over the life of a client relationship and need to be taken into consideration in pricing.

Manufacturing companies must do considerable up-front work before they can begin producing a product. Marketing and design engineering people work on the product concept and specifications, process engineers and tool makers develop manufacturing methods, purchasing people spend time arranging for sources of material and components, and quality control people test and verify that samples comply with the intended design. All of these efforts constitute fixed costs that are independent of sales volume.

The math for this highly simplified example is conceptually very easy. If a product incurs $100,000 of fixed costs and $1.00 of variable unit costs, then the cost is $100,001 to make one unit, $101/unit to make 1,000 units, $11/unit to make 10,000 units, and $1.01/unit to make 10 million units. We can see a graph of this relationship in Exhibit 1.1.

In the real world, costs exhibit a behavior that is much more complex. Today's activity-based costing (ABC) uses a cost assignment network to recognize that costs may be fixed, variable, or step-variable, exhibiting behaviors that may be related to products, customers, distribution channels, or other factors. In this book, cost behavior will often be described in simplified terms to create easy to understand examples. However, to be really effective in pricing, a company must thoroughly understand the cost side of the profit equation using ABC.

The authors of most of the leading books on pricing primarily have marketing backgrounds. Although those books sometimes exhibit a wonderful understanding of customer behavior and the effects of price on volume, they generally provide little insight into how costs fit into the profit equation. The marketing professors who have authored many of these books express confidence in the quality of cost accounting data that they encounter in the real world. Unfortunately, this confidence is often unwarranted. The author of this book, whose firm does consulting work in both pricing strategy and turnarounds, has found that many turnaround clients were in their precarious position because they had significantly underbid work

Exhibit 1.1 Relationship between unit cost and volume

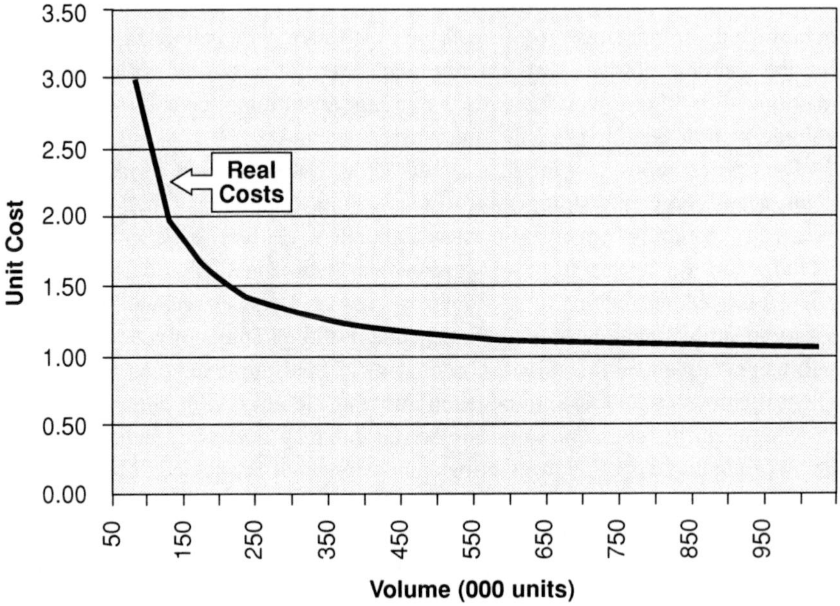

Note: Real cost per unit for most products has a predictable relationship with volume. Shown is the cost per unit for a product with $100,000 of fixed costs and $1 of variable costs for volumes between 50,000 and 1 million units.

thinking that it would be profitable. In the real world it is not uncommon to find companies that have products that are priced at one half of real cost. In a company whose pretax profit target is 5% of sales, it takes only one such "dog" product to wipe out the effects of ten profitable jobs. How could a product be priced at one half of costs? The root causes of these errors include the following:

- Lack of qualified cost accounting personnel
- Lack of communications between cost accounting and pricing personnel
- Use of inadequate, old-fashioned cost accounting techniques

Having an old-fashioned understanding of costs is not restricted to any particular industry. Many cost accountants are still using costing methods that bear little resemblance to how real costs behave in the real world. Traditional cost accounting methods provide a high-level quantification of average costs for average products. These old-fashioned techniques may do an adequate job for preparing financial statements, but they invariably fail in identifying cost for the many companies that have few products that are truly average.

Traditional cost accounting methods concentrate on the variable unit costs of materials and labor, throwing all other costs into vast pools called overhead. Overhead is then allocated to products on a per-unit basis, often using labor as the allocation factor. Because traditional cost accounting assigns all cost based on the number of units produced, it characterizes cost as a constant over some relevant range. Exhibit 1.2 shows a difference between real costs and traditional cost accounting costs of 9% at high volumes and 250% at low volumes. If this graph were drawn to show a wider range of volumes, the difference between the two methods would approach 20% at very high volumes and would become ridiculously far apart as volumes decreased. As volumes decrease, even accountants trained in traditional methods at some point abandon the old-fashioned allocation approach for a more common-sense method. The rough methods of traditional cost accounting are not adequate in twenty-first–century business. A more extensive discussion of traditional cost accounting methods is presented in Chapter 4.

Many companies have a handful of products where they really "lose their shirts." Solving that problem alone would be a great accomplishment. Although no single

Exhibit 1.2 Traditional costs versus real costs

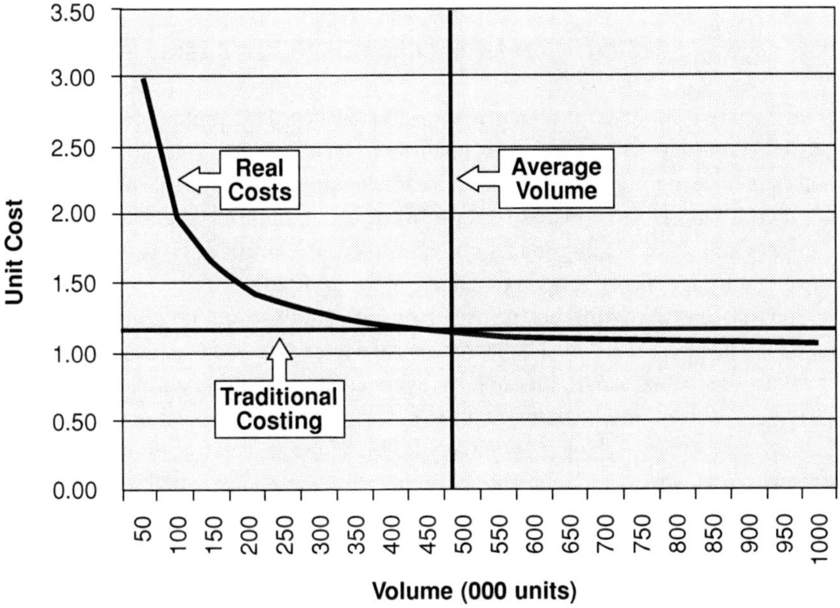

Note: Traditional cost accounting does not take sales volume into account in calculating cost. As a result, it assigns too much cost to high-volume products and too little cost to low-volume products.

technique can completely eliminate pricing mistakes, the methods presented in this book will drastically reduce their occurrence.

It is not the position of this book that costs should determine price. The position of this book is that too many companies establish their prices with an inadequate knowledge of their costs, thereby setting price at a point that would be irrational if they knew their real costs. It would be irrational for a company to set its price at half of its real costs, yet in the real world this happens all the time. It would also be irrational for a company to set its price well above its real costs in a direct competitive bid against a well-qualified competitor because it would be unlikely to make the sale. Due to a lack of knowledge about product costs, this, too, happens all the time. In too many companies, the people who are charged with establishing price are equipped with inadequate tools and incomplete information about the company's cost structure. As a result, the company makes bad decisions based on a lack of good data.

Although cost-plus pricing may be suitable in some situations, the purpose of this book is to present activity-based pricing (ABP) as a tool that will supplement, not supplant, the existing wealth of knowledge about pricing developed by marketers and economists. Activity-based costing has been added to the pricing toolbox to provide better assurance that additional revenue really will result in additional profit.

USING COSTS TO PLAN FOR PROFITS

If the goal of a company's management is to achieve a 10% pretax profit, a logical starting point toward achieving that goal would be to determine the company's full real cost for every item that was sold and then apply a 10% profit margin to that number. Anything more than a 10% profit for any product would be a bonus. The company might keep any product not earning a 10% profit only as long as there was not an opportunity to sell something more profitable.

Activity-based costing has provided us with a new, more common-sense approach to thinking about cost behavior. It seeks to understand the cause-and-effect relationships between activities and the events that cause those activities to occur. In ABC, machine maintenance is much more than an overhead cost. Machine maintenance occurs because a company has machines. Each type of machine that the company owns may have very different machine maintenance requirements. One product may use machines that require a lot of maintenance; another product may not use any machine maintenance time at all.

Activity-based pricing is ideally suited to companies that compete in competitive bid environments. Companies that competitively bid for their sales usually work with very thin margins. When a company prepares a competitive bid, the objective is that profit will be increased if it wins the bid. The company knows that if it submits a bid that is too high, another company will get the work, and its effort in preparing and submitting the bid will have been wasted.

If ABC is accepted as a representation of a company's real costs, then there are important lessons that can be learned by comparing the results of ABP to prices determined by other methods. Examining the differences between traditional cost accounting and ABC is illuminating. Because traditional cost accounting and ABC both tend to use actual historical results to derive their data, costs derived using traditional methods and costs derived from ABC should be on average the same. Of course, few products are truly average. Some products will be produced in higher than average volume, and others in lower than average volume. Some products will heavily use the resources of key departments, while other products will not use those departments at all. For some products ABC will assign higher than average costs, while in other cases it will assign lower than average costs.

Sales volume is only one of many factors that may cause traditional cost accounting and ABC to arrive at different costs for a product. Activity-based costing recognizes factors that cause a product to consume more or less than an average amount of the company's resources. These factors are described at length in Chapter 6. Some companies will experience few substantial differences between the two accounting methods. In other companies, differences of 50% to 300% may occur on 30% of the company's products.

When large differences in cost exist between traditional and activity-based methods, they do not tend to follow a normal statistical distribution. In Exhibit 1.3, 11 products have the same costs as those described in Exhibits 1.1 and 1.2. Five products have above-average costs and five have below-average costs. These 11 products each have \$100,000 in fixed launch costs and \$1 of variable unit costs. At low volumes, the percentage differences in cost between ABC and traditional methods may be huge, but for high volumes the price differences are fairly modest. The bottom-line impact of making a bad pricing decision for a product selling only 1,000 units may be similar in magnitude to making a good pricing decision for a million units.

It is possible to take a sample of products and determine the average cost of an average product using each costing method. Because both costing methods generally use the same historical costs as their basis, the average cost of a large sample of products should be exactly the same under the two methods. If we look at the distribution of costs around these averages, however, we would normally find that the variation from average (i.e., the standard deviation for those who are statistically inclined) would be much less using traditional cost accounting methods than using ABC. This occurs because traditional cost accounting throws great pools of costs together and comes up with an average overhead rate. Activity-based costing may identify differences in costs that do not show up using traditional

Exhibit 1.3 Behavior of traditional costs and activity-based costing (ABC) at different volumes

Sales	Unit Cost		Extended Cost		Difference	
Volume	ABC	Traditional	ABC	Traditional	Extended	%
1,000	$101.00	$1.20	101,000	1,200	99,800	8,317%
9,000	12.11	1.20	109,000	10,800	98,200	909%
50,000	3.00	1.20	150,000	60,000	90,000	150%
240,000	1.42	1.20	340,000	288,000	52,000	18%
350,000	1.29	1.20	450,000	420,000	30,000	7%
500,000	1.20	1.20	600,000	600,000	—	0%
550,000	1.18	1.20	650,000	660,000	(10,000)	–2%
700,000	1.14	1.20	800,000	840,000	(40,000)	–5%
850,000	1.12	1.20	950,000	1,020,000	(70,000)	–7%
1,000,000	1.10	1.20	1,100,000	1,200,000	(100,000)	–8%
1,250,000	1.08	1.20	1,350,000	1,500,000	(150,000)	–10%
			6,600,000	6,600,000	0	0%

Note: Sales volume can be one of the major sources of differences between traditional cost accounting and ABC. For a truly average product, the two methods will yield exactly the same cost. However, ABC will provide a somewhat lower cost for high volume products and a cost that may be many times higher for low-volume products.

methods. For instance, if three products had the same direct costs and the same cost per setup, traditional cost accounting would say that they had the same cost even though they may be produced in radically different lot sizes and radically different volumes. Activity-based costing is geared to identifying these factors that produce these very real differences in cost.

NEED FOR SOLID COSTING INFORMATION

Traditional cost accounting data can be translated into price in many different ways. Most commonly, traditional cost-based pricing methods will calculate costs at the gross margin level and then apply a markup to cover administrative costs and profit.

Activity-based pricing generates a volume-sensitive model that defines what costs will be in various situations. Based on a knowledge of the full real costs of producing a product at any given volume, management can then establish a pricing strategy for the product. Other factors such as the price elasticity of customer demand, customer buying habits, competitive products, and the value received by the customer must be taken into consideration

In theory, prices derived from traditional and activity-based methods should reflect the same variations as the cost accounting methods on which they are based. Although there may be considerable variation in price on any individual product, the average price of all products combined should be exactly the same using the two methods because both methods draw from the same pools of costs as the basis for their data. Observations in the real world do not prove this theory. Real-world observations show that companies using traditional cost accounting often add "fudge factors" when pricing their products. Fudge factors may be applied in many different ways through increased cost, increased margin, or an arbitrary discount. Although the author knows of no study analyzing these differences, it is generally thought that these fudge factors drive the average quoted price higher than ABP-derived prices.

There is a logical reason why fudge factors are so prevalent in pricing. Traditional costing methods generate "accounting" costs that are scattered all around real costs. Suppose that there are two companies that have identical cost structures, and one company (Company T) uses traditional pricing methods and the other company (Company A) uses ABP. Suppose these two companies are asked to quote three products, as shown in Exhibit 1.4. These three products have the same material cost at $1.00 per unit and direct labor content of 1 hour per 100 pieces. Company T's traditional cost accounting methods would say that products X, Y, and Z have identical costs at $1.50 per unit. Because Company T would like (although it has not recently achieved) a 10% pretax profit, it will mark up the quote by that amount. If costs were developed for these products at the same time it would not make intuitive sense that they should all have the same cost. In this case the estimator might adjust the quoted price. If costs were developed at different times, however, the estimator would probably not notice the inconsistency.

Because Company A uses ABP, it will more effectively use information than Company T to provide a quote. In addition to the information used by Company T, Company A would also want to know, among other things, the differences in volume and launch costs for these products. Even if it discovers that each product had the same launch costs, Company A will apply a different launch cost per unit because of the differences in volume between the three products.

Company T will win the competition for Product X with a bid of $1.65 per unit, substantially undercutting company A's quote of $2.64 per unit. Company T thinks its cost is $1.50 per unit, and its standard cost system will confirm this error. How-

Exhibit 1.4 Price competition between companies using traditional costing and activity-based costing methods

	Company T		
	Product X	Product Y	Product Z
Direct labor	100 pieces/hour	100 pieces/hour	100 pieces/hour
Labor and overhead rate	$50/hour	$50/hour	$50/hour
Labor cost	$0.50	$0.50	$0.50
Materials	1.00	1.00	1.00
Total cost	$1.50	$1.50	$1.50
Profit	.15	.15	.15
Selling price	$1.65	$1.65	$1.65

	Company A		
	Product X	Product Y	Product Z
Volume	10,000	100,000	190,000
Direct labor	100 pieces/hour	100 pieces/hour	100 pieces/hour
Labor and overhead rate	$40/hour	$40/hour	$40/hour
Launch costs	$10,000	10,000	10,000
Launch cost each	$1.000	$0.100	$0.053
Labor cost	0.400	0.400	0.400
Materials	1.000	1.000	1.000
Total cost	$2.400	$1.500	$1.453
Profit	.240	.150	.145
Selling price	$2.640	$1.65	$1.598

Note: Company T and Company A have the same cost structure. Company T uses traditional cost accounting, whereas Company A uses activity-based costing. Using traditional cost accounting, managers at Company T think that Products X, Y, and Z have the same cost, and they provide the customer identical quotes for all three products. Company A recognized the real differences in cost and quotes higher on Product X and lower on Product Z. Company T will win the bid for Product X and lose $0.75 per unit. Company A will win the bid for Product Z, earning $0.145 each.

ever, its real costs are $2.40 per unit. If Company T were able to create an income statement for Product X, it would look like this:

	Product X	
Revenue	$16,500	
Costs at standard	(15,000)	
Unabsorbed start-up costs	(9,000)	
Total costs	(24,000)	
Net loss	(7,500)	(45%)

Company A will win the competition for Product Z, with a price of $1.598, just 3% under the $1.65 quoted by Company T. Profit for Product Z will be:

	Product Z	
Revenue	$303,620	
Cost	276,070	
Profit	$ 27,550	+ 9%

On average, ABC and traditional cost accounting will yield the same results. Product Y happens to be an average product, and both companies have identified their costs as $1.50. The bid for Product Y should be a toss-up. Company A has quoted a lower price for Product Z, and Company T has quoted a lower price for Product X. Company A has won the contract for the highest volume product, what most operations people would identify as the "good" work, whereas Company T has received a low-volume contract that operations people will disdain. If both companies look for a 10% markup on full cost, Company A will earn a $27,550 profit on Product Z, whereas Company T will lose $7,500 on Product X. Results like this will occur repeatedly as the two companies compete against each other. Company T's financial statements will show a loss, and management will recognize that the cost base used for quoting does not translate into actual realized profits. As a result, in time Company T will add fudge factors to its quotes to shore up the income statement. The result is very predictable.

These fudge factors have the effect of raising price. Exhibit 1.5 shows that Company T has added 10 cents of extra costs to all three quotes. That money helps mitigate the loss on Product X, but it also gives Company A a clear advantage in the bid for Product Y and worsens the company's competitive position for Product Z. This phenomenon can lead a company to conclude that it could never make any money if it charged what cost accounting said were product costs and to abandon using cost accounting data altogether.

Exhibit 1.5 Effect of "fudge factors" on price

	Company T		
	Product X	Product Y	Product Z
Direct labor	100 pieces/hour	100 pieces/hour	100 pieces/hour
Labor and overhead rate	$50/hour	$50/hour	$50/hour
Labor cost	$0.50	$0.50	$0.50
Materials	1.00	1.00	1.00
Fudge factors	.10	.10	.10
Total cost	$1.60	$1.60	$1.60
Profit	.16	.16	.16
Selling price	$1.76	$1.76	$1.76

Note: By adding $0.10 of fudge factor, Company T has lowered its loss on Product X but will now lose the bid for Product Y to Company A.

PRICING FOR COMPETITIVE ADVANTAGE

Understanding cost is particularly important when price is competitively bid. This is especially true when the bid is for a custom-made, unique product that will incur fixed costs that do not benefit other customers. Whether an accounting firm bids to perform an audit, a contractor bids to build an office building, a manufacturer bids to make an automobile part, or a software company bids to provide an air traffic control system for the government—to all of these companies, volume is a matter of all or none.

The relationship between price and volume is an all-or-nothing proposition for businesses that competitively bid for their sales. When sales are competitively bid, the company either gets the entire contract, or none of it. A 1% difference in price may make the difference between winning or losing a contract, but if the winner is priced 10% lower than its competition, the extra 9% will make a 0% difference in the number of units that will be sold. When General Electric, General Motors, and General Mills request quotes from their vendors, it is the price of the jet engine, automobile, or box of cereal that will affect how many units are sold, not the price of the component part. When a plastic injection molder quotes the price of a toy to go in a cereal box, the volume that it sells will be all or none of General Mills's requirement. Companies that make parts for Corvettes know how many cars were sold last year and can make a fairly accurate estimate as to how many cars Chevrolet will sell in the upcoming year. Companies that make aircraft engine parts know in advance approximately how many planes their customers will sell.

An exact knowledge of volume is not necessary in the execution of an adequate pricing job. Unless a contract is for a specific quantity of goods, a company is never going to be able to project its sales to four significant digits. Getting the order of magnitude right is usually good enough. The difference in cost is probably not very much between 1 million and 1.2 million units (a 20% difference in volume). Costs may be very different, however, between 1,000 units and 10,000 units (a 1,000% difference in volume).

There is not a single right way to determine price in every situation. While there is a standard set of tools that apply to product pricing, not every situation will use all of the tools in the tool box just like no home carpentry project will use every tool in a well-equipped work shop. The intent of this book is not to provide a single right method of establishing price, but to enhance the quality of the tools available to people involved in the pricing process. In some companies this transition will be like going from a nineteenth century hand-cranked bit and brace drill to a precision laser cut hole.

This book pertains to manufacturing, retailing, wholesale, and service companies. One of the minor revolutions that has occurred in business over the last few decades is that various industries have taught each other new techniques. Manufacturing companies have learned important value-added techniques from service businesses. In turn, manufacturing was able to teach other industries valuable lessons about cost accounting. Each can learn from the other.

Many business people are slow to adapt tools that are not commonly used in their own industry. People in service businesses routinely tune out any discussion of techniques used in manufacturing, whereas manufacturing people may ignore techniques used in construction. This rejection is often ill conceived, because the accounting for manufacturing a custom piece of machinery in a job shop is very similar to constructing a building, which is in reality a form of manufacturing. Some modern ABC techniques were pioneered in the health-care industry when hospitals were cost reimbursed. However, health care and manufacturing seem to have developed these techniques independently without a lot of cross-fertilization. Despite the extensive service environment knowledge that ABC developed in the health-care industry, many service businesses seem to view ABC as a manufacturing technique that does not apply to them.

Many different situations exist when applying pricing strategy to the real world. In some pricing situations, strategy calls for a high price to be set initially, with many subsequent reductions. In other situations, the price must be set long in advance of the delivery of the first product, and that price is fixed for the entire duration of the contract. Some pricing situations are very tolerant of experimentation and guessing, whereas others require a detailed analysis up front because there is only one opportunity to determine a product's price. Although pricing defies a single formula approach, there are general principles that are easily transferable from situation to situation, from industry to industry.

This book includes examples from many different industries. Rather than repetitively say *product or service*, the term *product* will be used to mean all products, whether tangible or intangible. The readers of this book will work in many different industries. For this reason, the examples will often be for consumer goods such as food, clothing, and automobiles. Sometimes the examples will discuss tiny portions of those industries that the reader may never have thought about. Because many of the readers of this book will be financial types who have worked in public accounting firms, such firms will sometimes appear as service industry examples.

OBJECTIVES OF ACTIVITY-BASED PRICING

Although accounting techniques may never completely allow us to know our costs exactly, advances in ABC now allow companies using these techniques to have a distinct competitive advantage. Activity-based costing applied to pricing strategy is called activity-based pricing (ABP). The objective of ABP is not to establish price based on rote formula, but to provide a set of high-powered tools for the pricing toolbox.

The objectives of ABP are to:

- Establish price with knowledge of the full "real" costs to produce a product.
- Plan the amount of profit to be achieved at the time price is established.
- Never unintentionally sell a product at a loss.
- Optimize profitability by providing the management team with the information necessary to make good pricing decisions.

SUMMARY

The key points described in this chapter are listed below:

1. These things can happen when establishing price:
   a. Overprice: lose a sale that would have been profitable at a lower price.
   b. Underprice: make an unprofitable sale.
   c. Price appropriately: make a sale and make a profit.
2. Pricing is a science where the disciplines of marketing, cost accounting, business strategy, engineering, and economics converge.

3. Maximizing revenue does not maximize profit. Profit does not equal revenue.

$$\text{Profit} = \text{Revenue} - \text{Expenses}$$

4. Pricing is a multifaceted discipline, and companies get the best pricing results when they get input from people in various parts of the business.
5. Planning for profitable sales requires an understanding of the interrelationships between price and cost. Pricing for profitability requires that price is above full cost.
6. When companies sell to many customers, price affects the number of units that will be sold, which in turn affects the cost per unit. Price and cost are thus interdependent through sales volume.
7. Nearly every product has some costs that are fixed and some costs that are variable. The existence of fixed costs causes products to have progressively decreasing unit costs as sales volumes increase.
8. Traditional cost allocation methods assign all indirect costs into large pools called overhead. Overhead is usually assigned to products based on a measure of direct costs. The result is that traditional cost allocation methods treat all costs as variable costs and can provide only "average" costs for an "average" product. Traditional methods are only valid for assigning costs to large groups of products, not individual products.
9. Activity-based costing (ABC) provides a better measurement of "real" or "true" costs.
10. When companies do not know their real costs, the sales they make will be biased toward underpriced, money-losing products.
11. Activity-based pricing (ABP) integrates customer price response (demand) information with ABC data to find the combination of price and costs that maximizes profit.
12. Activity-based pricing provides a competitive advantage by allowing a company to confidently price lower on "good" profitable products, and to avoid selling unprofitable "dog" jobs.
13. The objectives of ABP are to:
    - Establish price with knowledge of the full "real" cost to produce a product
    - Plan the amount of profit to be achieved at the time price is established
    - Never unintentionally sell a product at a loss
    - Optimize profitability by providing the management team with the information necessary to make good pricing decisions

2

ECONOMICS AND DEMAND

Revenue does not equal profit. To truly determine how to maximize profit, a company must understand its cost structure

ORIGIN OF CAPITALIST ECONOMICS

Modern capitalist economics has its roots in the 1776 book *The Wealth of Nations* by Scottish economist and philosopher Adam Smith. Smith identified labor as the root of all value, pointing out that if it takes twice as much time to hunt and kill a beaver than a deer, that a beaver should logically be valued at twice the price of the deer.[1]

Smith identified the components of price as labor, rent, and profit. Commodities such as corn, he noted, would logically be priced based on the amount of labor that it takes to produce that corn and the amount of rent that must be paid for the land. Writing near the dawning of the Industrial Revolution, Smith noted that the price of corn compared with the price of labor had held nearly constant for a very long time, even though the price of corn had varied considerably when measured with respect to silver. Smith expected the relationship between corn and labor to hold constant for a long time in the future as well, not foreseeing that the Industrial Revolution would spread from English factories to farm production as well.

He believed that every commodity has a natural price. That natural price was based on the cost of the labor, rent, and profit necessary to generate the commodity. To his way of thinking, raw materials had value because of the labor necessary to obtain those materials. Land has a common rental value for its local area, and to the extent that business people employed labor, paid rent, or bought raw materials to produce a product, they were entitled to profits corresponding to the amount of capital that was used in the business. He was careful to point out that the owner of a business is also entitled to wages as an overseer, and the portion of the selling price of a product that corresponds to these wages should not be confused with profit.

Smith distinguished the "natural" price of a product from the market price. At any given time, the market price may be above or below the natural price. The natural price of a commodity is a cost-based price that represents the lowest price at which a product may be continuously sold over a long period of time. Although the market price may sometimes dip below the natural price, it will never do so for long. When market price is below the natural price, it necessarily means that the providers of labor, land, or capital must in turn receive less money than they could earn devoting their resources to other employment. Thus, if the market price dips below the natural price, supply of the product decreases as providers withdraw from the market.

The natural price, according to Smith, is a central point toward which the market price tends to gravitate. If the market price is above the natural price, more producers will emerge to take advantage of the larger than normal profits available in the business. He noted that although the market price will never be below the natural cost-based price for a long period of time, the reverse is not true. Impediments to competition may exist that may allow the market price to exist above the natural price for years, even centuries.

Smith's concept that the providers of money, or capital, are entitled to a profit on their investment stands near the center of economic theory today. Now in the twenty-first century we consider the concept of the *profit motive* as an obvious and natural requirement for a viable economic system; this was not always the case.

Like Adam Smith, German philosopher and economic theorist Karl Marx saw labor as the primary source of economic value. However, Marx saw profits as an immoral leftover of feudalism where capitalists exploited the working class. He viewed nineteenth-century industrial capitalism as a temporary historical stage. Eventually, he thought, all profits would be eliminated and everyone would live in a classless, stateless communist society where every person would be equal, each contributing according to their abilities, each receiving according to their needs. Although Marx's communism once engulfed much of the world and threatened the rest, today it is viewed as a failed economic system. Outside of the few countries where it is still practiced, communism is viewed as an anachronism that will eventually disappear due to its own ineffectiveness.

MODERN CAPITALIST ECONOMICS

Now, more than two centuries after the publication of *The Wealth of Nations*, capitalist economics has continually evolved and refined its terminology, finding more efficient ways to represent the concepts that Smith sometimes laboriously describes in detail. Although Smith described the economics of pricing in situations of direct competition, the majority of corporate strategy efforts today revolve around keeping our companies from falling beneath competition's heavy hand.

A basic premise of modern economics is that buyers and sellers act in their own *enlightened self-interest.* This means that both buyers and sellers are reasonably well informed about product features, product benefits, and alternatives to buying a particular product. Although twenty-first–century buyers have more information available than ever about the products they buy, today there is often too much information, rather than too little. Today buyers sometimes feel that there are too many product choices, there is too much information, and the mountain of information under which they are buried is often too technical to understand.

Measurement of the amount of goods that sellers are willing to sell and the pricing of those goods is called *supply.* Sellers have a *profit motive,* and economic theory says that if customers want to buy a product, sellers will be willing to supply that product, provided that the sale of the product will bring an acceptable selling price. That selling price is normally somewhere above cost, and the higher the market price is for a product, the more sellers will be willing to be in that business. Exhibit 2.1 provides an example of a supply curve.

Exhibit 2.1 Typical supply curve

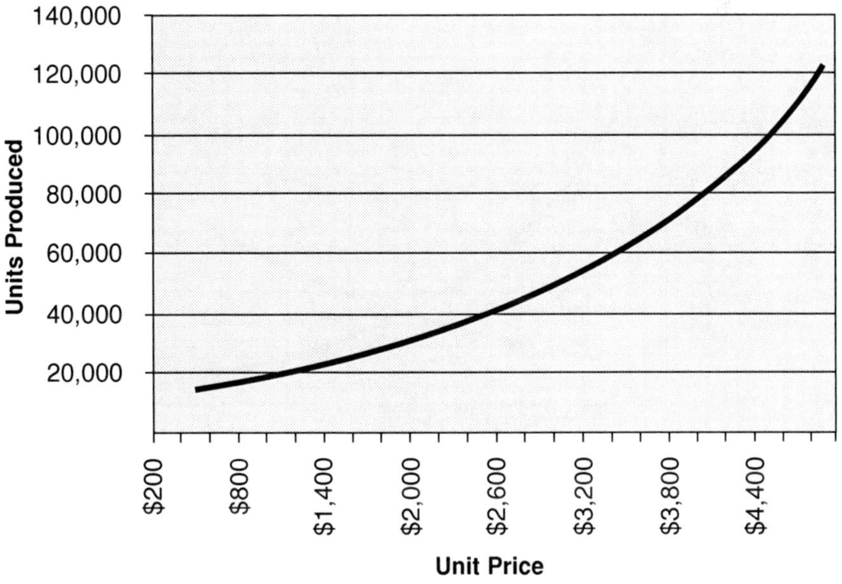

Note: The higher the market price is for a product, the more sellers will seek to be in that business.

Measurement of a buyer's desire for a product is called *demand*. Buyers have finite resources, and they continually make trade-offs in deciding how to spend their limited funds. In general, the lower the price of something, the more likely the buyer will be to buy it. Thus, as prices rise, some buyers will defer purchases, forgo purchases, seek substitutes for the product, or perhaps even make the product themselves.

A demand curve is shown on the same graph as the supply curve in Exhibit 2.2. In theory, the point where the supply curve and the demand curve intersect should reflect the market price of the product. The pure application of this theory, however, requires numerous conditions before it holds true.

The first condition is that the buyer must be able to get the product from more than one seller. If there was only one seller for a product, there would be no competition and thus the buyer must pay the price specified by the seller if they want the goods. Prices tend to be much higher when there is no effective competition. The term *monopoly* is used to refer to a market where there is only one seller. An *oligopoly* is a market served by only a few sellers who each hold a large market share. The term oligopoly is normally reserved for markets where there is little effective competition. Some businesses that are served by only a few sellers are

Exhibit 2.2 Supply and demand

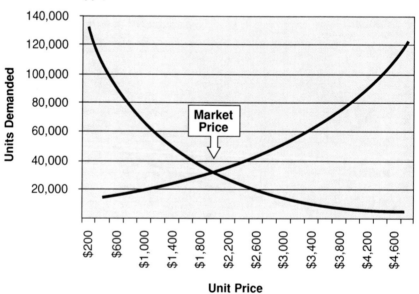

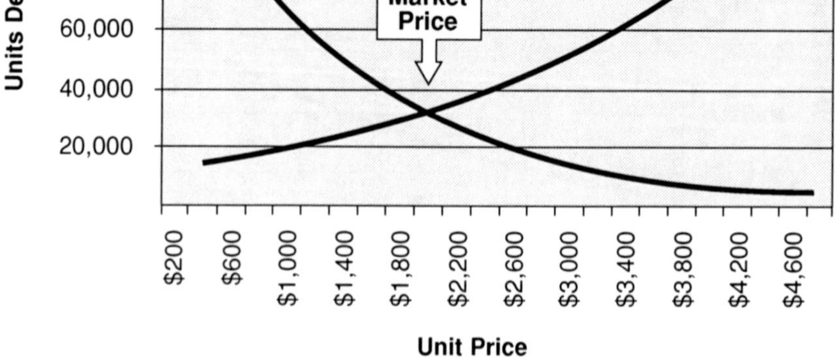

Note: The higher the price for a product, the fewer buyers will purchase it. The market will establish equilibrium at the price where supply equals demand.

very competitive. In many markets, the price of Coca-Cola and Pepsi is lower than bottled water due to constant price competition between these two soft drink makers.

The second condition is that the products available from the various sellers must be equivalent. When products are perceived to be identical, they are said to be *commodities*. Agricultural products, building materials, and chemicals are often thought of as commodities. Competition for commodities may be particularly fierce. A seller who prices his or her commodity product even slightly above the market price may experience a precipitous drop in sales. For this reason, all sellers competing in the same market often offer commodities at exactly the same price.

When many competitors offer their products at the same price, it is indicative of a fiercely competitive market. When similar products are available at a wide variety of different prices, it is an indication of a less competitive environment. Products are often sold at a variety of prices because sellers have successfully differentiated their products from other companies in their industry.

Airline travel is often viewed as a commodity. Most consumers cannot differentiate between the services of the largest airlines. Accordingly, the prices that these airlines offer tend to be identical on the same routes. If one airline raises its prices, the others may or may not follow the price leader. If other airlines fail to increase their prices in response to the actions of a price leader, the price leader will typically withdraw its price increase quickly.

Innovations in the airline industry have often been rapidly adopted by all of the major competitors. When American Airlines introduced their AAdvantage Frequent Flyer program, similar programs were quickly adopted by other airlines. When the concept of silver, gold, and platinum "elite" frequent flyer status was introduced, the other major carriers quickly adopted it. If one airline found a competitive advantage in serving hot chocolate chip muffins instead of peanuts, it is certain that all of the other airlines would be serving hot baked goods in short order.

If two sellers have products that are similar, but are not the same, some buyers will choose one product over the other, not on the basis of price, but on the basis of their preference of one product's features. To the extent that buyers perceive a product as being unique, no effective competition may exist. As we will see in Chapter 3, differentiation is an effective strategy to minimize price competition.

A third condition for pure competition is that competing products must be available at the same time and place. As a practical matter, two sellers with identical products can never be exactly in the same place at the same time, although they may be nearly so. Even two gas stations positioned diagonally across the street from each other may each have an advantage of location for certain customers. Because drivers will prefer to make a right turn into a gas station rather than a more time-consuming left turn across traffic, the station on the northwest corner may have an advantage in the morning when south-bound commuters pass on the way to the freeway. In the evening, that advantage will switch to the station on the southeast corner as commuters head north.

If all three of these conditions exist—(1) consumers can get the product from more than one seller, (2) products are equivalent (i.e., the customer is indifferent as to which of several competing products they choose), and (3) products are available at the same time and place—there is a state of pure competition. It should be obvious that these three conditions rarely exist simultaneously. Some products may be differentiated from each other in ways that are so subtle that many buyers are unable to comprehend why the product is worth a premium price to other buyers. In a blindfolded taste test, a chocolate lover may prefer candy from a Whitman's Sampler to a Godiva chocolate costing four times as much. However, given an opportunity to examine a box of Godiva's, a buyer understands that part of the price is for the visual experience of chocolate artwork. Important lessons may be learned by studying competition in the real world.

PRICE ELASTICITY

While supply increases as prices rise, demand increases as prices decline. If a small change in price makes a large change in buyer demand, price is said to be *elastic*, whereas demand is said to be *inelastic* if price increases have little effect on demand. The formula for price elasticity is defined as follows:

$$\text{Price Elasticity} = \frac{\%\ \text{Change in Unit Sales}}{\%\ \text{Change in Price}}$$

By definition, a product has elastic demand if the price elasticity ratio is greater than 1 and inelastic if the ratio is less than 1. Technically, price elasticity almost always has a negative value because a price decrease normally causes an increase in sales volume and vice versa. In practice, the negative value is ignored, and price elasticity is referred to as a positive number.

Price elasticity is often diagrammed as a straight line in economics and marketing texts, but a real-world market demand curve is usually much more complex. Exhibit 2.2 shows a demand curve for a hypothetical electronic device superimposed on the supply curve from Exhibit 2.1. If the device were very inexpensive, the company would sell many units and demand would be very elastic. As the price increases, demand decreases at a decreasing rate. If the price is set very high, demand becomes very inelastic because some buyers will place a very high perceived benefit on owning the product and need to have the product regardless of its cost.

In 1998, America Online (AOL) President Stephen Case feared mass customer defection when he increased the price of AOL's basic service by 10% from \$19.95

to $21.95 per month. To his amazement, there was no detectable effect on subscriptions due to the price increase. Case concluded that AOL was a service that people needed and that the demand for AOL service was very inelastic.

For products that are sold to many different customers, there is almost always a trade-off between price and volume. Except for those few situations where demand actually goes up when price is increased, real-world experience confirms the economic theory that fewer units of a product will be sold as prices are increased. Because revenue equals volume multiplied by price, revenue is maximized at the point on the demand curve where price times volume is maximized. This point occurs where the largest rectangle can be drawn from the origin of the axis to a point on the demand curve.

Revenue will be maximized at the price where price elasticity is exactly 1.0. This point on the demand curve is shown in Exhibit 2.3. At this point, any change in price provides an equal and opposite percentage change in unit sales. At any point to the left of this position, where price elasticity is less than 1.0, price can be increased, increasing revenue. Because revenue equals price times volume, revenue increases because the percentage decrease in volume is less than the percentage

Exhibit 2.3 Revenue maximization point

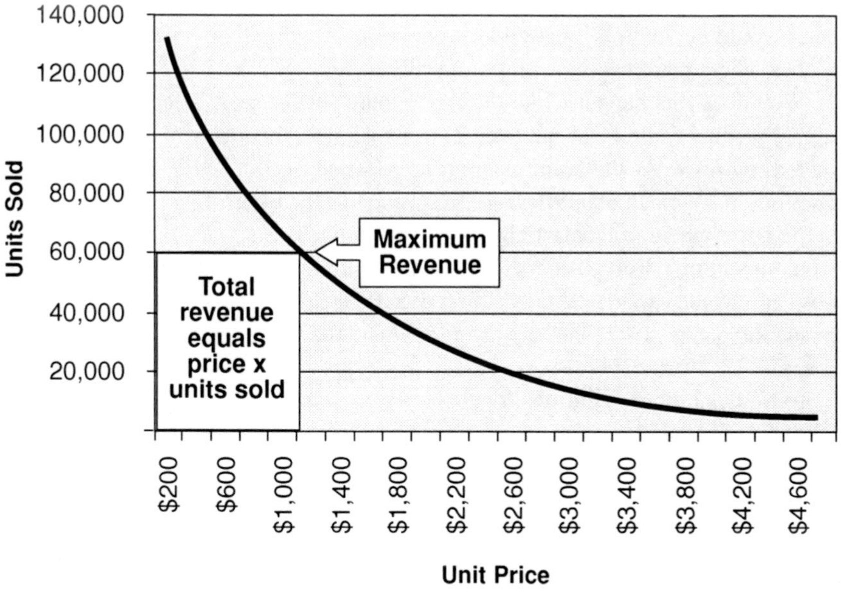

Note: Revenue will be maximized where the slope of the demand curve equals 1.0. At this point, the percentage change in price will generate an equal but opposite percentage change in unit sales.

increase in price. To the right of this position, where price elasticity is greater than 1.0, a decrease in price will also produce an increase in revenue. This is because the decrease in price is less than the percentage increase in volume. Graphically, Exhibit 2.3 shows that the point where price elasticity is 1.0 is the point on the demand curve that allows the largest rectangle to be drawn between the x and y axes.

MAXIMIZING REVENUE DOES NOT MAXIMIZE PROFITS

Some marketing and pricing books advise that profits will be maximized by setting price at the level where revenue is maximized, that is, where the price elasticity value on the demand curve equals 1. Any examination of cost information will prove that this assertion is not true. After all, Profit = Revenue – Expenses. Revenue does not equal profit. To truly determine how to maximize profit, a company must understand its cost structure.

Exhibit 2.4 illustrates total revenue, cost, and profit for the electronics product from the previous discussion. Here, fixed launch costs have been set at $25 million, whereas variable costs are $500 per unit. The company would maximize its sales at a selling price of about $1,200 per unit, generating sales of $69.2 million and profits of $15.4 million. At a 50% higher selling price of about $1,800 per unit, sales would be $5.5 million (8%) lower, yet profits would be $5.7 million (37%) higher. These data may be seen graphically in Exhibit 2.5.

Why does this happen? Intuitively, it would seem that if revenue were good, more revenue would be even better. The answer is in the trade-off that is made by increasing price. At the point where price elasticity is 1.0, a 1% change in price does not make much of a difference in revenue. If the price of an item were $1.00 at the point where price elasticity were 1.0, then a 1 cent price increase to $1.01 would result in a drop in sales from 1,000,000 units to 990,000 units. Total sales, however, would experience only a drop of $100, a difference of 1/100 of 1%. What would happen to cost? Fixed cost would remain the same, but variable cost would decrease by 1%.

Exhibit 2.6 shows the resulting change in profitability if fixed costs were $200,000 and variable costs were $0.70. A small increase in price provides a small drop in sales but provides a big boost to profitability.

This is an important insight into profitability. The price that maximizes revenue and the price that maximizes profit may be far apart. For a company to truly maximize profit, it must understand not only customer demand but also the cost behavior of the product. It is not very hard to find combinations of customer demand and product cost structure that are unprofitable at the price that maximizes revenue but provides a reasonable return on sales at a higher price.

Exhibit 2.4 Revenue and cost behavior at various prices

Unit price	$1,000	$1,200	$1,400	$1,600	$1,800	$2,000
Demand	67,861	57,682	49,029	41,675	35,424	30,110
Elasticity	0.88	1.06	1.24	1.41	1.59	1.35
Revenue	67,860,813	69,218,029	68,641,212	66,680,034	63,762,783	60,220,406
Cost	(58,930,406)	(53,840,845)	(49,514,719)	(45,837,511)	(42,711,884)	(40,055,102)
Profits	8,930,406	15,377,183	19,126,493	20,842,524	21,050,899	20,165,305

Note: This table shows the total revenue, cost, and profits for the product shown in Exhibit 2.3. This product has $25 million in fixed launch costs and $500 of variable costs. While revenue is maximized at a price of about $1,200 per unit, profit is maximized at about $1,800 per unit.

Exhibit 2.5 Maximum revenue versus maximum profit

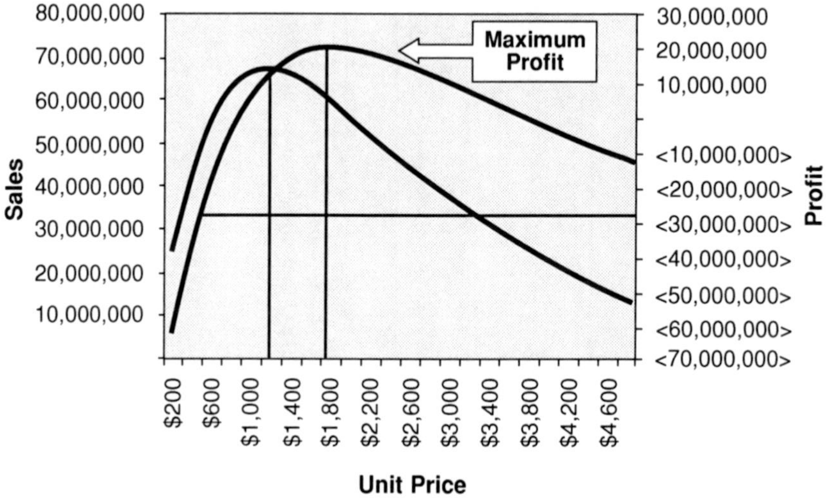

Note: For most realistic customer demand and cost structure situations, profit (scale on right) will be maximized at a price that is higher than the price that maximizes revenue (scale on left).

Exhibit 2.6 Maximizing revenue does not maximize profit

	Price Elasticity		
	@1.0	Above 1.0	Difference
Units sold	1,000,000	990,000	(10,000)
Selling price	$1.00	$1.01	1%
Revenue	1,000,000	999,900	(100)
Fixed cost	(200,000)	(200,000)	—
Variable cost @$0.70	(700,000)	(693,000)	7,000
Profit	$100,000	$106,900	$6,900
Profit increase			6.9%

Note: Revenue is maximized at the point where price elasticity equals 1.0. At this point, a 1% increase in price equals a 1% decrease in units sold. In this example, a 1% increase in price results in a 6.9% increase in profits. Except for products with no variable costs, profit is always maximized at a higher price and lower sales volume than the price that maximizes revenue.

To maximize profit, it is not enough to merely study customer demand. Cost behavior must also be understood as well. Cost structures can be very complicated. In the examples given thus far, relatively simplistic representations of cost behavior have been used. Costs come in many more flavors than "fixed" and "variable." Most businesses have many factors that cause cost. Modern cost accountants sometimes say that, in the long term, all costs are variable, whereas in the very short term, all costs are fixed.

Many factors can make a single product deviate far from the average product. These factors can include product complexity (or lack of it), unusually low or high volumes, and many other factors. Some costs have nothing at all to do with producing products, but have everything to do with having customers. Understanding cost behavior is key to profitability and an effective pricing strategy.

Cost behavior in the real world may be complicated with many variables. Some costs may be associated with the number of company locations. Other costs may depend on the number of products, the number of batches produced of that product, or the number of units produced. Yet other costs will be associated with the number of units in a box. All of these factors could undoubtedly be described by a long algebraic equation based on all of the relevant parameters that would allow a company to solve for a single price, which would (in theory) maximize profit. In practice, modern activity-based costing software uses a sophisticated cost assignment network to represent real-world cost behavior.

It is doubtful that many companies will routinely price their products by solving a single algebraic equation that determines the single best price for a product. The reason for this is that it is worthwhile to "play" with various pricing scenarios to obtain a deeper understanding of the customer demand curve and the cost–volume curve to understand the profit sensitivity if everything does not happen as planned. Pricing analysis today is most often performed on computer spreadsheet models. These models are likely to continue to play a key role in pricing due to their ease of use and flexibility.

Using computer spreadsheets, costs may be analyzed for many different points along the customer demand curve. Once price can be localized into a general neighborhood, management can analyze the cost structure of the product to find more cost-effective methods of production at the general planned volume. These changes to the cost structure may be significant enough that the planned price will be changed once again to a more profitable point on the customer demand line.

Cost behavior will be discussed more in Chapters 5 through 8. First, customer demand should be discussed in more depth.

ESTIMATING CUSTOMER DEMAND AND PRICE ELASTICITY

There are four basic ways of estimating customer demand and price elasticity for a product:

1. Expert judgment
2. Customer surveys
3. Price experimentation
4. Analysis of historical data

Expert Judgment

Expert judgment is a relatively inexpensive way to estimate customer demand. The experts that this method uses will often consist of personnel within the company who are experienced with sales of similar products. Through interactions with customers, salespeople often have a good sense of the values that customers place on existing product features as well as their desire for product features that are not available. Experts might also include loyal customers or distributors who resell the company's product.

The closer a new product resembles the look, features, and function of an existing product, the more reliable expert judgment is likely to be. It is often difficult to evaluate the value of a new product or of a new product feature to a customer, and experts often grossly underestimate the value of products and product features that are truly innovative.

IBM once hired the consulting firm of Arthur D. Little to evaluate the possible acquisition of Haloid Corporation. Haloid had developed a concept for a new office machine. Because IBM was the leading manufacturer of typewriters, this machine might fit nicely into IBM's product line. Arthur D. Little did not think that there would be much demand for the technology because the process was essentially a substitute for carbon paper. Carbon paper was very inexpensive. It cost almost nothing and it could be used over and over again. They figured that worldwide demand would not be any more than 10,000 units for this expensive "photocopy" process. Haloid, being rebuffed by IBM, decided to go it on their own. Recognizing that their name sounded like chemicals, not office machines, they made up the name Xerox and proved many more than 10,000 times over that the experts did not know everything.

Ten to twenty expert opinions are commonly used to estimate a customer demand curve. Experts are normally asked to provide price estimates and the corresponding sales volumes for three or more points. These three points might be:

1. The highest realistic price
2. The most likely or expected price
3. The lowest realistic price

The Delphi Method is one technique used in synthesizing the opinions of experts. This method involves polling experts, tabulating the results, and then having those experts examine the data, discuss their answers, explain their rationale, and then arrive at a consensus opinion. It may be a good idea to have the panel of experts moderated by a neutral party to minimize potential political bias in the process. Sales managers might be reluctant to express an opinion that a new product "won't sell at all" if their boss was a key supporter of the new product. Getting people from different levels of the organization or obtaining the participation from people outside of the organization may improve the quality of the data by introducing people with different paradigms and biases into the process.

Expert judgment has the advantage of being relatively fast and inexpensive. The downside is that the panel of "experts" really may not be all that in touch with the market. Particularly with inside experts, each person's opinion may have come from the same flawed source, perhaps from an earlier feasibility study or the opinion of an executive. Dissention and diversity on an expert panel is good because they cause reexamination of prejudices that may have no basis in fact.

Customer Surveys

Getting the opinions of customers should provide more accurate data than polling in-house experts. After all, it is the customers who will be buying the product. Market research firms may use focus groups, surveys, or other methods of accumulating customer data. Gathering data through customer surveys has many advantages and disadvantages. Surveying customers may be costly and time consuming. The quality of the information may be very good or very bad. The survey process has the potential to strengthen the bond between the company and its customers or make them really angry for wasting their time.

Customer surveys may take many forms. Many companies collect survey information through their product registration forms. Market research firms may mail surveys to potential customers or may do customer surveys over the phone. Most customer surveys consist of a structured set of questions designed to discover answers to specific things that the company wants to know about a product.

Getting good data from a customer survey can be a difficult task. Most people have a limited tolerance for filling out survey forms and an even lower tolerance for telephone surveys. Unskilled temporary phone personnel who have little familiarity with either the product or the potential customers for that product often perform surveys. Although people may tolerate a few questions from a market researcher, they are likely to excuse themselves and hang up if the questions begin to try their patience.

A focus group is a group of people who have been contacted because they meet the demographic profile of the target customer group. Members of a focus group may be paid for their efforts or they may receive a free sample of the product for their efforts. One common use of a focus group is to gather 10 to 12 focus group members in a room, demonstrate or describe the product concept, and then generate a discussion about the product, its features, functions, and price.

A member of the market research firm normally conducts the focus group, but client managers often observe the discussion through one-way glass. The focus group also may be tape recorded or videotaped for later analysis. A key advantage of a focus group is that it provides a forum where reactions to the product are revealed that never would have been revealed by structured survey questions.

One particularly effective method of customer survey is a trade-off analysis (also called conjoint analysis). A trade-off analysis is designed to place a value on key attributes of a product. The method involves providing customers with a series of two choices and asking them to choose between the two. Implicit in each question is a trade-off between the choices that allows the researcher to assign a value to each product attribute.

If a real estate developer were studying the value that yuppie condominium buyers ascribed to potential properties, they might seek to know the value of a second garage space, separate breakfast and dining room areas, additional bathrooms, and outdoor deck area. The value of each of these features can be determined by asking potential customers to make a series of carefully designed choices.

Trade-off analysis surveys are most often performed on a personal computer. Using the computer has the advantage of allowing the survey to be adjusted based on the responses given by the respondent. A major downside of this technique is that it is difficult to design, administer, and interpret the data. Companies that use this technique successfully usually administer the test using only highly trained market researchers who are well versed in the methodology.

Trade-off analysis is particularly effective for providing information about the value that customers place on various product features. The results of trade-off analysis often differ dramatically from what respondents say using other survey techniques. For instance, automobile buyers may say that it is very important to have a car that is environmentally friendly. However, when a trade-off analysis determines the amount of money that buyers are willing to pay for environmental features, trade-off analysis has shown that car buyers are willing to pay a little extra for such features.

Price Experimentation

Price experimentation involves changing the price of the product and observing customer reaction. This may be done on a broad basis or by doing a localized study. Dayton, Ohio, is reputed to be a frequent locale for price experiments. Dayton, it turns out, is a fairly average American city demographically. In addition to its demographics, Dayton's proximity to Cincinnati, home of consumer products giant Proctor & Gamble, makes it a convenient place to test consumer price reactions.

The basic technique for price experimentation is fairly straightforward. The company sells the product at one price for a period of time, notes how much product they sell and then changes the price again. The company will do a series of price changes, noting the effect of price on volumes each time. In theory, the company should be able to plot the price–volume relationship, drawing the customer demand curve from the data.

Extraneous factors may muddy the data. A new product may have a natural trend of constantly increasing volume that is independent of price. Seasonal buying trends may increase or decrease sales in ways that have nothing to do with price and differences in advertising or promotional efforts may disguise the real effects of price on customer demand.

A negative aspect of price experimentation is that a price experiment may train customers to expect prices to change frequently or that the product may sometimes be available at a much lower price. Customers who are exposed to a one-time deep discount may wait for another deep discount to occur again, stocking up when the price is low. Price experimentation also may set off an unfavorable reaction among competitors, who may fail to recognize the price experiment for what it is, setting off a price war.

Price experimentation requires an existing product. The company must invest time and money in product development, product launch, and product promotion before running a price experiment. Because this may be an expensive proposition, other methods of determining customer demand will be necessary for a new product.

Analysis of Historical Data

Analysis of historical data works in much the same manner as price experimentation. If the company has a history of having sold its products at different prices from time to time, historical data may provide insight into customer price elasticity. Historical data have the advantage that they are already available and can usually be inexpensively analyzed. If the company has not routinely varied its price, however, there may be no meaningful data to analyze. In addition to the other variables that must be eliminated from a price experiment, historical pricing data often cover many years and must be inflation adjusted to give a true picture.

DEMAND FOR COMPETITIVELY BID PRODUCTS

For many companies there is no such thing as a demand curve for their products. Many companies produce unique, one-of-a-kind products that have a single customer. Manufacturing companies often fall into this category. A large portion of manufacturing companies produce products that are component parts for larger products that their customers assemble together. For some products there may be three or more tiers of suppliers before a finished product is sold to an end user.

Ford Motor Company is in the business of assembling automobiles. Ford does not manufacture seats for automobiles, but instead purchases seats from companies like Lear Seating or Johnson Controls. These Ford suppliers may in turn assemble seats from components that were purchased from other companies. How will price affect the sales volume of the company that makes the plastic button that drivers press to make their seats go forward or backward on their Ford Taurus? How will price affect the number of seats that will be sold? When it comes right down to it, the demand for these manufactured parts is completely dependent on how many cars Ford sells. For the company making the seats, customer demand is an all-or-nothing proposition. They either get the whole contract with Ford or none of it.

SUMMARY

1. Modern economics traces its roots back to Adam Smith's 1776 book *The Wealth of Nations*. Smith described the effects of supply and demand and thought that every product had a natural cost-based price.
2. Capitalist economics is based on the concept that sellers of goods have a profit motive and that buyers and sellers interact based on an enlightened self-interest.
3. In a stable market, supply and demand reach an equilibrium at the price and volume where the supply and demand curves intersect. The price at this point is called the market price.
4. The pure operation of economic theory requires:
   - That there be many buyers and sellers for a product.
   - That the products available from various sellers be equivalent.
   - That the products be available at the same place and time.
5. Demand is said to be elastic when a small change in price leads to a big change in demand. Price is said to be inelastic when a large change in price results in only a small change in demand. A measure of customer sensitivity to price is called price elasticity.
6. A measure of customer sensitivity to price is called price elasticity.

$$\text{Price Elasticity} = \frac{\%\ \text{Change in Sales Volume}}{\%\ \text{Change in Price}}$$

7. Revenue is maximized where the price elasticity is 1.0.

8. Maximizing revenue does not maximize profit. Profit is often maximized at a considerably higher price and lower volume than the price that maximizes sales.

9. There are four basic ways of estimating customer demand:

- Expert judgment
- Customer surveys
- Price experimentation
- Analysis of historical data

NOTE

1. Adam Smith, *An Inquiry into the Nature and Causes of the Wealth of Nations* (1776, reprinted by Prometheus Books, New York, 1991), p. 50.

3

COMPETITIVE STRATEGY AND PRICING

> You do not merely want to be considered just the best of the best. You want to be considered the only ones who do what you do.
>
> Jerry Garcia, the late leader of The Grateful Dead

IN SEARCH OF COMPETITIVE ADVANTAGE

People invest money in businesses to make more money and increase their wealth. The process of turning money into more money is referred to as earning a financial return. Money can be invested in many ways. One way is to deposit money to a bank. Banks will pay a low rate of interest to use money, but that money is relatively safe. Alternately, that same money could be invested by buying an ownership interest in a business with the expectation of receiving the higher rate of return associated with a higher level of risk. There are many ways to invest money in a business. Among these, a person could start a new business, buy an entire existing business outright, buy part of a business with partners, buy stock in a publicly traded company, or buy stock in many publicly traded companies through a mutual fund.

A key objective of anyone investing in a business is to generate a superior financial return. After all, if the investment in a business cannot return more money to the stockholder than putting money in a less risky savings account, the rational action would be to invest in the savings account where the money is relatively safe. In many companies, company executives are the owners. However, even in companies where top management does not own the company, the owner's objective of achieving a superior financial return becomes the objective of the management team.

To achieve a superior financial return, management seeks ways to have buyers prefer their company's products to the products of their competitors. After all, having the highest revenues should equate to having the highest profits. Conventional wisdom says that if all other things are equal, buyers will prefer the product that has the lowest cost. Conventional wisdom also says that having the lowest cost is dependent on having the highest market share. Thus businesses are driven to continually increase market share and lower cost in pursuit of higher financial returns.

Even though many company presidents continually drive their companies to decrease costs and increase market share, there is more to earning a superior financial return. For every high-profit/high–market share success story like Microsoft, there is a contrary low-profit/high–market share example such as General Motors.

High market share is not what business owners really want most. Given a choice, most company owners would rather have the most profitable company in the industry rather than the company with the largest market share. Company objectives that create value for ownership more directly than high market share include that the company:

- Operates profitably.
- Has positive cash flow.
- Has a strong return on investment.
- Is otherwise successful as measured by normal accounting conventions.

The achievement of each of these objectives is dependent on having customers who pay an adequate price for the company's products.

Each management team views financial success in comparison with their own frame of reference. Some companies, particularly start-up companies, may sacrifice short-term profitability to gain market share in the belief that market share will generate higher profits over the long term. High market share does not necessarily lead to profitability, yet many companies blindly seek to increase market share year after year, never achieving either market dominance or a satisfying profit.

In developing corporate strategy, managers seek a combination of factors that will give their company a superior financial performance. Harvard University Professor Michael E. Porter calls these factors *Competitive Advantage* in his book by the same name.[1] Porter avoids defining the specific financial measurements that should define financial success, saying that competitive advantage is any factor that allows superior financial performance as measured by conventional financial means.

CORPORATE STRATEGY

Strategy Defined

The word *strategy* comes from a combination of two Greek words, *stratos*, meaning an army, and *agein*, meaning to lead. Hence, Strategos means the leader of an army, or in English, a general. The first definition of strategy in a modern dictionary would read something like this:

- *Strategy* is the *positioning* of troops before a battle, specifically distinguished from *tactics*.
- *Tactics* is the *maneuvering* of troops after the battle begins.

With military strategy, generals plot where to position their troops, which troops to put in each position, and the timing factors related to that positioning. Business strategy has many parallels. Company executives decide the who, what, when, where, and how of producing and selling their products. In short, management's job is to use the company's scarce resources to earn a financial return by profitably serving customers. Developing strategy is a basic function of management.

Evolution of Corporate Strategy

Although business people have probably plotted the positioning of their enterprises for thousands of years, formal strategic planning took a long time to develop as a discipline. Henry Fayol advocated business planning in the late nineteenth century. In the early twentieth century, Frederick Taylor[2] advocated "scientific management," whereby companies would plan their every move in excruciating detail, including the repetitive daily motions of their lowest level employees. After H. Igor Ansoff's 1965 book *Corporate Strategy*[3] appeared, it became fashionable for the best and the brightest from North American business schools to go to work in the strategic planning departments of big publicly traded companies like General Electric.

In the decades that followed Ansoff's book, the strategic planning process evolved rapidly. Original research into corporate strategy focused on strategic planning as a process. Everyone recognized that some businesses achieved spectacular growth and spectacular financial results through cleverly conceived strategies. The basic theory of the time was that if management could only duplicate the process that these businesses went through, then any management team could improve their performance by following the same formula. Thus, the outcome of extensive strategic planning research was that academics and practitioners alike focused on the development of detailed work programs to lead them through the process of strategic planning.

Further research was geared to quantifying the performance improvements of companies preparing strategic plans. Intuitively, everyone was sure that businesses that had a formal process for developing strategy must do better. However, study after study showed "cookbook" strategic planning to be a wasted effort and a failure. Two major reasons for this failure were strategic planning's basic suppositions that strategy could be condensed into a work program and that strategy should be separated from tactics. Clever new ideas do not come from filling in the blank boxes in a work program. New ideas come from rearranging the boxes, throwing some out, and making new ones.

Relationship of Tactics to Strategy

The separation of strategy and tactics was also an obstacle. It is difficult to tell in advance when some seemingly trivial operational detail will provide a company with a competitive advantage. For instance, when it comes to customer services, quirky little nuances in the way that service is delivered can provide a real strategic advantage, particularly if those nuances make service very fast. Outback Steakhouse advertises that there are "no rules, just great tasting food" at their restaurants. The servers at Outback are encouraged to be friendly with the patrons and to help make their meal memorable. A server at Outback may slide into the booth across from the customer to explain the specials and take the order. This action breaks down the barriers between customer and server and leaves the customer with the impression that Outback is a "nice friendly place." Such seemingly small operational techniques can be very strategic.

The distinction between strategy and tactics is important to the evolution of corporate strategy. If the definition of strategy and tactics is taken literally, strategy is the responsibility of the generals and their staffs (top management), whereas tactics is the responsibility of the colonels and captains (middle management) who maneuver their troops in the field. There is a strong implication that strategy refers to big important things while tactics are mere details.

World War I seems to have cured military thinkers of the idea that strategy and tactics should be separate. In *The Rise and Fall of Strategic Planning*,[4] Henry Mintzberg described the planning and conduct of the 1917 Third Battle of Ypres, which focused on the village of Passchendaele in West Flanders, Belgium. The British high command decided that a three-pronged attack on German lines was necessary to break the stalemate that had lasted since 1914. Critics of the British planning of the battle maintain that no senior officer in the battle ever set foot on the battlefield during the 4 months that the battle was in progress. As the battle progressed, the heavy rains and the artillery's destruction of the area's ancient drainage systems made the terrain increasingly muddy. No man's land was such a quagmire that ammunition-laden soldiers would slip into mud-filled shell holes and disappear without a trace. At first, daily reports on the conditions of the battlefield were ignored, but when front-line officers pressed their reports with increasing urgency, they were ordered to discontinue filing battlefield condition reports.

After 4 long hard months of fighting, Canadian troops captured Passchendaele. The total cost of the battle was some 250,000 casualties. Mintzberg quotes J.L. Stokesbury's *A Short History of World War I:*

> [A] staff officer . . . came up to see the battlefield after it was all quiet again. He gazed out over the sea of mud, then said half to himself, "My God, did we send men to advance in that?" after which he broke down weeping and his escort led him away.[5]

World War II was won, in part, because General Dwight D. Eisenhower and other allied leaders understood the importance of tactics and the even more mundane science of logistics. *Logistics* is the moving, supplying, and quartering of troops. Preparation for the June 4, 1944, invasion of Normandy, although strategically sophisticated, was perhaps the most complicated tactical and logistic effort ever attempted by mankind in either time of war or time of peace.

As General Norman Schwartzkoff described the reasons for the quick allied victory in the Persian Gulf War, "Mediocre generals talk strategy, great generals talk logistics, and Saddam Hussein is not a great general."[6]

Like military strategy, corporate strategy initially took the attitude that strategy was important work done at a high level and that strategic plans were not meant to include seemingly trivial operational considerations. Although military thinking changed prior to World War II, it took business management until the 1980s to understand the importance of using strategy and tactics together.

In the days when business strategy and tactics were separate, imagine the top managers of a large corporation carefully crafting the annual revision to their strategic plan. They are proud of the bold new direction in which they are going to steer the corporation and have taken great pains to describe the new strategy in a formal strategic plan, bound in a three-ring binder that is to be distributed to all managers in the company (grade 7 or above). Imagine the interest that those middle managers might develop each year, as they anticipate receiving their copy of the strategic plan that will tell them of the brilliant strategy that their leaders had conceived.

Such a middle manager might be Joe, a grade 7 process-engineering manager in charge of a team that is responsible for launching new products. A 15-year "company man," Joe has actually reserved his Saturday morning to sit in the lounge chair in his back yard and read the strategic plan with a pot of coffee. What would be Joe's reaction when he comes across provisions in the company strategy that look completely unrealistic from his engineering perspective. "Don't those guys at headquarters know how our products are made?" he thinks. "Besides, even if we could do this, is it what our customer really wants?"

Joe might think that top management is a bit out of touch. Were he not so dedicated to the company, the word *incompetent* might cross his mind when thinking of the top management authors of the strategic plan. Of course, top management will be thinking the same thing about middle management when they fail to execute their brilliant strategic plan.

Today in both military and business strategy it is widely acknowledged that the often mundane details of running any enterprise can be very strategic. Many successful businesses have as their foundation the nuts-and-bolts details and the logistic nuances of getting generic undifferentiated products to customers quickly and dependably.

If we were to try to come up with the one single word that was the closest synonym for strategy, whether in the military or business, it would be *positioning*. Here positioning means that each company must define itself in terms of its customers, competitors, core competencies, technologies used, geographic areas served, and other factors that allow the company to focus its resources effectively on serving its customers.

SOURCES OF COMPETITIVE ADVANTAGE

In *When Lean Enterprises Collide,*[7] Robin Cooper describes competition in terms of three factors: price, quality, and functionality, which he calls "the survival triplet." Although Cooper diagrams the survival triplet (Exhibit 3.1) on a three-dimensional x-y-z axis, he notes that there may be many aspects to the functionality of a product. An automobile, for instance, represents different things to different people. To one person, an automobile may be just transportation, to someone else it may be an expression of their station in life, and to another it may be a mobile listening room for music. Each customer may have very different expectations of the functionality of the products that they buy. Conceptually, then, the functionality axis of the survival triplet may itself actually be of many dimensions.

Using Cooper's concept of the survival triplet, it is obvious with any analysis that companies within an industry might differentiate themselves to stake out their own territories with different combinations of price, quality, and functionality (Exhibit 3.2). One company might choose to produce a low-price generic product with average quality and average functionality, whereas another company might choose a high-price, high-quality, and high-functionality position. Many different positions may be available for many companies in the market for a single product. The functionality parameter alone provides many opportunities for differentiation.

Exhibit 3.1 Survival triplet

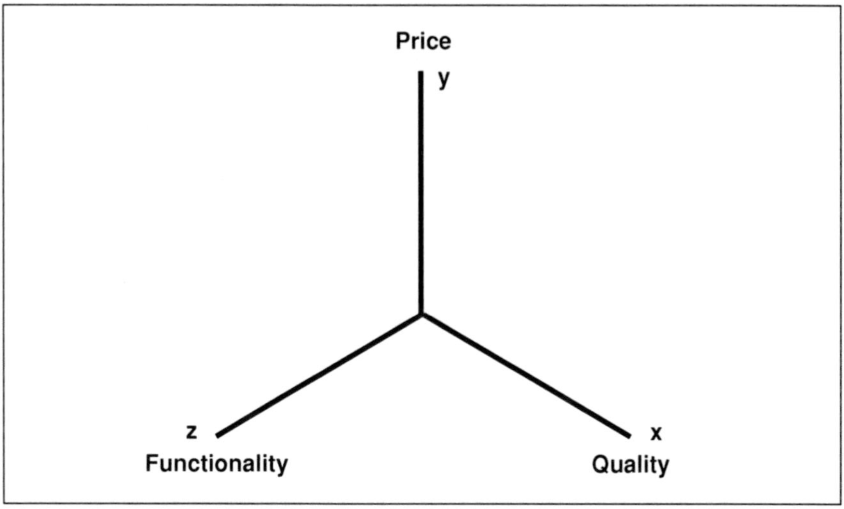

Source: Adapted and reprinted by permission of *Harvard Business Review* from "When Lean Enterprises Collide" by Robin Cooper. Copyright © 1995 by the Harvard Business School Publishing Corporation.

Exhibit 3.2 Differentiation strategies

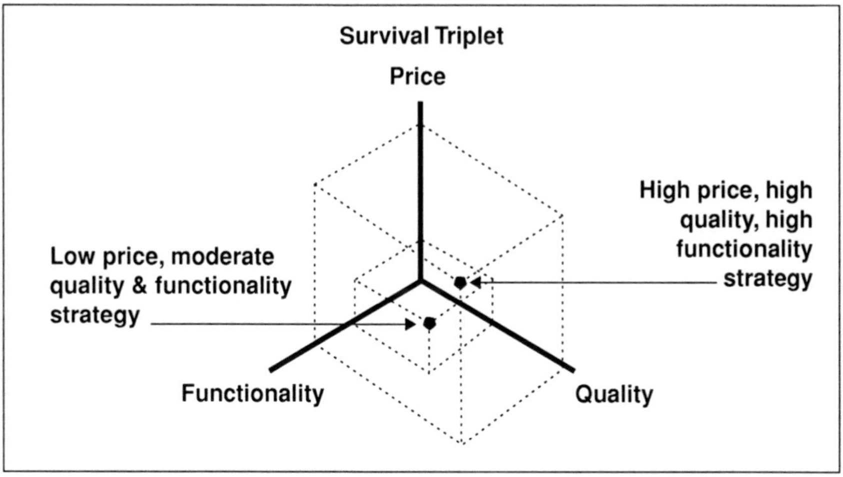

Note: The survival triplet, showing two products competing using different strategies in the same market.
Source: Adapted and reprinted by permission of *Harvard Business Review* from "When Lean Enterprises Collide" by Robin Cooper. Copyright © 1995 by the Harvard Business School Publishing Corporation.

In *Competitive Advantage*, Michael Porter contends that competitive advantage comes from only two sources: low cost and differentiation.

Porter argues that if there are only two sources of competitive advantage, cost leadership and differentiation, then a company could pursue either a broad market strategy or a focused strategy. Although it might seem that this approach would result in four generic business strategies, Porter defines only three generic strategies for achieving competitive advantage, with the third of these strategies having two substrategies. These are the generic competitive strategies that Porter defines:

1. Cost Leadership
2. Differentiation
3. Focus
    a. Cost Focus
    b. Differentiation Focus

Porter conceptualizes these strategies as shown in Exhibit 3.3.

Exhibit 3.3 Porter's generic competitive strategies

Porter's Generic Competitive Strategies		Competitive Advantage	
		Low Cost	Differentiation
Competitive Scope	Broad Target	1. Cost Leadership	2. Differentiation
	Narrow Target	3a. Cost Focus	3b. Differentiation Focus

Source: Adapted with the permission of The Free Press, a Division of Simon & Schuster, Inc., from *Competitive Advantage: Creating and Sustaining Superior Performance* by by Michael E. Porter. Copyright © 1985, 1998 by Michael E. Porter.

COST LEADERSHIP STRATEGIES

The first source of competitive advantage is cost leadership. Because the laws of supply and demand say that buyers prefer products that have a lower price, cost leadership becomes an important source of competitive advantage. Because sellers seek to provide fewer products and buyers seek to obtain more products as the price goes down, markets normally establish equilibrium where prices are relatively stable. It allows a cost leader to price its product lower than competitors and still make a profit. It would be futile then for a company that did not have the lowest cost structure to attempt to compete based on price because the cost leader can sell at a price level that provides it with a profit but generates a loss for competing companies. Eventually, one of the competing companies will run out of financial resources if they continue the price war.

Economics theory says that when products are perceived to be identical, the buyer will prefer the product with the lowest price. Having the lowest cost provides a competitive advantage because buyers prefer a product that costs less if all other factors, such as features, quality, and service, are equal. A buyer does not need to perceive that two products are identical, only that there is proximity between the two products. Products have proximity when the buyer perceives that two products are roughly equivalent in those features that matter.

Many factors may affect a buyer's perception of product quality. At one time the words *made in Japan* printed on a product were synonymous with poor quality. In the two decades following World War II, Americans associated Japanese manufactured goods with the little umbrellas that came in fruity cocktails such as a mai tai or piña colada. Today, this impression is reversed. Many buyers prefer Japanese automobiles and electronics today because they perceive that the quality is better than that of domestic alternatives.

Relationship Between Cost and Volume

How can one company have lower costs than other companies? One common way is to be the high volume producer. Virtually any product or service has some fixed cost associated with producing it. Thus, the high-volume producer has a cost advantage because there are more units of product over which to recover fixed costs. The first company to market a product may become the cost leader, but the cost leader is most often the first company that produces the product using high-volume techniques.

The Ford Model T provides a good example of a product that was sold using a cost leadership strategy.[8] Henry Ford did not invent the automobile. Karl Benz built the first commercially successful automobile in 1885 in Germany, and Charles Duryea produced the first one in North America in 1893. The longest surviving

North American automaker was Oldsmobile, which began producing Oldsmobiles in 1897. The Oldsmobile brand name will be discontinued in the 2002 model year. Ford produced his first automobile in his garage in 1896 but was a relative latecomer to the industry when he incorporated the Ford Motor Company in 1903.

Ford began producing his Model T in 1908. He realized that by using mass-production techniques he could produce an automobile at a cost low enough to be affordable by the average American family. The Model T was basic, no-frills transportation. Originally an open touring car, there were few options. A customer could buy a Model T in "any color, as long as it was black." Ford's Highland Park, Michigan, plant began producing Model Ts on an assembly line in 1913 and immediately put severe pricing pressures on the rest of the industry. By 1921, Ford was capable of producing thousands of automobiles a day, far more in one day than the annual production of many competitors.

The year 1921 began with the Model T priced at $440 at a time when the median household income was $1,500. The price of this automobile would be the equivalent of about $12,000 in 2001 dollars. Considering that this vehicle had no seatbelts, airbags, electric starter, radio, or heater, the price does not seem like such a bargain in today's terms. The Model T was more similar to a late twentieth-century golf cart than a twenty-first–century automobile.

General Motors (GM), which had a 14% share of the North American automotive market in 1921, was one of those companies that relented to the price pressure. Among the price reductions that General Motors made was to lower the price of its bottom-of-the-line single Chevrolet model to $645. Because this Chevrolet was the most direct competitor to the Model T, Ford responded by dropping its price to $415. GM Vice President of Operations Alfred Sloan rationalized that the $230 price differential was not really as big as it seemed because the electric starter and demountable rims that were standard on the Chevrolet were extra on the Ford, making the real price differential only about $95. The automotive industry's first price war was now underway. Chevrolet responded to the $25 Ford price decrease with another price decrease of its own of $20 to $625. At this price GM's accountants figured that Chevrolet was losing $50 per vehicle. The market had still not found the bottom as Ford lowered the price of the Model T another $60 to $355 in September 1921. When 1921 ended, Ford had a 62% market share of the 1.6 million vehicles sold. Chevrolet finished the year with a tiny 4% market share and an astronomical $8.7 million loss.

In retrospect, the folly of trying to compete with Ford in 1921 is all too obvious. For every product there are certain costs that are fixed and independent of volume. For instance, tooling and design cost for a Ford and a Chevrolet were probably similar. Suppose that these tooling and design costs were $50 million for both companies and that a design would be sold for 5 years, roughly the time between major automobile redesigns today. If Ford sold 990,000 units per year and

Chevrolet sold 65,000 units per year, then the tooling and design cost for the Model T would be $10.10 per vehicle versus $153.85 for the Chevrolet. The effect of those fixed costs may have actually been more lopsided than this hypothetical example because the Model T was produced for 18 years between 1908 and 1926. The GM models of this era were redesigned about every 7 years.

Badly beaten, GM pursued a differentiation strategy, making its cars stylish and offering closed sedans to compete with Ford's open coupe. New advances in color paint technology from Dupont shortened the drying time from days or weeks to nine and one-half hours. The shortened drying time made it more practical to produce cars in colors. GM's Oakland division adopted the new Dupont Duco lacquer in 1924, and most of the industry adopted the new paint in 1925, with Ford as the major exception. Ford was stumbling badly. With a market share reduced to 28% in 1926, Henry Ford shut down his company's automotive production for 19 months while he personally redesigned a new product for his company, the Model A. General Motors' differentiation strategy worked, making it the dominant automaker in the world. Paradoxically, as Ford nears overtaking GM as the world's largest automaker in the dawning days of the twenty-first century, it is Ford that is pursuing a well-defined differentiation strategy, whereas GM seems to be pursuing a cost leadership strategy, if any strategy at all.

When Size Does Not Provide a Cost Advantage

Although high unit sales generally confer low unit costs, this is not always the case. Organizations that produce high volumes of a product are often geared to producing only high-volume products. Whether in a service, retail, wholesale, or manufacturing business, companies that produce products in high volumes invest money up front on systems and methods that allow that product to be cost-effectively delivered at those volumes. A large catalog retail company, for example, often has expensive customer support software so that any person who answers the phone may be able to access information about the customer. Its computer system may use caller ID to identify the customer from the company's data base. The software will be able to tell the status of the customer's last order, how much the customer has bought from the company, and something about the customer's buying habits. Problems with previous orders may be identified. This system may have cost a lot of money, but is cost effective considering the large number of transactions that the system processes.

Small companies usually cannot afford such expensive up-front expenditures. However, small companies may be much better structured for dealing with customers who have special-needs, out of the ordinary requirements, or seek to purchase a product in low volume. Small companies may not be able to afford expensive customer support software, but their customer support people may very effectively service their customer base through a direct personal knowledge of their customers.

Size may actually provide a cost disadvantage when customers demand highly differentiated or customized products. When large companies invest money in equipment that allows them to produce a product in high volume, that investment may commit them to a particular process that is hard to change.

If a child's birthday cake is purchased at the supermarket, that cake was not baked at the store but at the cake-baking factory at one of the store's vendors. The customer gets a generic cake with a limited choice of "girl's birthday or "boy's birthday" styles. The store may be able to add the word *Bob* under the words *Happy Birthday* that were already there, but as far as customization goes, that is it.

To get a truly custom cake, a birthday cake has to be ordered from a bakery or restaurant unless it is made at home. At the bakery, instead of just a choice of chocolate or yellow cake, they can make chocolate marble, carrot cake, or some other flavor chosen by the customer. The bakery will decorate the cake to the customer's specifications.

Are the bakery and supermarket competitors? Although they both sell cakes, they are each catering to very different market segments. The supermarket's customers are people who "need to buy a cake" while the bakery customers "want to buy a very special cake." A supermarket birthday cake may sell for $9.99. The bakery could never sell a cake for that price, but it does not need to because the cake factory cannot make a custom cake for the mere $35 that the bakery would charge. The cake factory is not geared to making cakes one at a time and if asked to do so, it would respond that it just does not do that kind of baking.

DIFFERENTIATION STRATEGIES

The second source of competitive advantage is differentiation. Differentiation is when a company produces products that are different in some way that is valued by buyers. Differentiators receive a premium price for their distinctive difference, but to be successful, the premium price must be more than the cost of differentiating.

Differentiation is successful because it makes a product relatively more attractive to those customers who value the difference. The difference may be in the product itself or the service associated with the product. Examples of differentiated products include the following:

- Flame broiled taste of the Burger King Whopper
- Free FedEx delivery and free monogramming with the L.L. Bean Visa Card
- Optional keypad entry on Lincoln-Mercury automobiles

- Strong robust taste of Vernor's ginger ale
- Superior design of Weber barbecue grills
- Colorful Apple computers
- Unique taste of Hawaiian brand bread

Because direct competition is costly for the combatants, companies usually avoid direct competition by differentiation. In essence, there is a tacit agreement between companies that "I will not go after your market segment if you do not go after my market segment." Although each company may test out their competitors by occasionally attempting to enlarge their market segment, direct competition on all fronts is normally avoided.

The airport in Kalamazoo, Michigan (population 82,000), is served by six airlines without a single dominant carrier. The few places that you can fly to out of Kalamazoo are the hub cities of these six airlines, and a large portion of the passengers originating in Kalamazoo are probably making a connection at these hubs to fly to their final destination. One would think that six airlines would cause a lot of competition for so few Kalamazoo area passengers. However, the airlines have avoided direct competition by each specializing in its own niche. Only Northwest Airlines flies to more than one location out of Kalamazoo, and the only duplication of routes is to Chicago, which is served by both United and American:

Airlines Service from Kalamazoo, Michigan

Airline	*Destinations*
American	Chicago
Continental	Cleveland
Delta	Cincinnati
Northwest	Detroit and Minneapolis
United	Chicago
U.S. Air	Pittsburgh

Both Chicago and Detroit are about 120 air miles from Kalamazoo. If pricing to these two cities were based on the cost of flying a plane, the tickets to both destinations would be expected to be about the same. Someone who understands competition, however, might speculate that it would cost more to go to Detroit than Chicago. After all, both American and United Airlines fly directly to Chicago, while only Northwest flies directly to Detroit. In actuality, the reverse is true. Northwest's cheapest fare is $134 from Kalamazoo to Detroit, whereas the cheapest fare from Kalamazoo to Chicago is $213. How can this be?

The answer may lie in the alternatives to purchasing an airline ticket. Kalamazoo, Detroit Metropolitan Airport, and O'Hare International Airport are all situated close to Interstate Highway 94 (I-94). The 120-mile drive from Kalamazoo to Detroit is an easy 2 hours through mostly rural farmlands with little potential for traffic jams and hardly any sections where the 70 miles per hour posted speed is not realistic. Most travelers who need to get to Detroit to catch a flight to their ultimate destination, particularly nonbusiness travelers paying for their own ticket, would choose to drive to the Detroit airport rather than pay the $134 air fare.

Because Lake Michigan sits between Kalamazoo and Chicago, the drive around the bottom of the lake makes this trip farther, about 160 miles. Between Kalamazoo and the Indiana/Illinois border, the traffic on I-94 is also likely to go very quickly. Then the driver reaches Illinois. The Chicago area is notorious for congestion and long construction delays. During rush hour the 40-mile drive between the Indiana state line and O'Hare Airport could take 3 hours. Many travelers, even nonbusiness travelers, would willingly pay $213 to avoid spending 3 hours in Chicago area traffic. Accordingly, the real competition for flights out of Kalamazoo may be alternative methods of transportation and not other airlines.

FOCUSED STRATEGIES

Although companies often think of their competitive position with respect to their industry, the entire industry may not be the relevant market in which a company competes. Marketing people use the term *market* very broadly, thinking in terms of all customers for a broadly defined group of products. They realize, however, that a market may actually be subdivided into several major segments, and each segment may be divided into tiny niches. Clothing might be defined as a market, clothing for professional women as a market segment, and clothing for pregnant executives as a market niche.

A market segment is a subset of a market. The same rules and considerations apply to a market and a market segment. The only difference is that by focusing on only a portion of a market, the competitive universe is smaller. Segmentation is possible when customers perceive that some products in a market are not really suitable for them, and the customers focus their attention on only a portion of the products available when making a buying decision. Markets may be segmented in many ways.

A market niche refers to a specific position in a market and is often so narrowly defined that only one company occupies the market niche. The word *niche* comes from the Old French word for nest and means "a place or position particularly suitable for the person or thing in it." The concept of niches is borrowed from biology, specifically the theory of Charles Darwin, which he described in his 1859 book *Origin of Species*.[10] Darwin said that organisms, both plants and animals, compete for food, water, light, and shelter and that no two organisms could occupy the same ecologic niche and both survive long term. In business, a niche is a narrowly focused position in a market.

There is no strict demarcation line between a market, a market segment, and a market niche. A company that chooses to compete in only a portion of a market is said to have a focused strategy. Each subdivision of the market may have habits that distinguish it from the others. Products sold to one segment of the market may be unsuitable to buyers in another market segment. Some buyers' needs are so narrowly focused that even in a huge market such as clothing, there are only a few companies' products that can satisfy their needs. Within each focused portion of a market there are opportunities for a company following a focused cost leadership strategy and potentially many companies pursuing focused differentiation strategies.

Focused Cost Leadership Strategies

Focused cost leadership strategies are possible when one company is capable of segmenting a market and producing products for that segment more cost effectively than other companies. Rather than attempting to produce all products for a market more cost effectively than other companies, focused cost leaders restrict their efforts to become the cost leaders catering to a specific market segment.

Most of us have baked something that came from a box. Today there are dry boxed mixes for cakes, cookies, brownies, muffins, biscuits, pancakes, bread, pizza crust, and just about any other kind of baked good that you can imagine. The market for cake mixes in the United States is dominated by the Betty Crocker, Duncan Hines, and Pillsbury brands, which are all owned by companies with over $1 billion in annual revenues.

It was not that way when Mabel Holmes invented baking mixes in a rural Michigan village. One day in the 1920s, Mabel's twin sons, Howard and Dudley, brought home from school for lunch two of their classmates who had no mother. Mrs. Holmes looked at the lunch that their father had made them and was appalled by the dry, hard biscuits he had included in their lunch. She did the only thing that a self-respecting woman would do. She threw the biscuits out; fed them a proper lunch; and after the boys went back to school she set to work on solving a problem. She resolved to figure out a way to make biscuits "so easy that even a man could do it."

Mrs. Holmes concocted a mixture that only needed the addition of water and an egg. Her family had owned the flourmill in Chelsea, Michigan, since 1887, so she was not handicapped with the lack of production facilities like many inventors. Soon her baking mixes were available for purchase by men and women all around the country.

You may recognize Mabel's mixes, sold in a blue and white box that has changed little in years. Reflecting on her childhood, Mabel remembered how her father loved hot biscuits and would announce when he came home, "Mabel, I'm in a hurry."

Gulla, the cook, would chuckle as she called from the kitchen, "Now, Miss Mabel, you tell your father them good hot biscuits will be ready in a jiffy." And so, Jiffy became the brand name of America's first baking mix.

As is often true of the first company to market a product, the Chelsea Milling Company staked out a cost leadership strategy early on. Jiffy issues no coupons and has no marketing department, and its sole advertising is for goodwill in its local communities such as sponsorship of the church page in the local newspaper. Even with Dun & Bradstreet estimated sales of $75 million in sales, they keep costs down by using only 35 salaried employees. Compare the wholesale prices of Jiffy with competitors (Exhibit 3.4). Jiffy fruit muffin mixes are $0.0521 per ounce, whereas Betty Crocker mixes are $0.082. Jiffy baking mixes are $.0290 per ounce, whereas Bisquick mixes are $0.0505. The Chelsea Milling Company has thus thrived through a cost leadership strategy that has a narrow focus on only a portion of the boxed baking mix market. Although each of its competitors produces a broad array of choices of baking mixes, the Jiffy product line contains only 19 items heavily focused on muffins. The company claims a 57% market share for boxed muffin

Exhibit 3.4 Wholesale price comparisons for dry baking mixes

Product Category	Size	Case Cost	Cost per Ounce
Biscuit Baking Mixes			
Jiffy	12/40 oz.	$13.90	$0.0290
Bisquick	15/40 oz.	$30.30	$0.0505
Pioneer	12/40 oz.	$24.60	$0.0512
Corn Muffin Mixes			
Jiffy	24/8½ oz.	$6.70	$0.0328
Martha White	24/7½ oz.	$6.80	$0.0378
Betty Crocker	24/6½ oz.	$7.15	$0.0458
Fruit Muffin Mixes			
Jiffy	24/7 oz.	$8.75	$0.0521
Martha White	24/7 oz.	$14.31	$0.0852
Duncan Hines	12/18.9 oz.	$17.16	$0.1021
Betty Crocker	12/18.25 oz	$19.96	$0.0911
Fudge Brownie Mixes			
Jiffy	24/8oz.	$8.55	$0.0445
Pillsbury	12/21½ oz.	$14.40	$0.0558
Betty Crocker	12/19.8 oz.	$14.40	$0.0606
Gold Medal (General Mills)	18/10¼ oz	$12.44	$0.0674
Martha White	18/10¼ oz.	$13.16	$0.0713
Duncan Hines	12/23.7 oz.	$19.08	$0.0671

Source: Chelsea Milling Company, February 1999.

mixes, including an 85% share of corn muffin mixes. Jiffy brand has no lower than a one-third market share place for any individual product.

How can a single-location company with 350 employees compete with the likes of General Mills ($6 billion in revenue), which has a sophisticated marketing department and an advertising budget larger than their smaller competitor's total revenue? The Chelsea Milling Company dominates the market for boxed muffin mixes for the same reason as most cost leaders. Like most cost leaders, Jiffy brand baking mixes were the first to be produced using high-volume techniques. Although the cost leader in an industry is not always the first to market, the cost leader is often the first company to produce a product using high-volume techniques. Cost leadership is a compelling competitive advantage.

When they incorporated in 1901 as the Chelsea Milling Company, it was one of 488 gristmills in Michigan; today five mills remain, including the Chelsea Milling Company, run by Mrs. Holmes's grandson. The makers of Jiffy remain a private family-owned company.

Because high volume production provides such a strong competitive advantage, many products have been the cost leaders in their market segment for decades. Examples include Ivory soap, Campbell's soup, Coca-Cola, Tide laundry detergent, Ford pick-up trucks, and McDonald's hamburgers.

Focused Differentiation Strategies

Small companies survive (and often thrive) by choosing a tiny part of a market and making it their own. The author has twice been involved with making a major improvement in the fortunes of small companies by identifying narrow market niches that those companies would serve.

Choosing a market niche is all about efficient use of company resources. No company has the resources to be all things to all people. A company trying to sell to everyone must advertise everywhere, but a company that defines its customers as "duck hunters" only has to advertise in *Ducks Unlimited* magazine. Remember this jingle from the 1960s?

Drop in and look,
Shop from the book
Give Sears a ring
Sears has everything.

Over its history, Sears has sold automobiles, tractors, paint, clothing, sporting goods, hardware, and prefabricated homes, but they did not last as the number one company in retailing when companies like Kmart, Wal-Mart, L.L. Bean, and Land's End each successfully went after parts of Sears's domain.

Successful small companies differentiate themselves from their competition. In 1983, James E. Lozelle, President of Edgewood Tool & Manufacturing Company in Taylor, Michigan, would describe his company as a "general stamper." His company would use their stamping presses to make just about any kind of part that a customer might need to be stamped out of a coil of steel, mostly auto parts. That year, Lozelle's company had 110 employees and $7 million in sales. One of those employees, his new controller, a University of Michigan MBA and future author of a pricing strategy book, observed that their small company was likely to have problems competing in the future against the huge international conglomerates that were its competitors. The controller told him, "What we need is a niche, something that we can be better at than anyone else." Much to his credit, Lozelle saw the wisdom of this advice. "What's more," Lozelle said, after thinking it over for a few days, "if we are going to have a niche, there is only one niche that makes any sense for us: hood hinges."

Edgewood Tool manufactured only four kinds of hood hinges in 1983. They made the hood hinges for the Ford F-series pick-up truck, the Ford Ranger pick-up truck, the Ford Thunderbird/Mercury Cougar, and the Chrysler Fifth Avenue. Unlike architectural hinges, which are relatively simple affairs, the engineering for a hood hinge may be very sophisticated. Hinges need to have tight tolerances to prevent the hood from hitting and damaging the quarter panels. A hood hinge may need to have a gooseneck shape to accommodate mounting surfaces on the hood and the firewall, which may be far apart. Most important, in a crash, the hood must buckle, rather than sheer the pivot points on the hinge, go through the windshield, and decapitate the driver. That would be very bad for auto sales.

Edgewood Tool grew dramatically by specializing in hinges. By 1994 it was a $70 million a year company and merged with a company of similar size to go public as Tower Automotive. Becoming a $2 billion company by 1998, there was $50 million in hinge business alone when Tower spun that part of its business off to Dura Corporation in 1998.

That controller was to prove his worth as a strategist again in 1991. Now Vice President–Finance, Lozelle sent him to evaluate a former joint venture in Windsor, Ontario, that had experienced significant losses and a 40% drop in sales. Perhaps Lozelle's rationale for sending a finance guy to Canada was "who better to deal with the bankers when liquidating a business?" The "finance guy" recognized that this company was not going to be competitive producing high-volume automotive parts anymore. However, he saw an opportunity for that company to do well in a low-volume niche. His plan for the future was to go to Ford and tell them, "We want to be your low-volume heavy truck parts supplier."

The strategy worked, and that business survives today having enjoyed a four-fold sales gain and strong profitability in the following 7 years.

The lesson in these stories is simple. Strategic success depends on becoming better than anyone else at doing something that customers want. Each company must figure out what it is going to be really good at and concentrate its resources on that goal. The niche occupied by a small company may be so miniscule that the market leader does not even know that the niche exists. Being the very best at doing one narrowly focused skill makes the issue of price secondary if customers really need those skills.

To quote Jerry Garcia, the late leader of The Grateful Dead: "You do not merely want to be considered just the best of the best. You want to be considered the only ones who do what you do."[11]

LEAN COMPETITION

Although cost leadership provides a competitive advantage, businesses should avoid competing on price. Even for the winner, price competition can be very costly. For this reason, it is common to see competing companies set their published prices exactly the same as those of their competition. In retailing, products are commonly sold at price points. Thus, men's shirts might be found at $24, $29, $34, or $39. Higher end retailers often price their products in whole dollars, whereas other retailers commonly append 95 or 99 cents to their prices. Although a shirt might be priced at $29.00, $29.95, or $29.99, it would be unusual to see one priced at any price that was not a common price point.

Robin Cooper described his studies of competition in *When Lean Enterprises Collide*.[12] In the 20 Japanese companies that he studied, Cooper found that each of the companies and all of their competitors had quality levels that exceeded the expectations of their customers. Accordingly, he concluded that in the industries represented, competition did not occur based on quality. Because these companies' products were sold at specific price points, he concluded that real competition was not based on price or quality but based on the features and functionality that was available at a particular price point. In his observation, competition was not based on who had the lowest price, but which product provided the best features at $29.95.

In this environment, Cooper observes, a new product feature may provide a competitive advantage. These advantages were usually short-lived because companies are quick to imitate the newest and best features of their competitors. Therefore, no competitive advantage is sustainable for very long. It was also rare, he observed, for new product features to be a surprise to competitors at the time of introduction. The driver's side sliding door on Chrysler minivans is an example of a feature that provided a temporary competitive advantage. Chrysler was the only company to offer this feature for almost 2 years and enjoyed strong sales because of it. Other minivan manufacturers were slow to react, not because they lacked forewarning of this innovation, but because they did not think that it would be a big selling feature. Even Chrysler was caught by surprise by the demand for the driver's side sliding door. Initially thinking that about 20% of the market would want this feature, they were surprised when some 80% of all new minivans were sold this way.

Informal networks exist within industries, such as between former college classmates that cause news of innovations to travel very quickly. Thus, the company with the latest and greatest features available at a particular price point will have the advantage in sales at any given time. Cooper concluded, therefore, that the key to competitiveness is how fast a company can innovate and how quickly a company can adapt the latest innovations of competitors.

STRATEGY OF COMPETITIVE BIDDING

Many companies competitively bid for all or most of their sales. Most companies can point to several other companies who do similar work. There are literally thousands of companies in North America who make metal stampings, provide accounting services, build commercial buildings, or produce plastic injection molded parts. Service businesses come in all shapes and sizes, from giant accounting firms to one-person house-painting companies. A cursory study of economics might lead a seller to conclude that price is everything in a competitive bid situation.

The buyer would seem to have the upper hand in negotiation with so many potential vendors from which to choose. After all, the buyer could request many qualified vendors to quote on their business and simply select the vendor with the lowest price. However, the problem with asking lots of businesses to bid on your work is that vendors perform a cost–benefit analysis in their heads, if not on paper, to determine whether it is worth the effort to even prepare a quote. This analysis examines the number of vendors known to be quoting, the cost of preparing a proposal, and the likelihood of getting the work at a good price. Those vendors that are best at what they do are busy all of the time. Companies that have more work than they know what to do with have limited time to respond to any proposal that does not have a reasonable chance of generating a good profit. Faced with many competitors, some vendors will decline to even prepare a proposal when faced with a strong probability that it will be a wasted effort. When faced with many competitors, those companies who prepare a proposal may give the proposal process only the briefest effort, and the list of companies submitting a bid may consist of only underqualified vendors who lack enough work to gainfully occupy their time.

Attempting to compete based on price is generally only an effective strategy if a company is the low-cost producer. However, if it were always true that the low-cost producer would win all bids, then one company should consistently come out on top. If the low-cost producer always won every bid, then there would be little point for the other companies to waste their time submitting a bid. In the real world, there are often marked differences between the competitive bids of different vendors. These differences may appear to occur for no rational reason. It is very normal for a 20% spread to exist between high and low bids, and 100% spreads between bidders are not all that unusual.

There are some common reasons for the differences in competitive bids. One is a difference in methods used to produce the product. Some companies are better suited than others for doing specific tasks and thus their costs may be lower. Another difference may be the workload at the time of the quote. One bidder may have all the work that they can handle, thus bidding high to assure a really good profitability if they should get work that they do not really need. Another bidder may be short of work, bidding low to increase their chances of getting the work. Companies that are short of work often bid below their full costs in order to fill excess capacity.

Another major reason that competitive bids may be far apart is differences in quoting and costing methods. Many companies use estimating methods that do not accurately reflect their real costs. Using inaccurate cost accounting data can have the disastrous result that the company wins lots of big, new contracts priced well below cost. The author of this book was personally involved in trying to turn around one manufacturing company whose chief executive officer had personally prepared a large number of quotes priced at only 50% of full cost. Rather than improve his company's profitability with increasing sales, he tripled the already rapid rate at which the company was losing money.

Accountants have long known that traditional methods of cost accounting lead to cost distortions in many circumstances. Today, we know that traditional cost accounting provides a result that is a good approximation much of the time, but is grossly inaccurate often enough to cause real problems for companies that use those costs as a basis for pricing.

The accuracy of traditional cost accounting can be thought of in terms of a normal distribution. On average, traditional cost accounting provides a number that is exactly the same as "real" costs. Perhaps 70% of the time, traditional costs are close to real costs. It is the 15% of the time that traditional cost accounting is too high and the 15% of the time that traditional cost is too low that gets companies in trouble.

Traditional cost accounting methods tend to undervalue complex and low volume "bad" jobs while overvaluing easy, high-volume "good" jobs. Accordingly, any company that has a better handle on its real costs, through activity-based costing, would have a competitive advantage. That competitive advantage is often sizable enough to offset the cost differential of the low-cost producer.

A company that is not the low cost producer may effectively compete based on price when it has a superior knowledge of its real costs. This can occur when a cost leader fails to capitalize on its cost advantage through the failures of traditional cost accounting. Because traditional accounting methods produce distortions for products that are not "average," a company that does not know its real costs often adds "fudge factors" to its pricing calculations to make up for the deficiencies of its accounting systems. These fudge factors have the effect of raising the company's quoted price and eliminating any price advantage that the company may have. Traditional cost accounting tends to assign too much cost to easy or high-volume products and not enough costs to difficult or low-volume products. As a result, these companies overprice the "good" work and underprice the "bad" work, leaving an opportunity for smaller competitors who know their real cost to grab the best work by offering a lower price.

Companies using traditional cost accounting are at a terrible disadvantage when competing with companies using activity-based pricing. Because they most often win "bad" lower volume and complex work, losing money at it, their cost structure gets progressively worse without them even understanding what is happening. Activity-based pricing can provide a strong competitive advantage.

SUMMARY

The key points described in this chapter are listed below:

1. Many companies seek low costs and high market share as a means of achieving superior financial return, even though there are many examples of high–market share/low-profit companies.
2. The word *strategy* originally meant the positioning of troops before a battle, specifically distinguished from *tactics,* which is the maneuvering of troops after a battle begins. Business strategy is best described as positioning the company in terms of its customers, competitors, core competencies, technologies used, geographic areas served, and other factors that allow the company to focus its resources effectively on serving its customers.
3. It is often difficult to know in advance when an operational consideration can have important strategic implications.
4. Michael Porter contends that the only sources of competitive advantage are low cost and differentiation.
5. If products are equivalent, customers will choose a product that costs less because it allows them to spend their limited resources on other things.
6. Customers may choose a differentiated product at a higher price because it is better suited to their particular needs.
7. Robin Cooper describes competition in terms of the "survival triplet":
   - Price

- Quality
- Functionality

Because many products are sold at price points and quality exceeds customer expectations, Cooper maintains that most competition is based on the functionality that products offer at a particular price point. Cooper calls this environment lean competition.

8. Lean competition is based on which company has the best features at a particular price point. The most important factor in this environment is how fast a company can innovate.

9. Porter identifies these generic competitive strategies:

- Cost leadership
- Differentiation
- Focus
  - Cost Focus
  - Differentiation Focus

10. Companies are often unaware of the real profitability of their various products and customers. This is illustrated by the often widespread differences found in competitive bid situations. A company that is not the low cost producer may gain a competitive advantage through superior cost information using activity-based costing.

NOTES

1. Michael E. Porter, *Competitive Advantage* (New York: Free Press, 1985).
2. Frederick W. Taylor, *The Principles of Scientific Management* (New York: Harper & Row, 1913).
3. H. Igor Ansoff, *Corporate Strategy* (New York: McGraw-Hill, 1965).
4. Henry Mintzberg, *The Rise and Fall of Strategic Planning* (New York: Free Press, 1994), p. 187.
5. Ibid.
6. Norman Schwartzkoff, Cable News Network, January 15, 1991.
7. Robin Cooper, *When Lean Enterprises Collide* (Boston: Harvard Business School Press, 1995), p. 14.
8. For background about the Model T and its effect on competitors, see Ed Cray, *Chrome Colossus—General Motors and Its Times* (New York: McGraw-Hill, 1980), pp. 195–208.

9. All airfares mentioned here are from *www.Travelocity.com,* September 23, 2000.
10. Charles Darwin, *The Origin of Species* (1859, reprinted by Prometheus Books, New York).
11. As quoted by Tom Peters, *Lessons in Leadership* Conference at Dearborn, Michigan, January 21, 1997.
12. Robin Cooper, *When Lean Enterprises Collide* (Boston: Harvard Business School Press, 1995).

4

UNDERSTANDING PRICING STRATEGY

Smart companies that are not in a cost leadership position pursue some type of differentiation strategy.

STRATEGY CONSIDERATIONS

The economic laws of supply and demand would suggest that a company should charge as high a price for its products as the market will bear. This strategy might be particularly tempting when the company has a new, unique product that is available from no one else. The trouble with this strategy is that in the absence of *barriers to entry*, other companies will also be motivated to enter the market, seeking to earn high profits on any product that can be produced and sold at a high premium over cost.

Many strategic considerations come into play in determining price. These include:

- Customers
    - Customer perceptions of value
    - Elasticity of demand
- Cost
    - Cost structure
    - Effect of volume on cost
    - Expected learning curve effects
- Competition
    - Current competition
    - Potential for future competition

- Substitutes for the product
    - Features and usefulness of substitutes
    - Pricing of substitutes
- Legal and ethical constraints

Pricing strategies are situation specific. A strategy that works well in one situation may completely fail in another. This chapter will discuss various pricing strategies and when they are most appropriate.

ETHICS OF PRICING

> The man who holds that every human right is secondary to his profit must now give way to the advocate of human welfare.
>
> Theodore Roosevelt[1]

Each society has its own view of the ethics of pricing. These views have shifted with the passing of time. Each society has its own concept of a "fair" price and the circumstances that must exist for the price to be fair. In *The Strategy and Tactics of Pricing*, Thomas Nagle and Reed Holden[2] described five levels of ethical constraint on pricing as shown in Exhibit 4.1.

Exhibit 4.1 Ethical constraints on pricing

Level	The Exchange is Ethical When:	Implication/Proscription
1.	Price is paid voluntarily.	"Let the buyer beware."
2.	Price is based on equal information.	No sales without full disclosure.
3.	Price does not exploit the buyer's "essential needs."	No "excessive" profits on essentials such as life-saving pharmaceuticals.
4.	Price is justified by costs.	No segmented pricing based on value. No excessive profits based on shortages, even for nonessential products.
5.	Price provides equal access to goods regardless of one's ability to pay the price.	No exchange for personal gain. Give as able and receive as needed.

Source: Adapted from *The Strategy and Tactics of Pricing* by Nagle and Holden. Copyright © 1995. Reprinted by permission of Pearson Education, Inc., Upper Saddle River, NJ 07458.

Most people would place some ethical limits on pricing. The first level of ethical constraint is that the exchange between two parties is voluntary. Any price is too high if sellers have the ability to force their price on an unwilling buyer. Today's society rejects out of hand monopoly powers that deny consumers a choice of products. In the nineteenth century some companies in the United States and Europe used secret agreements and predatory pricing tactics to eliminate their competitors. Legislation such as the Sherman Antitrust Act in the United States now prevents companies from obtaining monopoly powers, although the 2000 case involving price fixing by the auction houses of Christy's and Sotheby's proves that some companies still attempt to gain an unfair pricing advantage through illegal acts. Even when the seller is the government itself, people condemn government's monopoly power to charge for services through taxation unless those people feel that they have the power to influence the terms of the relationship with the government through the ballot box. The cry of the American Revolution, "Taxation without representation is tyranny!" illustrates this concept.

The second level of ethical constraint is that the buyer and seller both share equal knowledge about the product to be exchanged. "Let the buyer beware" once characterized commercial law in much of the world. Unscrupulous sellers could once make false claims of their product's benefits, sometimes selling unwholesome or dangerous products to unsuspecting consumers. A common principle of fairness today is that the buyer has access to truthful information about the product. Today, making false claims about a product or withholding relevant information about a product is considered fraud. Consumers in the United States are protected from false claims and unequal information by legislation such as the Pure Food and Drug Act.

A third level of ethical constraint is that sellers shall not profit from other people's adversity. This ethical constraint limits the seller's profit on "necessities." Examples of this principle would include the pricing of life-saving drugs, generators during a power outage, or even of bottled water during a hot baseball game. Sometimes this ethical constraint limits the seller to a fair profit, at other times no profit at all. Although this ethical constraint usually lacks the force of law, breaking this basic principle will frequently generate an outcry from buyers. A store that raises prices during a weather emergency risks creating enormous bad will with their customers.

A basic concept of fairness is that profits bear a reasonable relationship to the cost of producing a product or service. Although the third ethical constraint limits profits on necessities, the fourth ethical constraint carries the third ethical constraint to all products. This ethical constraint evaluates fair profit from the perspective of the cost of the inputs such as labor, materials, and rent that are required to make the product. From this viewpoint, a fair price for a product would resemble the *natural price* described by Adam Smith. Service businesses sometimes have to deal with the perception that their hourly rates are priced unfairly high. Few business people think that their law firm is reasonably priced, contributing to the perception by many people that lawyers are unethical.

A second part of this fourth ethical constraint is that all customers are charged the same amount for the same product. A common marketing strategy is to segment a market by offering variations on a product to different market segments at different prices. This ethical constraint views segment pricing as fair and permissible only in situations where there are real differences in the costs of serving different market segments.

The fifth most restrictive level of ethical constraint was once a basic part of the belief systems of the majority of the people in the world. In this concept of fairness, it is immoral to profit from making a sale. Furthermore, according to the philosophy of communism, each person should give according to their abilities and receive according to their needs. Today this concept of fairness is quickly fading as history has taught the world that the profit motive is a desirable and necessary creator of value for society.

PRICING LAW IN THE UNITED STATES

Development of National Commerce

Prior to the development of railroads, transportation of manufactured goods was slow and inefficient. Shipment of manufactured goods from the Northeast to ports along the Atlantic coast was relatively fast and efficient, but shipment to the interior of the country over narrow, primitive roads was slow and inefficient. The practical matter of transportation limited commerce to smaller localized industries. The Erie Canal opened the Great Lakes region to settlement and commerce from the East, but it was not until the age of the railroad that large, national companies began to define commerce in the United States.

Railroads radically changed the face of American business in the nineteenth century. Railroads allowed goods to be efficiently transported long distances, changing basic business economics and providing scale economies that encouraged increasingly larger businesses to develop.

The railroads and the bankers that often owned them wielded enormous power over commerce. Railroads often had monopoly power over transportation services to or from any particular location, and they strengthened their grip on commerce by developing arrangements of interlocking ownership and corporate directorship designed to limit competition and control prices. The interlocking business arrangements were often accomplished through *trusts*. In this arrangement, the owners of the major companies in an industry would give their stock and voting rights to the directors of a trust in exchange for trust certificates and regular dividends. The result was that the companies controlled by the trust had monopoly powers. These trusts used unethical tactics to maintain their dominant market positions, often to the detriment of their customers as well as their competitors. Depressions in the 1870s and 1880s caused blame to be focused on the trusts, and by the election of 1888 public outcry caused both American political parties to unite to limit monopoly powers.

The Sherman Antitrust Act

The Sherman Antitrust Act of 1890 (Sherman Act) might have been called the Sherman Antimonopoly Act had the large business combinations of that time been organized in a different manner. The Sherman Act made it illegal to conspire to restrain commerce or to monopolize trade. Most of the trusts simply changed their legal structure to corporations. Because these corporations dominated their industries, there was no longer a need to *conspire* to set prices. The Justice Department lost six of the first seven antitrust cases that they prosecuted, proving that the law was difficult to enforce.

Today the Sherman Act is most often used to prevent a large firm from gaining market share through acquisition. In recent years, the Justice Department has used the Sherman Act to control consolidation of the airline industry. Proposed acquisitions by United and American Airlines have been scrutinized and impeded, and Northwest Airlines was forced to divest shares of Continental. Microsoft, the world's leading software producer, has been repeatedly the subject of Sherman Act scrutiny. When Microsoft, the maker of the number 2 personal financial software MS Money, sought to purchase Intuit, the maker of the industry-leading Quicken personal finance software, the threat of a Justice Department review caused Microsoft to abandon the proposed acquisition.[3]

Later Pricing Legislation

Antimonopoly efforts gained teeth during the 1901 to 1909 administration of Theodore Roosevelt, who secured passage of the Hepburn Act in 1906 that prevented abuses in railroad shipping rates. Although known as a "trust buster," Roosevelt attempted to provide both business and consumers a "square deal." The Pure Food and Drug Act, which was passed during his administration, provided consumers protection against adulterated food and helped change the previous "buyer beware" market ethic.

Because the courts seemed unwilling to use the Sherman Act to prevent what were widely regarded as widespread unfair business practices, Congress enacted a series of legislation over the next few decades to police competition and pricing practices.

The Federal Trade Commission (FTC) was established in 1914 by an act that empowered the FTC to prevent "unfair methods of competition in commerce." The Clayton Act, in the same year, eliminated a list of specific business practices that included interlocking directorships among competitors and the now-prohibited practice of forcing a consumer to purchase one product when buying another. This law was later used to prevent phone companies from requiring their subscribers to rent phones from the company.

The 1936 Robinson-Patman Act was popularly known as the "Chain Store Act" because it protected "mom and pop" retailers from the purchasing power of large chain retailers. The Robinson-Patman Act targeted companies that sold to chain stores, requiring that sellers must charge all customers *in commerce* the same price except:

- To meet a competitive price.
- When there is a cost justification for differential pricing.

Today, the companies that are most often litigated under the Robinson-Patman Act are manufacturing companies that are suppliers to "big box" retailers that give deep discounts to high-volume customers such as Wal-Mart, Kmart, Best Buy, Borders, or Office Max. These suits are often brought by groups of small retailers that lose business when these large retailers open up nearby. Small booksellers recently used the Robinson-Patman Act to attack pricing arrangements with large booksellers Barnes & Noble and Borders Books.

Manufacturers sued under the Robinson-Patman Act have a choice of two defenses. The meeting-the-competition defense applies when a manufacturer learns from one of its customers that a competitor is offering the customer a better price. The manufacturer, if it reasonably believes the customer's information, is entitled to meet the competitor's price, even if the customer's assertion later proves to be false. This exception to the law is designed to allow a company to meet specific competitive threats relating to a single customer and cannot be used to justify overall discriminatory pricing schemes.

Attorney Carl A. Person[4] notes that most small companies, when thinking about discriminatory pricing schemes, assume that volume discounts are lawful because they are cost based. He says that few companies sued under the Robinson-Patman Act use the cost justification defense because they are unable to justify 100% of the discriminatory discount. The treble-damage penalties provided under the Robinson-Patman Act can be just as much when defendants can justify part of the difference as when they can justify none of it. The burden of proof in a price-discrimination lawsuit is on the defendant. Because the seller must show that it carefully studied its cost *before* arriving at a price differential, this requirement prevents many sellers from using the cost justification defense.

Because volume price breaks are a common business custom, what can companies do to protect themselves against Robinson-Patman Act litigation? For a company that is not the market leader, one obvious approach is to document the pricing schedules of the market leaders. As long as a company's pricing schedules are not more discriminatory than the market leaders, this should afford a good level of protection. Perhaps a better approach is to develop pricing schedules that are cost based. Traditional cost accounting will not work well for this exercise because it essentially treats all overhead costs as variable and unit based. When a cost defense is used, the court must be convinced that the categorization of costs is reasonable. In the case of *American Can v. Bruce's Juices*, the court ruled for the plaintiff because American Can's costs were "tainted with the inherent vice of too broad averaging." [5] The ideal tool to support cost differentials is activity-based costing (ABC). Activity-based costing can recognize differences in cost at the market, customer, batch, and order level. The use of ABC for the development of pricing will be explored in Chapter 7.

What if ABC shows that the commonly accepted volume discount schedules of your industry do not reflect the real economics of your business? The author's experience in auto parts, for instance, shows that automotive parts suppliers routinely underprice low-volume parts and overprice high-volume products. Therefore, a company that uses activity-based pricing would have a competitive advantage in obtaining desirable, high-volume work when competing against a company using traditional cost accounting.

Interestingly, Carl Person's experience with companies selling to large retailers indicates that the opposite is true. He found that manufacturers often underprice high volume sales to big box retailers. He makes a living litigating on behalf of small retailers who are being charged an unjustified differential from the price paid by their larger competitors. If a company is in an industry where the competition is giving large customers discounts that are unwarranted by cost, the logical strategy is to target sales to the smaller retailers that the competitor is overcharging.

There is no violation of the Robinson-Patman Act if a business charges different prices to customers who are not *in commerce* (i.e., businesses). Many businesses that sell to consumers such as restaurants, theaters, or other entertainment venues often differentiate in their pricing. Ski resorts often customize their lift ticket prices according to age. There may be one rate for skiers between ages 25 and 55, and a lower rate for senior citizens. Students 12 to 25 may receive a discounted rate, children 5 to 11 a lower rate still. Children under 5 may ski at no charge at all. Many bars have "ladies night" where there is no cover charge for women or women receive their drinks at a discount. Because pricing law covers only sales to customers who are in commerce, such price discrimination is perfectly legal. Customized pricing by age and sex still provides an opportunity for legal trouble if the customers who receive a preferential price are not a protected group under civil rights law. Providing a discounted drink price on "men's night" that is not available to women would be an invitation for a lawsuit.

Case Law

Much of the law governing pricing today comes from precedent established in court rulings in individual cases. Although the following paragraphs will attempt to provide an overview of the major rules that case law provides, a thorough discussion of this topic is beyond the scope of this book. Any company that seeks to explore the fringes of acceptable pricing practice should consult an attorney who specializes in this area.

Price Fixing

The pricing practice most likely to result in an unfavorable court ruling is conferring with a competitor to obtain an explicit agreement about price. The courts have long held this practice, known as "price fixing," as unacceptable when companies with a large market share collude to control market price. The exchange of information alone is not illegal, per se. Courts have allowed the exchange of pricing information when it was to bring about uniformity in pricing through the operation of economic law. Indeed, when small competitors exchange pricing information in a sparsely concentrated market, the exchange may be viewed as pro-competitive.

Differential Pricing

Pricing law prohibits discrimination in price for goods of like grade and quality. This restriction has been interpreted very narrowly, including only tangible goods and not services. A seller may produce goods that are only slightly different and meet the requirements of the law. In one case Borden sold identical milk under both the Borden brand and a private label. The court held that because the consumer valued the Borden brand more than the private label and was willing to pay a premium price for the Borden brand, the price differential was therefore legal.[6]

Predation

Predation is a strategy whereby a firm sets its price very low in an attempt to discipline a competitor or drive the competitor from the market altogether. Unlike a cost leadership strategy whereby a company uses its superior cost structure to gain market share, a predatory price is a price that is set below a level that would provide an adequate financial return for the predator. Although the predatory price hurts the predator, the intent of the strategy is to hurt the competitor even more.

Predatory pricing cases usually involve a national company that attempts to weaken a strong competitor in a local geographic market. The predator will lower the price in one geographic area but not in others. Predatory pricing strategies are rarely attempted and are rarely successful. A successful predator must have the financial resources to be able to sustain a predatory price for a long period of time. Even if one competitor is eliminated, the predator may be so weakened itself as to be vulnerable to a competitive challenge by yet another firm. In recent years the courts have taken the general stance that competition is good, making predatory claims very difficult to win. Recent court cases have relied heavily on analysis of the relationship between cost and price. A defense solidly grounded in ABC data would make a very convincing argument if it showed that the incremental volume associated with a price decrease was cost justified.

PRICE-BASED COMPETITION

Having the best price can provide a competitive advantage. If two products are perceived to be the same, a rational buyer will choose the product that has the lowest price. After all, paying a lower price will enable buyers to conserve their resources, which will allow them to save or have additional resources to buy other things. All buyers have limited resources. Even the U.S. government has far less money than Congress has uses for tax money.

Price is a signal of value. A buyer's perception of value may be affected by brand name, packaging, previous purchasing experiences, and many other factors. Price will be more important in signaling value when a customer has little or no experience with a product category. A customer planning a meal for a dinner party is more likely to choose a more expensive brand of an unfamiliar ingredient rather than compromise the quality of the meal. Experienced customers are better able to evaluate product value and make price–value judgments. Buyers are more likely to choose the lower priced item if they are knowledgeable and perceive the lower priced item to be at least as good in quality and functionality.

A company that has a lower cost structure than its competitors may effectively compete based on cost. Cost leadership is usually associated with a company that is the high-volume producer of a product. Almost any product in any business has some portion of costs that are fixed and independent of volume. Sometimes those fixed costs are very large; sometimes those fixed costs are very small. Product development costs are a common example of fixed costs. Pharmaceutical companies invest huge sums of money to develop each drug, rejecting far more "molecules" than they are ever able to market. Manufacturing companies must invest in molds or tooling for the products that they make. Even an ice cream store must invest in a soft serve machine before it can sell its first chocolate-vanilla twist cone. Because fixed costs are the price of admission to an industry, the higher the fixed cost, the bigger the advantage the high-volume producer enjoys.

Suppose that two companies dominate an industry for a product that normally sells for $99. Company A has a 40% market share, and Company B has a 20% market share. Their cost structure is shown in Exhibit 4.2. Both companies are earning a good return on sales. Because buyers should prefer a lower priced product, Company B might be tempted to try to increase its market share by decreasing its price to $95. This strategy might work if Company A maintained its $99 price. However, few market leaders will so willingly cede market share. One response that Company A might make is to lower its price to $95 as well, as shown in Exhibit 4.3. The result of this maneuver would be that both companies would have significantly reduced profits.

Either company might retaliate with a further price reduction as shown in Exhibit 4.4. At $90, Company A's profit would have dropped by 64%, but it would still have profits of 6% of sales. Company B's profits would be entirely gone. Because the relative price of the product is the same for each company, neither company has gained any market share. Market-dominant Company A has been hurt far less than Company B, but the only real winner is the buyer who now enjoys a lower price as a result of the price war.

Attempting to gain market share based on price does not make sense for a company that is not the cost leader. Company B is in a weaker position. Having the

Exhibit 4.2 Market share and profitability before price competition

	Company A	Company B	
Market share	40%	20%	
Unit sales	4,000,000	2,000,000	
Revenue	396,000,000	198,000,000	Selling price $99/unit
Fixed costs	20,000,000	20,000,000	5-year product life with $100 million in fixed cost
Variable cost	320,000,000	160,000,000	Variable costs $60/unit
Profit	56,000,000	18,000,000	
Percentage of revenue	14%	9%	

Note: Profitability for two market-leading companies before Company B lowers its price.

Exhibit 4.3 Market share and profitability after a price decrease

	Company A	Company B	
Market share	40%	20%	
Unit sales	4,000,000	2,000,000	
Revenue	380,000,000	190,000,000	Selling price $95/unit
Fixed costs	20,000,000	20,000,000	5-year product life with $100 million in fixed cost
Variable cost	320,000,000	160,000,000	Variable costs $60/unit
Profit	40,000,000	10,000,000	
Percentage of revenue	11%	5%	
Decrease in profits	16,000,000	8,000,000	
Percentage decrease in profits	29%	44%	

Note: Company B attempts to gain market share by lowering price. Company A responds by also reducing price. As a result, Company B does not gain market share and both companies have a substantial decrease in profits.

Exhibit 4.4 The results of a price war

	Company A	Company B	
Market share	40%	20%	
Unit sales	4,000,000	2,000,000	
Revenue	360,000,000	180,000,000	Selling price $90/unit
Fixed costs	20,000,000	20,000,000	5-year product life with $100 million in fixed cost
Variable cost	320,000,000	160,000,000	Variable costs $60/unit
Profit	20,000,000	—	
Percentage of revenue	6%	0%	
Decrease in profits	36,000,000	18,000,000	
Percentage decrease in profits	64%	100%	

Note: If either company responds further by decreasing price again, both companies suffer without gaining market share. In this case, Company B's profit has been entirely eliminated.

lower cost structure, Company A has the ability to price its product at a level that is unprofitable for Company B. If buyers perceive no difference between the products of these two companies, Company A has the ability to hurt its competitor badly anytime it chooses. This is not an enviable position for Company B, which is the reason that smart companies that are not in a cost leadership position pursue some type of differentiation strategy. Presented with a selection of differentiated products, some buyers will be willing to pay more for the product features that match their own preferences.

When buyers perceive real differences between products, competition becomes less direct. Some buyers may be willing to pay $99 for Company B's product, even if a similar product is available from Company A for $95. In "smart" industries, each company stakes out its own territory, avoiding direct competition with the core businesses of the other major players in the industry. In smart industries, competition tends to be based on product features and functions rather than based on price. Although companies may compete fiercely around the periphery of their chosen market segment, smart competitors avoid attacking the core business of a major competitor.

The members of the airline industry in the United States have had particular problems differentiating their services from one another. Southwest Airlines is the only major U.S. airline that has successfully differentiated its service. Southwest is known for its no-frills boarding process, the quirky banter of the flight attendants, and running its airline like a reliable European train. All of the other airlines use similar airplanes, provide the same choice of pretzels or peanuts to eat, have the same requirements about carry-on luggage, offer similar frequent flyer programs, and recite the same canned safety instructions at the beginning of the flight.

The hub system has allowed the major airlines to delineate their core markets geographically, limiting direct competition. Each of the 10 major airlines operates one or more hubs from which their operations radiate. With Chicago's O'Hare Airport the most notable exception, each major airport is generally the hub to only one major airline. A table of major airline hubs is shown in Exhibit 4.5. Most flights begin, end, or pass through one of these hubs. Sometimes an airline will completely dominate service at its hub. For example, Northwest Airlines flies some 75% of all flights out of Detroit Metro Airport. Because the hub airlines offer the most choices of flights from the hub city, flyers will most likely find a flight that fits their time schedule by flying on the airline that has a hub at their city of origin or their destination city.

For example, a traveler flying from Dallas to Minneapolis would most likely choose American Airlines or Northwest Airlines because direct flights are available with a choice of departure times. American Airlines maintains a hub in Dallas, and Northwest is headquartered in Minneapolis. A round-trip ticket on either of these airlines is $253.50 with a 2-week advance purchase.[7] Travelers flying between these destinations have a choice of spending slightly less to fly on lesser known airlines such as Sun Country, Vanguard, or American Trans Air. They can

Exhibit 4.5 Major airline hub airports

Airline	Hub Cities
Alaska Air	Anchorage, Seattle
American	Chicago, Dallas (DFW), Miami
America West	Columbus, Phoenix
Continental	Cleveland, Houston, Newark
Delta	Atlanta, Cincinnati, Salt Lake City
Northwest	Detroit, Memphis, Minneapolis
Southwest	Dallas (LUV)
TWA	St. Louis
United	Chicago, Denver, Washington (Dulles)
U.S. Air	Charlotte, Philadelphia, Pittsburgh

Note: The companies in the airline industry have largely been unable to differentiate their services from their competitors in the eyes of their customers. The hub and spoke system has reduced airlines' costs while reducing direct competition.

also spend $50 less and fly United Airlines with a stopover in Chicago or Denver. The $50 difference represents the price of the convenience of a direct flight or the perceived superiority of flying a better known airline.

Hub strategy also affects pricing at smaller, nonhub airports. High portions of travelers flying from a spoke into a hub airport make a connection and fly elsewhere out of that hub. Airfare pricing schemes provide a lower fare if all of the flight segments are purchased together. By providing a cheaper fare when four flight segments are bundled together, the airline encourages customers to fly its entire itinerary with the same airline.

Geographic specialization makes a lot of sense. By operating flights out of a few major airports, the airlines can significantly improve the cost efficiency of their ground operations. This scheme has allowed the airlines to minimize the competitive damage that they do to each other in an industry where customers heavily price shop.

Companies that pursue a differentiation strategy do not necessarily always have a higher price than the market in general. A focused strategy may allow a company to pursue a cost leadership strategy in a narrowly defined portion of the market. Red Lobster is not the least expensive place to go to dinner. Denny's, Shoney's, Big Boy, and others are more cheaply priced. Compared with other seafood restaurants, however, Red Lobster is inexpensively priced. The key is specialization. By avoiding competition with Outback, Lone Star, Ruby Tuesdays, and Bennigan's, Red Lobster has endured in its selected niche.

In some industries, particularly for products that are sold business-to-consumer, pricing is public information and visible for all to see. Pricing of consumer goods is readily available in newspapers, catalogs, the Internet, or by visiting retail stores.

Consumer goods are particularly susceptible to open market forces that provide pricing feedback through each day's sales reports. Suppose that the two major companies in an industry are Company A, which uses ABC, and Company T, which uses traditional cost accounting. Company A has a reasonably good knowledge of its costs but Company T is using cost data that is significantly high or low for 30% of its products. Traditional cost accounting tends to underassign costs to low-volume products and overassign costs to high-volume products. This will cause Company T's cost reports to show that low-volume products cost less than they really do and high volume products cost more than they really do.

In a business that is market driven, either company might initiate price increases or decreases to the market price. If Company A tends to lead in establishing price, its tactics may perplex Company T. Because Company A knows that costs are much lower on high-volume products, it may offer these products at very attractive prices, leading Company T to conclude that it is "giving away" the business. Company T may meet the low price or cede this desirable portion of the market to Company A, thinking that it is not cost competitive. Company T may have the market to itself on the lower volume products. Understanding its costs on low-volume products, Company A may cede this portion of the market to Company T. These differences in cost information may eventually dictate that Company A deals with mass-market products and Company T sells only a low-volume niche.

In an industry where price is market driven, a company may be better off with no cost information than flawed traditional cost accounting information. In the absence of good cost information, Company T would have little choice but to set its price based on the prices of the other companies in the industry. Although Company T would remain at a competitive disadvantage compared with competitors with good cost information, the company might avoid some of the major damage that bad cost information can inflict.

Price competition in industries that use competitive bidding leaves little room for error. In an industry where sales are made through competitive bid, a company cannot wait to see what the competitors will do. A company that attempts to compete in a competitive bid environment without good cost information is at a significant competitive disadvantage. Good cost information can allow a small firm to successfully compete against an industry cost leader if that cost leader is armed with inferior cost information. This topic will be discussed in more detail throughout the remainder of this book.

MARKET SKIMMING

Occasionally, a company will introduce an innovative new product that is unlike anything that anyone has sold before. New products often incur high development costs prior to their introduction. Development costs are true fixed costs because the amount that was spent on development has usually been incurred before the first shipment is made and will be independent of the eventual sales volume. Initial production of a new product is frequently undertaken in low volumes because market acceptance may be uncertain. If many units will be sold over the life of the product, the fixed cost per unit will be very low. However, if the product never really catches on, the fixed cost per unit will be very high.

For many new products there are some customers who are willing to pay a lot of money for the product. When videotape capabilities first became available, the technology was too expensive for the budgets of most individuals. However, many businesses purchased video technology because the high price tag was justified by the benefits they received. For example, instead of flying students or instructors all around the world, accounting firms could produce videotapes and have their staff view training films in their own local offices, avoiding airfare, hotel bills, and travel time.

Market Skimming is a strategy that is frequently used when a company has a new, unique product. Market skimming is a practice whereby the price of a product is set at a relatively high rate to attract only high-end buyers who are willing to pay a premium price. New products frequently use *sequential skimming*, a strategy whereby the initial price is set relatively high but is then progressively reduced as the product matures. Many examples of this practice can be seen in the consumer electronics industry. Early cellular phones cost several thousand dollars each. In those days, only a few executives and salespeople who did a lot of business traveling had them. As more cellular phones were produced, unit costs came down, as did unit price.

Sequential skimming is the strategy of choice for new, innovative products with moderate to high barriers to entry for competitors. A logical application of this strategy is to reduce price as production capacity (of both the company and its competitors) increases. A skimming strategy might be combined with a market segmentation strategy so that as capacity increases, the company maintains a high price on the high-end version of the product, but offers lesser products at a lower price to capture a larger portion of the potential market.

The electronics industry often uses an interesting method of implementing a skimming strategy. New designs in cameras are often introduced at the highest price point in a company's product family. As a particular model loses its innovative edge, the product will be moved to a lower price point as a new camera is introduced. In this manner, the manufacturer can obtain a premium price from a high-end buyer who wants the latest features while still selling a lesser product to consumers who are more price sensitive.

Some products use a market skimming strategy to target high-end customers without the intent to lower price later. This is a form of differentiation strategy that must be accompanied by some product feature that allows the company to charge a premium price. Campbell Soup's Godiva Brand Chocolates is an example of a product that uses a skimming strategy. Godiva chocolates are able to command a premium price through a visually appealing product, expensive looking packaging, attention to quality, and smart marketing.

Market skimming is effective in two very different situations:

1. Customers who are unfamiliar with a product category often use price as an indicator of product quality and product value, sometimes choosing a product just because it costs more.
2. A portion of the market understands the benefits of the product and is willing to pay a premium price for those benefits.

Some innovative new products have a hard time gaining market acceptance because the potential customers for that product lack an understanding of the benefits that a product will provide. When demand for a product needs to be created, a market penetration strategy may be more effective.

MARKET PENETRATION

Market penetration is a strategy whereby price is initially set low in hopes of generating buyer demand (and market share) through a low price. If the market is price sensitive (demand is *elastic*), then the strategy should attract buyers, allowing for increased production volumes and lower unit costs.

Market penetration is used in several different situations. It is sometimes used for a new product to gain market visibility and market acceptance, and to build a user base. This strategy has frequently been used by Internet start-ups that will sell their products at a loss to gain market share and attract investors. The strategy also may be used for a new product as a defensive measure to prevent other companies from entering the market. This might occur when there are low barriers to entry in the market. More commonly, market penetration is a strategy used by a company that is not the market leader (a *market follower*) and is trying to increase its market share.

For a market follower, the downside of a market penetration strategy is that it may induce the market leader to lower price as well, initiating a price war. Subsequent to the 1978 deregulation of the airlines industry, many new entrants to the industry had tried to carve out a niche as a low-fare airline. The predictable result when a new airline introduces a low fare on a route that is already serviced by another airline is that the existing airline will lower its price to meet the new competition. When a brand name airline offers the same low fare as a start-up, there is little incentive for customers to switch. As a result, new entrants to the airline industry have often failed to attract enough passenger volume to become profitable.

Market penetration is generally not the strategy of choice for a market follower. Most companies attempting to compete against a larger competitor with superior financial resources should pursue a differentiation strategy, avoiding competition based on price.

LOSS LEADER (PROFIT LEADER)

A *loss leader* (also called a profit leader) is a product whose price is set low to attract buyers for the company's other products. This practice is often seen in grocery retailing. For example, by setting the price of whole frozen turkeys very low, or even giving them away with a minimum purchase, a grocery store may entice customers to do all of their Thanksgiving grocery shopping at their store. Some accounting firms view their audit department as a loss leader to attract more profitable tax, financial planning, and management advisory services work.

The effectiveness of a loss leader strategy is dependent on the customer's buying habits. For a loss leader to be effective, customers also must purchase other products from the seller. The seller must raise the price of other goods in order to sell the loss leader at a discount. Because of this, the company may not be cost effective on other products if other companies do not follow the practice. The strategy is not effective if the customer comes to the store to purchase only the product that is on sale. If the customer buys the loss leader from one store but buys the rest of the associated products from another store, the strategy is ineffective. The loss leader strategy works best for lower cost products such as groceries where the cost of shopping around is high compared with the value of the products that are being purchased.

COMPLEMENTARY PRICING

Complements are products that are normally sold alongside another product. For instance, patrons of a concert or sporting event might purchase parking, food, drinks, and souvenirs along with their tickets. The sponsor of one of these events might get $40 for a ticket, $10 per car for parking, and another $15 per person for food and drinks. Because the event itself is a fixed-cost proposition, if the event is not sold out, the sports team or concert promoter might be better off giving away the remaining tickets a few days before the event to increase the profits on food, souvenirs, and parking. The potential problems with executing this approach are:

- How to give those tickets away without angering those people who actually paid money to attend the event?
- How to prevent giving a free ticket to someone who would otherwise pay?

Elias Brothers Restaurants, formerly the franchiser of Big Boy Restaurants, was the concessionaire at the Pontiac Silverdome, the stadium used by the Detroit Lions. Both the stadium authority and the Lions were interested in maximizing food and drink sales because they each received a large cut of the concession revenue. One afternoon, an accountant who had just taken a job with Elias Brothers got a phone call from an Executive Vice President of the restaurant chain that went something like this:

VP:	John, you're involved with the Cub Scouts, aren't you?
Accountant:	Yes, I'm an Assistant Cubmaster
VP:	The Lions are playing Jacksonville Sunday. Could you use some tickets for the scouts and their families?
Accountant:	Sure, that would be great.
VP:	How many would you like?
Accountant:	How many can I have?
VP:	Could you use 500?

This was an ideal way for a losing sports team to fill up the empty seats for their preseason game. They could not give tickets away to just anybody, because the people who had paid full price for their tickets would be angry. By giving tickets to a youth group, this revenue enhancement technique upset no one and looked like a charitable contribution. Cub Scouts were an ideal recipient for these football tickets. By giving tickets to the Cub Scouts, the football team was also exposing their product to young potential buyers who might be patrons for years to come.

Complementary pricing may be used for other products as well. Companies that sell shaving equipment earn more money selling razor blades, which are purchased frequently, than by selling razors that may last a decade or more. Because not all razors and razor blades are interchangeable, the type of razor determines the type of razor blades that a customer will buy for years. In order to lock a customer into buying a particular type of razor blade, the company might give away the razor or at least sell it at a discounted price.

Some automobile dealerships view new car sales as a loss leader that attracts customers to their service business. Although the new car business is very price competitive, where customers get their cars serviced is strongly influenced by where they bought them. Although the base car itself may have a relatively low profit, options, financing, and service agreements may improve the profit on the transaction considerably.

MARKET PRICING

For some products, the market determines the price. When a company has a relatively small share of the market and is unable to differentiate its products from its competitors, the company is characteristically unable to charge any price higher than the prevailing rate in the market. Corn, wheat, soybeans, and other commodities are priced based on swings in the market caused by periodic changes in supply and demand. Although it may seem that there is little that a company can do to differentiate the agricultural products that they sell, Perdue and Tyson brand chickens, Butterball brand turkeys, and Honeybaked brand hams have proved that it can be done.

When a company feels that it has no control over its selling price, understanding the relationship between cost and price becomes particularly important. If a company produces only one product, it is easy to tell at the end of the year if that product was profitable. However, when a company sells 3, 6, 10, or 100 products, some of those products are likely to be sold at a profit and others sold at a loss.

Companies that sell more than one product are not always good at everything that they do. Sometimes one or two products provide all of the profit. Sometimes one or two products prevent any profit at all. Even in a market-pricing environment, profitability comes down to understanding the relationships between price and cost. A company that makes a "full" product line of five different variations on a product might profitably produce only two of the five items. To improve profitability, the company might discontinue producing three of the five items, devoting its resources to specializing in the high-end portion of the market. Alternately, the company might purchase items that it cannot make profitably, from another company. The two companies might reach an agreement to alter their product lines so that the two are complementary, with both companies benefiting from increased economies of scale.

In the long term, a company can choose whether or not to compete in a price-driven market. Farmers decide annually what to plant, sometimes growing corn, sometimes wheat, sometimes rye or soybeans. Withdrawal from the market for a particular product is one way of preventing a loss if the company has the ability to switch capacity to producing something more profitable. Some products have regular swings in price that seem to be due to a bad mix of psychology and economics: "*The price of corn was great last year so I'll grow even more this year and make a good profit.*" Unfortunately, when many producers think this way, the predictable result is an increase in supply, causing a corresponding decrease in price.

The basic reality of a market price environment is that the laws of supply and demand are alive and in full force. When there are many sellers and an undifferentiated product, a company must be really good at what it does to earn a superior financial return.

SATISFICING

Satisficing is a pricing strategy whereby the seller sets the price at a level that will provide an adequate financial return. Satisficing is a cost-based defensive strategy. This strategy may be used by a seller to effectively preempt competition from entering the market by establishing price at a level that will give an adequate, but not attractive profit.

Satisficing reflects the strategy used in most competitive bid situations. Except in cases where bidders collude to illegally agree on a high price, each company involved in a competitive bid is usually ignorant of the price that will be submitted by the other potential vendors. Bidders know that if they bid too high, they will lose the sale. They are also conscious that a low bid could gain the sale but cause them to lose money on the work. Accordingly, companies submitting a competitive bid normally select a price that provides only a modest profit.

The success of a satisficing strategy is dependent on good cost information. Companies with poor cost information are particularly vulnerable in a competitive industry. These ill-informed competitors will sometimes bid way too much for a contract and sometimes bid much too little. These companies inevitably flounder because they will receive none of the overbid work and the losses on a few jobs that are significantly underbid can completely erase any profits on the few jobs with modest margins. When money-losing companies seek new work, additional sales often accelerate their losses due to bad cost information.

VALUE PRICING

Value pricing refers to a strategy whereby price is set based on the value received by the customer. Although this strategy has received considerable attention in recent years, it is only effective in a limited set of circumstances. Value pricing is most effective for differentiated products in situations where there is limited competition.

Although few companies have a policy of pricing all of their products using this method, companies often adjust the price of their work up or down based on the value that the customer received. An accounting firm that has put a lot of effort into solving a client's problem may not charge the client the full rate if the client will receive less benefit from the solution than the cost of the problem. Lawyers' contingency fees are also an example of value pricing. Attorneys receive a very high fee if they provide a high benefit to their client; or they could receive nothing.

In the everyday world of product pricing, value pricing most often comes into play in situations where there is not head-to-head competition such as when a company has a unique expertise. In these situations, the customer may be willing to pay a premium price in order to obtain services that they cannot otherwise obtain. A common example of this is when an existing customer needs a special product on an emergency basis. In this situation it would be common to charge some sort of a premium for the service. Many people have noticed that their plumbing, heating, and cooling emergencies always seem to occur on holidays, weekends, or outside of normal business hours. In return for missing Sunday dinner or watching the last game of the Stanley Cup finals on TV, a plumber will charge time and a half or double-time to come abate the flood in a customer's basement.

The buyer's *value chain* is a complex set of factors relating to how the buyer uses a product. In choosing among competing products, the buyer evaluates the various trade-off that will maximize the product value and minimize the buyer's cost. The same product may be sold at considerably different prices at different places or at different times. A soft drink may sell for $0.35 (in a 12-pack) at a supermarket, but for $0.75 in a vending machine in the same shopping plaza. The same product may sell for $1.00 at a filling station across the street because the $0.65 difference in cost is not worth the effort involved in crossing the street and waiting in a supermarket checkout line.

Value pricing has its limitations. Naturally, the value that a customer receives must be higher than the product price in all situations in order for the seller to make a sale. However, even if the customer gets a huge benefit from a product, the existence of a lower priced competitor will effectively preempt a value pricing strategy. People with allergies can be miserable at certain times of the year. For an allergy sufferer, the ability to get rid of the runny nose and itchy eyes associated with hay fever may be worth any amount of money. Some allergy medicines are very expensive. If the allergy sufferer has a choice between an expensive prescription drug and an over-the-counter medication that works almost as well, the over-the-counter medication may very well get the sale.

MARKET SEGMENTATION STRATEGIES

Exhibit 4.6 shows a customer demand curve for a product. If the seller sought a single price that would maximize revenue for this product, it would be found at a price of about $350 and a sales volume of 1.5 million units generating $525 million in revenue (where the price elasticity equals 1.0). The demand curve shows that some customers would be willing to pay much more than $350 for this product but other customers would only buy the product if it sold for much less. Although high-end buyers would not knowingly pay more than someone else for an identical product, they might gladly pay for an enhanced product with better features. In theory, profit would be maximized if the company could sell a product to each customer for an amount that represented the maximum amount that the customer was willing to pay, hence the concept of product lines.

Instead of selling a single version of a product, it would be possible for the

Exhibit 4.6 Segmenting markets by price

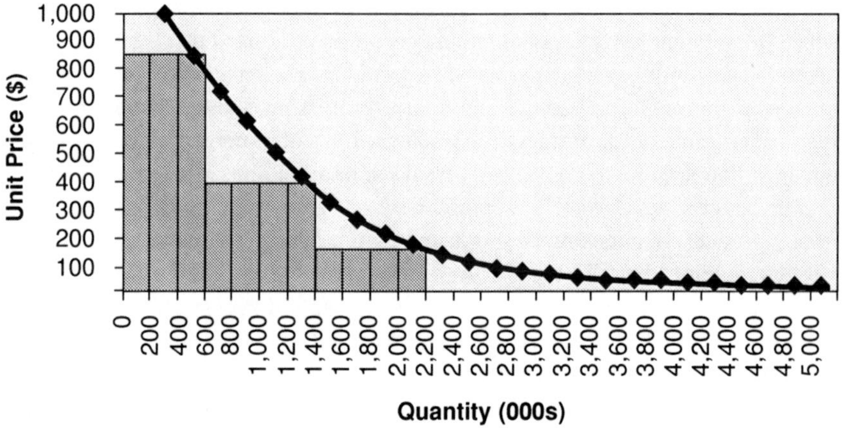

Note: Companies are able to increase revenue and profits by segmenting a market so that customers with different budgets and product requirements are able to choose differentiated products positioned at different price points. Shown here are products priced at $849, $399, and $189.

company to create three different versions of the product geared to customers with different needs and budgets. The bars on the graph in Exhibit 4.6 show the sales that could be made at price points of $849, $399, and $189. Market segmentation would allow unit sales to increase from 1.5 million to 2.4 million units and from $525 million to $1.2 billion in revenue.

Markets may be segmented in many ways. Consumer products are often sold at three levels that are categorized as "good-better-best." Customers, depending on their needs and means, have a choice between a generic serviceable product, an upgraded product with more features, or a product that is "top of the line." Buyers tend to avoid extremes in their purchasing decisions. Accordingly, a company that has two levels of choices in its product might enhance its profitability by introducing a third higher grade. Although that higher priced option may not gain substantial sales, its existence may substantially increase the average sale by increasing the portion of sales for the middle-level model.

Many examples of product families can be seen in the hotel industry. Marriott brands include Marriott, Renaissance, Courtyard, Residence Inn, and Fairfield Inn. Choice Hotels International operates under the names Comfort Inn, Quality Inn, Clarion, Sleep Inn, Rodeway Inn, Econolodge, and Mainstay Suite. Holiday Inn also offers Crown Plaza Hotels and Holiday Inn Express. These chains often put two or more hotels right next to each other, effectively segmenting a market according to traveler tastes and budgets.

In the consumer electronics industry, it is common for a company to position its "latest and greatest" product as the top of the line. As new models come out, the company will continue to sell one or more of the older models, moving them to a lower price point under the same brand name. When the venerable Hewlett-Packard 12C financial calculator was introduced in 1982, it was the expensive top-of-the-line model. Today, Hewlett-Packard has priced the 12C at $59.95, less than half of Hewlett-Packard's most expensive and feature-rich model. Hewlett-Packard provides financial calculator buyers a choice of products in four different price ranges, with the 12C and the even less expensive 10B taking the bottom two positions. This product positioning strategy provides electronics manufacturers such as Hewlett-Packard a much longer product life than if a product was specifically developed for a particular price point.

Cost is an important issue in a market segmentation strategy. Because a seller must differentiate its product in some way to segment the market, there will be costs associated with producing multiple product variations. A segmentation strategy makes sense when the scale economies of increased sales volume exceed the incremental cost associated with the increased volume and the creation of product variations.

A frequent problem in managing product line strategies is that customers often have trouble differentiating between products within a product family. General Motors long had this problem with its Buick, Oldsmobile, and Pontiac product lines, eventually deciding to eliminate the century-old Oldsmobile brand. Without clear product differences, a company merely expends funds creating product variations that the customer does not understand, appreciate, or want to pay for, thereby decreasing profit potential. At one point in the late 1990s, General Motors' stated strategy for Buick was to target the brand to women drivers, yet women never perceived anything special that Buick did to target their vehicles to them. A market segmentation strategy does little good if the customer does not perceive that the product is well suited for them.

Pricing law, and most people's concept of fairness, prohibits selling the same product to different customers at different prices. However, in some cases it may be possible to sell similar products at different prices to different groups of customers. It makes sense for a business to customize its product offerings to satisfy the varying needs and budgets of different customers.

Campbell's soup has attempted to create a high-end line of soup under the Campbell's Select name but has had little success in getting the customer to understand its strategy. These ready-to-serve soups are sold in a larger pull-top can whose label includes a large close-up picture of the product. Despite all of these efforts, the Select product line is not sufficiently different from Campbell's regular product line for most customers to be aware of the differentiation. In the meantime, Campbell's efforts to market high-end soups under their Pepperidge Farms brand name has never really gotten off the ground. This failure may relate to a lack of genuinely high-end soup products to be sold under either brand name. Customers seeking lobster bisque, bouillabaisse, or another high-end soup for their dinner party are likely to find such a product unavailable in their local supermarket.

PROVIDING VALUE TO THE CUSTOMER

Customers buy for complex and diverse reasons. Price may play an important part in the customer's buying decision, or it may be an insignificant factor. Many supermarket shoppers are familiar with the prices for only a few of the items that they purchase regularly. Some shoppers may choose a supermarket based on the prices of representative items. Other shoppers may prefer a particular store because it is clean, well lit, or otherwise visually appealing. The store that a customer chooses may be directly related to the brands or selection available or may be specifically related to a single product that the customer can find no place else.

The tangible, physical product may be a very small part of what provides value to a customer. Here is an example of a restaurant that has managed to sell much more than food and beverages.

> The Dakota Inn sits on John R. Street in Detroit, a run down area consisting of boarded up storefronts and run-down houses. Many people would not go into that part of Detroit even if someone paid them, yet this restaurant has a loyal following of regulars. Inside, the décor is vintage German beer hall, with long tables surrounded by Tyrolean style chairs. The menu is simple German fare: bratwurst, sauerkraut, weinerschnitzel, and hot potato salad. There is a pipe organ with music in the evenings, and many of the patrons sing along as they drink beer. A fixture at the Dakota Inn for many years was an elderly man known to most patrons only as Basil. Quiet and unassuming, Basil would shuffle in by himself on Saturday evenings and nod to the organist on his way to the bar. Wearing an old gray suit, he would thoughtfully take long draughts from a mug of thick German beer and listen to the music from the old country. The regulars all recognized Basil and might point him out to their novice guests. Basil and the organist knew the routine, so there was no need for words. When Basil was ready he would shuffle to the side of the organ. When this happened, the organist knew which songs to play and Basil would sing soul-warming old-world tunes in a wonderful baritone voice. Here in this little corner of the world, Basil was a celebrity.
>
> The prices at the Dakota Inn are very reasonable, but price has nothing to do with why people come here. This restaurant is not really selling beer or food or entertainment. Although some customers may come to satisfy their urge for bratwurst or German potato salad, the Dakota Inn is really in the travel business. This restaurant is selling trips to Europe. While you are inside, you can imagine that you are somewhere near the German-Austrian border. Outside, the

Alps loom high above. It is cold outside and there is a great deal of snow on the ground, but inside there is good food and music that touches the soul. Compared with a trip to Munich or Innsbruck, the Dakota Inn seems very inexpensive indeed.

Time is money. Too often companies mistakenly emphasize cost cutting in an attempt to lower their cost, when the effect is that they also lower the value that the customer receives.

The first introduction contact that many companies make with a new customer is over the telephone. Some companies present themselves very well over the telephone. A call to catalog retailer L.L. Bean is likely to be picked up on the first ring by a real person. That person is likely to be pleasant, well informed and eager to take an order. Best of all, because Bean uses caller ID to look up their customer's records, the order taker already knows who the customer is if they call from their own phone. Most companies want their customers to have a pleasant experience when they call, yet so many companies cause their customers considerable frustration and grief when they call with a question or even to place an order.

Some retailers unintentionally make it difficult for their customers to make a purchase. Many travel web sites contain sophisticated, high-resolution moving graphics such as a plane that moves across the screen. Although such features look great to a user who is equipped with a high-speed data line and a new computer with lots of memory, the home user trying to purchase an airline ticket on a 5-year-old computer across an ordinary phone line is having a frustrating experience. Slow download time greatly decreases the utility of a website. Given the choice between nice graphics and quick response time, customers would likely choose getting their business done quickly. It would be interesting to know how many potential Internet buyers simply give up rather than endure slow response time from an Internet commerce website. A slow download from a website is equivalent to being put on hold on the telephone.

Conventional business wisdom contends that it costs 10 times as much to obtain a new customer as it does to retain an existing customer. If this is true, why do so many businesses seem to go out of their way to avoid dealing with their existing customers after the sale? The customer service help lines at many companies should more accurately be labeled customer abuse lines because of the frustrating process that customers must go through to get their questions answered. The offenders include companies of all sizes in many industries. When customers have trouble reaching a real live customer service representative, those customers usually feel like they are being ignored. For many people, nothing makes them angry faster than being ignored. When a customer is angry, there may be no amount of discount to get them to buy from the offending company again.

The critical success factors for a business depend on its market strategy. Two seemingly identical businesses may be competing for very different customers using very different strategies. Here is the story of how a small town restaurant-bar has differentiated itself from its better situated competitor a block away.

> Hidden away on a side street in Albion, Michigan is Charlie's Tavern. Like many Michigan bars, Charlie's is long and narrow with knotty pine paneling on walls that are darkened from decades of cigarette smoke. In one corner is an early 1980s vintage Pac-Man video game that still works. If someone had been away from Charlie's for 20 years and returned for a visit, they might not notice any change other than a few more sports mementos hung on the walls and the addition of a big screen TV.
>
> A block away, situated in the middle of downtown, Cascarelli's has a better location and is far less crowded for lunch. Most people would also concede that Cascarelli's also has better food, yet at lunch time on any weekday, business is so good at Charlie's that there are always a couple of place settings ready on the Pac-man in case tables are in short supply. How can this be?
>
> Speed is very important for lunchtime restaurant customers. Some people only get a half hour for lunch and other people do not want to spend a whole hour. Service at Charlie's is seat-yourself, but a waitress may be at your table before you even have a chance to sit down. Charlie's has printed menus, but the regulars do not use them because they know that the specials are posted on the walls. Every day there is a choice of four entrées that usually consist of sandwiches and several soups. There is a basket of crackers on the table, but before a patron is through with their first packet of crackers, their soup and drink is likely to be sitting in front of them. Before the soup is finished, the sandwich will be there, too. If someone needs to be through with lunch at Charlie's in only half an hour, it is not going to be a problem, whereas lunch at Cascarelli's around the corner is likely to be an hour-long affair. Price is not a major consideration in this purchasing decision. Charlie's provides value to its customers by serving a good lunch quickly.

SUMMARY

The key points described in this chapter are listed below.

1. Ethical constraints limit pricing decisions. Although not all societies have the same ethical standards about price, each of the following have been common ethical standards at one time:
   - No one is forced to make a purchase.
   - Buyer and seller have equal knowledge about the transaction.

- Seller will not profit from the buyer's adversity.
- Price is reasonable based on cost.
- Everyone pays the same price for the same item.

2. The major laws affecting pricing are the Sherman Antitrust Act, the Clayton Act, and the Robinson-Patman Act. These laws:

- Make monopolies illegal.
- Prohibit "price fixing."
- Limit the practice of charging different prices to different customers.
- Require compliance with "fair" business practices.

3. Common pricing strategies include:

- Price competition, where a company seeks to exploit a low cost advantage.
- Market skimming, where price is set high to attract customers who are willing to pay a premium price.
- Market penetration, where price is set low to gain market share.
- Loss leader, where the price of one product is set low to attract buyers to related products.
- Complementary pricing, where the purchase of one product is linked to related products.
- Market pricing, where the market sets the price of the product.
- Satisficing, where price is set to earn an adequate financial return.
- Value pricing, where price is set based on the value received by the customer.

4. Companies frequently segment the markets by offering several product variations geared to be sold to different buyers at different prices.

5. Customers buy for complex and diverse reasons that may have little to do with price.

6. The tangible, physical product may be a very small part of what provides value to the customer.

NOTES

1. Dr. Laurence J. Peter, *Peter's Quotations* (New York, Bantham Books, 1980), p. 428.
2. Thomas T. Nagle and Reed K. Holden, *The Strategy and Tactics of Pricing* (Englewood Cliffs, NJ, Prentice Hall, 1995), p. 384.

3. Kit Sims Taylor, *Human Society and the Global Economy (www.online.bcc.ctc.edu)*, p. 14.

4. Person's website (*www.lawmall.com/rpa/*) was a good source of information on Robinson-Patman Act issues. Unfortunately, that site no longer exists.

5. Ibid., Nagle and Holden, p. 379.

6. Ibid.

7. *www.Travelocity.Com* (December 16, 2000).

5

COSTS

> Allocations have long been a source of conflict between accountants, who knew that some form of cost apportionment was necessary, and their fellow managers, who knew that traditional cost allocation formulas bore little resemblance to what really caused costs.

USE OF THE WORD *COST*

The word *cost* is not uniformly used in the business world. At some companies cost means only operating costs shown above the gross margin. This definition of cost excludes selling costs, administrative expenses, and interest. At other companies, cost means only direct cost. Direct costs are costs that can be directly attributed to a single unit of production. In a manufacturing company, direct costs would include the cost of materials, purchased component parts, outside processing of the product, and direct labor. Direct labor is sometimes referred to under other names such as touch or contact labor and includes only labor that transforms materials into a product. In service businesses, direct costs are the costs of those efforts that can be directly associated with providing value to the customer. Examples would be an accountant's billable hours or the time that a repairperson spent working on a customer's washing machine. In a service business, labor is often the only direct cost. The benefits associated with direct labor may also be classified as a direct cost. Cost also may mean full cost, which includes all of the expenses that the company incurs, regardless of their nature.

Financial accounting conventions separate costs into three major categories:

- Cost of sales
- Selling, general, and administrative expenses
- Nonoperating expenses

This separation was historically an attempt to roughly classify expenses as variable, fixed, or those that did not directly affect operations on the income statement. By definition, a variable expense is one that increases or decreases as a function of business volume, whereas fixed costs do not change within a relevant range of business activities. In a low-technology, labor-intensive environment, operating expenses tend to be variable, and administrative expenses tend to be fixed. In these environments, the reader of a financial statement can use the cost of sales and administrative expenses to make a rough calculation of the companies' break-even points.

This book will use the term *cost* to mean all costs used to arrive at pretax income, excluding only income taxes from the discussion. Such cost is sometimes called full cost. The reason for not including federal income taxes as full cost is arbitrary. For most companies, there is no difference in the tax treatment of one dollar of pretax profit earned on one product from that of another product. Because of this, most companies using activity-based pricing concentrate on achieving a desired pretax profit.

RELATIONSHIP BETWEEN PRICE AND COST

Adam Smith observed that there was a natural cost-based price for all products and that where there was real competition in a market, the market price and the natural price would tend to be the same or close together over a long period of time. Exhibit 5.1 shows pretax profits compared with revenues for an unscientific sample

Exhibit 5.1 Pretax income as a percent of sales

	FYE 1999
AT&T	5.5%
DaimlerChrysler	3.8%
Hewlett-Packard	8.2%
Masco	12.9%
Merck	26.3%
Motorola	3.8%
Pactiv	–13.4%
Safeway	5.8%
Staples	4.3%
Wendy's	13.0%
Average	7.0%

Note: Most companies are not able to sell their products for substantially above costs as demonstrated by a comparison of pretax income to sales for 10 large publicly traded companies.

of 10 large publicly traded companies for 1999. The average pretax profit for all 10 companies is 7.0% of revenue. Only one of these companies had pretax profits that were more than 15%. Because profit represents the difference between revenue and expenses, this exhibit illustrates that the price and cost are normally close together.

Although every company would like to earn a higher profit, the heavy hand of competition usually keeps profit margins from climbing into a double-digit percentage. If companies in a particular industry were able to get consistently better profits, then other companies would attempt to enter that industry to take advantage of the high profit margins. This increase in supply would force profits down. Because of competition, the primary pricing strategy used by most companies in most industries is satisficing, where a company attempts to obtain an adequate financial return.

The prevalence of small profit margins dictates that not only should costs be considered when determining price, but really good cost data are also important when making this comparison. The 11.1% difference between selling a product at an $8.99 price point and a $9.99 price point is more than most companies' profit margins. For every product that generates a 25% pretax loss, the company must have another product that generates a 32% pretax profit to end up at a net of 7%. How often will competitors give enough breathing room to enjoy a 32% pretax profit on anything?

Making the presumption for now that a company could in some manner determine the full cost of all of its products, how would the profitability of the company's products be distributed? The natural inclination would be to think that the frequency of various profit rates would follow a normal distribution, as shown in Exhibit 5.2. Real world data do not look like this. Most companies have a few products that have highly negative profit margins as a percentage of revenue. These are often low-volume products. The products that generate the most profit for a company are usually sold in high volume, yet they may have a profit margin percentage that is not far above the average profit margin.

Exhibit 5.3 shows the profitability for 26 jobs for the Gale Manufacturing Company, a small company with $10 million in revenue and a 7% pretax profit. Gale Manufacturing's traditional standard costing system shows that all 26 of its products have a modest gross margin, but its president has a vague idea that three of its products may actually be losing money due to low volumes and high batch setup costs. In fact, if it were able to see the real cost of all 26 jobs, this company would find that six of its products were not profitable and three of those products had costs that were 30% more than their revenue (Exhibit 5.4). To make matters worse, it is not because of any inefficiency that these products are money losers. Production efficiency for these products is actually better than estimated. These products are unprofitable because the company did not take into consideration the extra material handling, administrative duties, and quality control requirements that make them

Exhibit 5.2 If profitable jobs followed a normal distribution

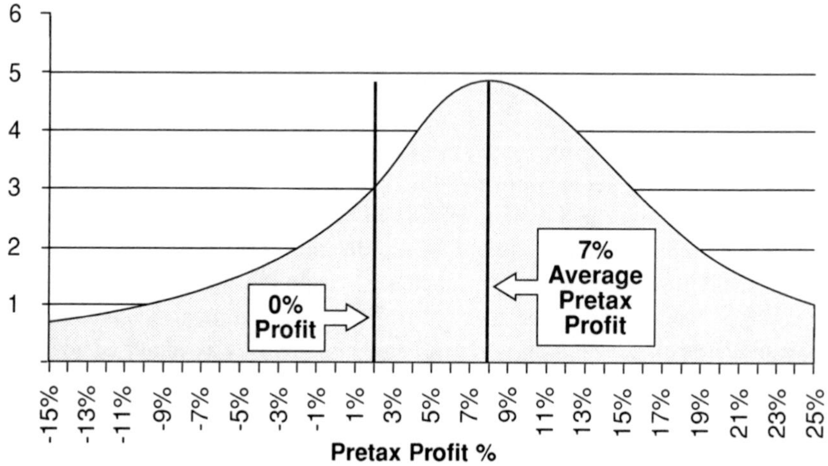

Note: In the real world, profit by product does not follow this normal distribution around the mean pretax profit. Most companies have a few products that would be way off the lower end of this graph. These unprofitable products often have low sales volumes, while high sales volume jobs are rarely far above average profitability.

significantly different from the other products that Gale makes. If the company had known the true cost of making these three products, it would have quoted a price that was considerably higher. Gale may not have made the sale at the higher price, but it would have avoided the drain on pretax profits that these products create.

It is interesting to note that three of Gale Manufacturing's products make up 61% of its profit. Elimination of the three most unprofitable products would increase profitability by $104,000, nearly a 16% increase over the current pretax profit of $656,000, as shown in Exhibit 5.5.

Price should not be set blindly as a markup on cost. Sometimes the market does not value a product enough to pay the cost that it takes to make the product. Sometimes the market will pay a great deal more for a product than its cost. Cost accountants should not decide prices. Likewise, salespeople, marketers, or engineers should not establish price. Pricing profitably is best assured when all of these disciplines collaborate to leverage their knowledge and gain synergies from their shared experience.

Getting good cost estimates early in product development may be very important to the profitability of a product. When a product is still in the design stage, all costs are subject to manipulation and adjustment. On paper or in the computer system, designs may be changed, material content may be altered, and product features may be added, deleted, or modified. Production methods may be changed in the planning stage because different levels of automation may be evaluated and

Exhibit 5.3 Common distribution of profit by product

Product	Units	Price	Revenue	Cost	Profit	% Profit	Cumulative Profit
A	320,000	$0.550	176,000	137,280	38,720	22%	38,720
B	35,000	$1.200	42,000	34,020	7,980	19%	46,700
C	610,000	$0.720	439,200	360,144	79,056	18%	125,756
D	892,000	$0.950	847,400	711,816	135,584	16%	261,340
E	332,000	$0.650	215,800	183,430	32,370	15%	293,710
F	440,000	$0.375	165,000	141,900	23,100	14%	316,810
G	890,000	$1.490	1,326,100	1,140,446	185,654	14%	502,464
H	720,000	$0.220	158,400	139,392	19,008	12%	521,472
I	400,000	$0.555	222,000	197,580	24,420	11%	545,892
J	185,000	$0.897	165,945	150,180	15,765	10%	561,657
K	738,000	$0.120	88,560	80,590	7,970	9%	569,627
L	1,250,000	$0.400	500,000	460,000	40,000	8%	609,627
M	620,000	$1.030	638,600	593,898	44,702	7%	654,329
N	80,000	$2.220	177,600	165,168	12,432	7%	666,761
O	545,000	$0.570	310,650	292,011	18,639	6%	685,400
P	270,000	$0.640	172,800	164,160	8,640	5%	694,040
Q	560,000	$1.670	935,200	897,792	37,408	4%	731,448
R	750,000	$1.540	1,155,000	1,120,350	34,650	3%	766,098
S	950,000	$0.890	845,500	820,135	25,365	3%	791,463
T	1,450,000	$0.497	720,650	713,444	7,207	1%	798,670
U	297,000	$0.760	225,720	234,749	(9,029)	–4%	789,641
V	264,000	$0.880	232,320	250,906	(18,586)	–8%	771,055
W	126,000	$0.490	61,740	72,236	(10,496)	–17%	760,559
X	49,000	$2.000	98,000	129,360	(31,360)	–32%	729,199
Y	42,000	$1.570	65,940	102,207	(36,267)	–55%	692,932
Z	12,000	$3.200	38,400	74,880	(36,480)	–95%	656,452
			10,024,525	9,368,073	656,452	7%	

Note: Shown is the profit by product for 26 products of Gale Manufacturing Company. The distribution of profit by job does not follow a normal distribution as some low volume products are very unprofitable while the most profitable jobs have a pre-tax profit that is much closer to the average product profit.

analyzed. Product features may be altered to enhance manufacturability. In the design phase, mistakes are cheap to correct, and time spent in error detection and prevention is usually very cost effective. Once the design of products and processes is complete, most of the cost of producing a product is set in stone. The product design determines material cost. The process design determines the amount of machinery, labor, and a substantial portion of the other costs required to make the product. The most effective time for a company to cut costs is at the time of design, not later once a product is in production.

Exhibit 5.4 Gale Manufacturing Company distribution of profit by product

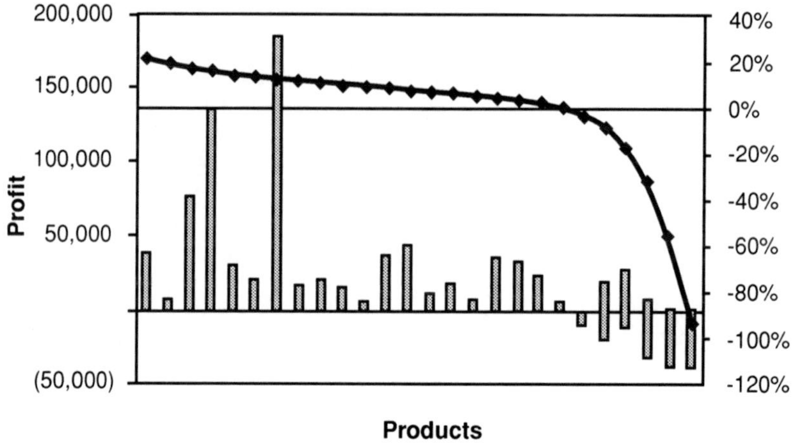

Note: The profit contribution of each individual product for Gale Manufacturing Company is shown on the left axis, while the pretax profit for each product is shown on the right axis. Products have been sorted by profit as a percentage of sales. Gale is typical in that no product makes a really large profit, but several products generate large losses as a percentage of sales.

Exhibit 5.5 Gale Manufacturing Company cumulative profit by product

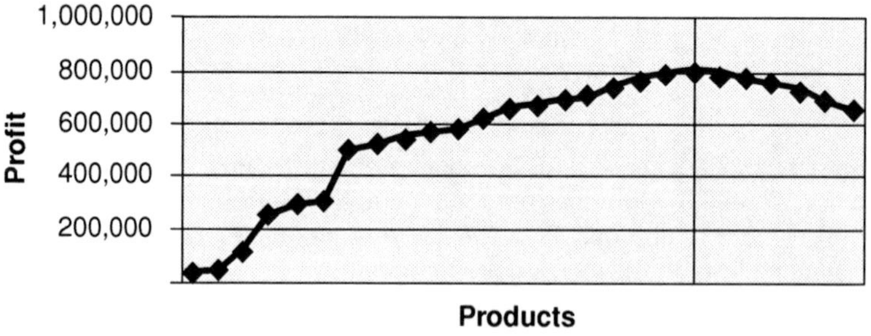

Note: Profit would be maximized if Gale Manufacturing Company could prevent producing the six unprofitable products shown on the right of the vertical line. For some companies the effect of their money-losing products is much more dramatic.

In many situations, a company has only one opportunity to affect price: at the time of the competitive bid. Accounting firms bid for multiyear contracts to perform an annual audit, construction companies submit proposals to build highways, manufacturing companies enter into contracts to sell to retailers, and hospitals enter contracts with insurance companies and preferred provider organizations. When an auto parts supplier enters a contract with an automaker, not only does it establish a base price for the life of the part, but it may also agree to decrease that price annually (cost downs) for the privilege of doing business with that customer. In all these situations, it is imperative that the seller know its costs in advance because there will not be an opportunity to raise the price later.

DEVELOPMENT OF COST ACCOUNTING

Humans have undoubtedly had methods for evaluating the profitability of their business propositions since long before the invention of money or the advent of the written word. Perhaps aboriginal tribes, meeting to trade with each other in the grasslands of prehistoric Africa, had a concept of value and profit. The website of the Association of Chartered Accountants in the United States provides a good history of the accounting profession.[1]

In Mesopotamia, the Code of Hammurabi, developed during the first dynasty in the city of Babylon (2285 to 2242 B.C.), specified that an agent selling goods for a merchant must give the merchant a price quotation under seal or face invalidation of a questioned agreement. Hundreds of Babylonian scribes were employed to draw up commercial transactions on clay tablets to assure compliance with the detailed legal requirements for record keeping.

Double-entry bookkeeping was developed in Italy in the fifteenth century. Many modern books trace the development of double-entry bookkeeping to Luca Pacioli's 1494 book *Summa de Arithmetica, Geometria, Proportioni et Proportionalita* (Everything About Arithmetic, Geometry and Proportion). Pacioli, born in 1445, was a true "Renaissance man," with a diverse knowledge of many subjects like his friend Leonardo da Vinci. Da Vinci helped him prepare drawings for a 1497 work *Divina Proportione*, and Pacioli in turn is said to have calculated the amount of bronze needed for da Vinci's statue of Duke Lidovico Sforza of Milan.

Bookkeeping was actually only one of five topics covered by Pacioli. *Summa* was translated into five languages in the first century after its publication, spreading "the Italian Method" of accounting throughout Europe. Pacioli himself did not claim to be the inventor of double-entry bookkeeping, instead crediting Benedetto Cotrugli, whose work *Delia Mercatura et del Mercante Perfetto* (Of Trading and the Perfect Trader) was published 36 years earlier.

When the Industrial Revolution began in Britain in the eighteenth century, a need arose for more accurate and formalized record keeping for the increasingly large companies of the nineteenth century. No doubt most readers will be familiar with the primitive record-keeping methods used at the counting house of Scrooge and Marley described in Charles Dickens's *A Christmas Carol.*

One of the key limitations to the development of both cost and financial accounting was the quality of the calculating devices available. The first practical device for doing multiplication and division used in western civilization was the slide rule, developed by Scotsman John Napier in 1614. This device, nicknamed "Napier's bones," consisted of scribe marks on sticks. Slide rules were never very precise, able to do calculations that were, at best, good to three significant digits. In the east, the abacus predated the slide rule by centuries and is still used in some parts of the world today. Thomas made the first mass-produced adding machine in 1820, and many refinements were made in the following decades. William Burroughs made major improvements to the adding machine in 1885, and by the 1920s comptometers made by Burroughs Corporation and others became a standard fixture in North American businesses.

Comptometers were bulky desktop machines that conventionally had columns of keys numbered 0 through 9 for each digit of the machine's 11-digit capacity. After punching in a number, the accountant or clerk would pull a hand crank to register the number on a paper tape. In some companies, operating a calculator was considered manual labor that was not cost-effective work for an accounting professional. Comptometer operators accompanied Certified Public Accountants on audits, and Arthur Andersen & Company continued to refer to such a position in its training manuals well into the 1970s.

By the first few decades of the twentieth century, formalized management systems were being implemented in many large companies led by DuPont in Delaware and General Motors in Michigan. Alfred Sloan, an engineer educated at the Massachusetts Institute of Technology, who became General Motors president in May 1923, was instrumental in initiating these changes.

In the labor-intensive 1920s, the cost structure of a typical company might be as follows:

Materials	40%
Direct labor	40%
All other	20%
Total Cost	100%

All other costs would include many different kinds of expenses normally referred to collectively as "Overhead." Overhead includes rent, depreciation, insurance, supplies, property taxes, administrative costs, selling costs, and numerous other expenses.

Material costs are relatively easy to calculate by hand or with a slide rule. If the amount of material in a batch is known, the amount of material per item is easily calculated by dividing by the number of pieces that were made in that batch. To the extent that a product is made up of more than one part, the material cost of the various components is simply added together.

Likewise, labor standards are easy to calculate. Labor standards may be calculated by dividing the amount of time that a person works by the output that was produced in that time. Labor content measured in hours can be converted to currency by multiplying by the cost per hour.

Italian mathematician and economist Vilfredo Pareto observed that 20% of the items in a natural statistical population make up 80% of the valuation of that population. Business people know Pareto's Law as "the 80/20 rule." Following this rule, business people have long recognized the wisdom of concentrating their efforts on those categories that make up 80% of business costs. Accordingly, for much of the twentieth century, accountants could do a reasonably effective job by concentrating on just labor and materials.

At just 20% of all costs, allocation of overhead was not necessarily a major concern or a cost-effective avenue for further investigation, particularly using the tools available before businesses commonly used computers. The practical and logical approach was to apportion overhead costs according to the consumption of some other resource, usually, based on labor hours. If total labor costs were $4 million and overhead was $2 million then a *burden rate* of $0.50 might be added to each $1.00. This would often be referred to as a 50% burden rate.

Some accountants recognized that portions of the overhead costs might have more to do with materials than labor. They also recognized that other overhead costs might have nothing to do with either labor or materials. Although the concept of allocating overhead based on the consumption of direct labor may have been conceptually faulty, the calculating capacity of slide rules, comptometers, and, later, 10-key calculators placed a practical limitation on a company's ability to do cost analysis on a large number of products. The cost of a product might simply be represented by two categories:

Materials, and

Labor and overhead.

William F. O'Brien, lecturer at San Jose State University, calls the "A" in allocation the "Scarlet Letter" of accounting.[2] Michael Maher, a cost accounting professor at the University of Michigan Graduate School of Business, used to open his lectures on cost allocation by asking the question, "Why allocate?" Allocations confound nonfinancial managers, who view traditional methods of allocation as arbitrary and without basis in reality. Allocations have long been a source of conflict between accountants, who knew that some form of cost apportionment was necessary, and their fellow managers, who knew that traditional cost allocation formulas did not accurately represent what really caused costs.

As the twentieth century progressed, increased automation began to reveal the faults of these standard cost accounting methods. As technology improved, many types of manufacturing equipment, such as plastic injection molding machines, could run without the full-time attention of a worker. One molding machine operator might be responsible for two, four, or even eight molding machines at the same time. In the 1960s and 1970s, business school professors challenged their students and the cost accounting conventions of the time by asking why overhead should be allocated to a machine that requires no labor. Obviously there were portions of overhead, such as depreciation, floor-space, utilities, and maintenance, that had nothing to do with labor and everything to do with the machine. Some astute practitioners began classifying overhead as machine-related overhead, labor-related overhead, and, sometimes, material-related overhead. It was the common-sense thing to do.

FINANCIAL REPORTING SYSTEMS

Because much of the data used by cost accountants begins with financial accounting records, the development of cost accounting was in part limited by the development of financial reporting systems. Prior to computers, financial accounting was done in ledger books filled with 11 × 14 inch ruled paper or on accounting machines such as those made by the Burroughs Corporation. Doing accounting in ledger books was a tedious affair. One book, called the *general ledger*, contained a page for each account that the company maintained, and another book, called the *general journal*, contained transactions that were posted sequentially. Other books might be used as well. For example, the company might maintain subsidiary journals for accounts receivable, accounts payable, and payroll. More often, records were kept on cards that accumulated the transactions related to each customer, vendor, or employee account. Subsidiary ledgers might also exist for the various entities owned by the corporation, complicating business record keeping.

Accounting was drudgery before computers. The process was error prone and required a mind-numbing tolerance for performing tedious work. Journal entries were posted from the subsidiary journals to the general journal and from the general journal to the general ledger. Sometimes an accountant would have an eight-line journal entry and post only seven lines to the general ledger. Sometimes they might post nine lines. Sometimes a credit would be entered as a debit or numbers would be transposed. For a month-end closing, half of the time might be spent looking for the posting errors that prevented the debits from equaling the credits.

There were many techniques that helped keep manual record keeping manageable. Astute accounting managers might "balance the books" several times a month to make error detection more manageable. Because posting errors expand exponentially with the number of general ledger accounts, accountants using manual books would use as few accounts as practical to minimize errors. They would also list the accounts in the order that they needed to appear on financial statements to ease the transfer of information from the general ledger to a typewriter.

Although these techniques minimized errors, they also limited the amount of useful information that could be derived from the financial records. With few general ledger accounts, many categories of costs would be lumped together. It was not unusual to see an account labeled "Factory Supplies" or "Payroll Taxes – Office." These expenses might cover many different kinds of expenditures under the responsibility of many different managers. Although wages might be categorized by department, various other expenses were normally lumped together in those precomputerized days. Without separation of expense by a responsible manager, budgeting was ineffective. This strongly impacted cost accounting because it was not easy to isolate all costs that pertained to a particular business function. Because like expenses for operating and administrative departments would be located in different parts of the chart of accounts, cost analysis that involved the whole company was sometimes difficult.

The introduction of computers into business gave accountants the opportunity to collect accounting data by department for the first time. Astute accountants began structuring their general ledger systems to match the organizational structure. This provided support for budgeting and responsibility reporting. By also grouping like expenses together, computerized general ledger systems also enhanced cost accounting. Although the number of general ledger accounts often exploded, the ability of the computer to sort and summarize hundreds of accounts in a variety of ways gave accountants the ability to answer questions that had never before been practical to attempt to answer. Now a financial manager could separate the cost of selling expenses from the rest of administration or distinguish how much of operating costs were for maintenance, setup, production, quality control, or shipping.

Large companies today often use specialized activity-based costing software such as that produced by ABC Technologies of Beaverton, Oregon, the company that dominates this market with three different activity-based costing products. For small companies, it is often possible to use standard accounting tools to develop activity-based cost data to determine pricing. If a small company's general ledger system has been well organized and if the company has good statistics regarding its major consumption of costs, it will be able to generate good costing data and an effective pricing model using electronic spreadsheets.

The remainder of this chapter will address techniques to assist with classifying and extracting activity-based pricing information. These techniques can be used either with or without specialized activity-based costing software. This discussion will include best practice methodology for setting up general ledger systems. Although such methods fall short of the capabilities available from specialized activity-based costing software, the techniques will provide adequate data for small and medium-sized companies. In addition, these techniques may provide ancillary benefits for companies through improved budgeting and financial reporting capabilities.

ORGANIZING FINANCIAL REPORTING SYSTEMS

Almost universally, accountants have never been taught how to set up a financial reporting system. There is little literature on this subject. Many of the conventions used today in computerized general ledger systems are left over from when financial accounting was done in manual ledger books. Financial reporting systems have the potential to provide an important tool for managing a business if they are well designed and well organized. A well-designed financial reporting system can provide the basis for strong financial control through the budgeting process. The financial reporting system can also provide the ability to extract data to answer "what if" questions and act as a starting point for cost analysis.

Structured Chart of Accounts

The best practice today for organizing a general ledger system begins with a structured *chart of accounts*. A structured chart of accounts is a highly organized method of developing a chart of accounts geared to support financial reporting, budgeting, and cost accounting. Although most organizations have adopted some structured techniques, few organizations have taken advantage of everything that this method has to offer.

Small and medium-sized companies often have poorly organized financial reporting systems. Most large organizations have reasonably well organized financial systems because it is virtually mandatory for a company with a complicated organizational structure. Most large organizations use a hierarchical account numbering scheme that is geared to allowing financial reports to be prepared for specific segments of the organization according to the needs of a wide audience of financial information users. Such structures often look something like one of these:

Company-Division-Location-Account	C-VV-LLL-AAAA
Company-Location-Department-Account	C-LL-DD-AAAA
Company-Account-Department	CC-AAAA-DD

Many organizations mistakenly create excessively long segments when creating their chart of accounts, particularly in the *account base* segment represented above with the character "A." Long account numbers or accounts with many significant digits create extra work and slow the processing of preparing and posting transactions. Having long segments is often rationalized as "to allow for growth." However, if a company expects to have significant growth, that growth will happen primarily in the number of divisions, locations, or departments that the company has and not in the types of accounts represented by the account base. As a company grows from $10 million to $10 billion in sales, it probably will only add one or two types of wage accounts to the account base. However, the company may increase the number of location-department-accounts base combinations that it has for wages by 1,000-fold. This growth will primarily come from increasing the complexity of the entity, not in types of expenses that are incurred. For this reason, growth should be accommodated in account segments other than account base.

General Ledger software and technical consultants who work for the software developer often encourage companies to use a long account base "in case you need it." Long account numbers are often the fault of redundant or unnecessary data. It is not uncommon to see a company use an account base of six digits, with meaningless digits in the middle of the account number. Nobody really needs a six-digit account base. A four-digit account base should accommodate even the largest company. No company is ever likely to need more than 9,999 accounts associated with a single department.

Most accountants prefer to see all accounts for the same location listed in numerical order on a trial balance. For this reason, account numbers are often organized so that the department code is last, facilitating this desired sort order. Some general ledger software packages also place restrictions on how account numbers are created, forcing account numbering schemes that are less than optimal. A few software packages are incapable of handling a structured chart of accounts all together. The acid test for a financial reporting system is that the company should be able to define its accounts in any way that it wants and show the accounts on financial statements in any order, summarizing them in any way or at any level that makes sense to them, no matter how illogical it seems to the computer programmer.

With manual books, companies could minimize the balancing time by using relatively few accounts. Financial statement preparation could also be made more efficient by numbering the accounts in the same order as they appear on the financial statements. Accordingly, a common numbering scheme still used by many companies follows:

1XX	Assets
2XX	Liabilities and equity
3XX	Revenues
4XX	Cost of sales—Purchases
5XX	Operations costs—Labor and benefits
6XX	Operations costs—Other
7XX	Administrative costs—Labor and benefits
8XX	Administrative costs—Other
9XX	Nonoperating costs

Use of the 1-Series for Assets and the 2-Series for Liabilities is almost universal. Equity is commonly in the 29xx or 3xxx series, and revenues are usually 3xxx or 4xxx.

Many companies that computerized in the 1970s and 1980s just converted their manual system to the computer, usually adding more digits because the computer would handle much of the work for them. As years passed, the Controller would add more and more accounts to accumulate additional desired detail. If the person setting up a chart of accounts was not familiar with both accounting methods and computer systems, the result was often a terrible mess.

For example, one large company had a chart of accounts where one of its cash accounts was 10210210. As in many companies, the first two digits, 10, meant Assets-Cash. When the company became computerized in the 1970s, its manual books had a cash account that was 102, for Cash Account 2. When it computerized, the computer programmer said that the number could be as long as they wanted, so the company just doubled its six-digit account number to get 102102. The final two digits got added on when the company installed a new general ledger system later on and went to an eight-digit account base. Even with this long number, this account failed to identify that this cash account was associated with a specific location. The three-digit location code was not used for balance sheet accounts, creating headaches for the company's tax manager, who got little help from the general ledger system in identifying which assets were associated with each state in which the company did business.

Today many companies use chart of account schemes that have not fully evolved from the days of manual books. Accounting literature suggests that some 90% of all financial information is used for internal purposes. Internal financial information requirements are generally more detailed than for external reporting. Computers make it easy to create greater levels of summarization from accounting data but make it very difficult to create greater levels of detail. Accordingly, companies should organize their general ledger systems to support internal financial information needs such as responsibility reporting and cost accounting.

Financial managers often need to present the same information many different ways. Sometimes users might want to know "How much overtime was worked in all departments for December?" At other times they might want to know "How much overtime was worked in the Sales Department?" or "What is the total cost of our Sales function?" (which must include overtime and all benefits). Depending on how the general ledger system is set up, these questions can be very time consuming or very easy to answer.

One common problem with financial reporting systems is that the organizational structure as expressed in the chart of accounts may not match the organizational chart or the information provided from the payroll system. Of course, in many companies the organizational chart has not been updated in such a long time that the organizational chart itself no longer matches the real organizational structure.

A company of 100 to 500 people may have 15 functional departments according to the organizational chart, 4 departments in the chart of accounts, 8 departments in the payroll system, and 17 departments in reality. The chart of accounts and the payroll systems should be reorganized to match the real organizational structure.

A common way to set up departments in the general ledger is to list all of the functional departments from the organizational chart in order of most direct to least direct and then number them with two digits by fives or by tens (10, 20, 30, 40, etc.). All zeros (00 or 000) are conventionally used for expenses not associated with a single department. For example, a year-end adjustment to accrued workers compensation insurance might be posted to department 00 rather than be apportioned among the actual departments.

In some instances, the company may want to create more "departments" on the chart of accounts than exists in the real organization for cost accounting purposes. If different groups of people in one department perform distinctly different kinds of work, those people might be separated into different general ledger departments even though they have a single supervisor. For example, an accounting department might be subdivided into accounts receivable, accounts payable, and general accounting groups. This separation would facilitate analysis to determine the costs of the various activities that fall under accounts payable and accounts receivable. This hierarchy might be reflected in the chart of accounts via a subdepartment account segment.

Although a company might create more departments in the chart of accounts than really exist, creating fewer general ledger departments is rarely advisable. Any time multiple areas of responsibility are mixed together, there is a loss of accountability for the managers of those departments. One common exception to this rule sometimes occurs in small companies where executive level management is included in an "administrative" department that includes miscellaneous personnel with a wide variety of functions.

If the company has multiple regions, locations, or divisions, the chart of accounts should recognize this structure while maintaining the same basic account-department scheme across all locations. Thus, if account 12-6000-90 (location-account-department) was Kalamazoo-regular wages-administration and location 94 was Battle Creek, then regular wages-administration for Battle Creek should be 94-6000-90.

A single location company might structure its chart of accounts in this manner: account-department = AAAA-DD. A big benefit of having a structured chart of accounts is to be able to publish financial statements for individual areas of responsibility. This is an important tool for department managers trying to live within their budget. Companies that use old-fashioned account structuring schemes often struggle with budgeting and financial control. If accounting is unable to provide financial reports to individual managers showing the budget-to-actual performance of their portion of the organization, then budgeting is unlikely to be effective.

A structured chart of accounts facilitates activity-based pricing by aggregating costs by business function or department. These functional categories often include the costs for several major related activities. Statistics are often available that allow functional costs to be reasonably separated into activity costs. Although these data should not be expected to be as accurate as what could be obtained by specialized activity-based costing software, they may be quite adequate for pricing purposes.

A common problem in smaller companies is that if accounts are numbered in the order in which they appear on financial statements, then the chart of accounts is not geared to answering "what if" questions. For instance, if the Chief Executive Officer goes to the Controller to find out the total overtime that the corporation paid last month, it is more difficult to extract that information from the computer if manufacturing overtime begins with "51" and administrative overtime begins with "71." The project is even more difficult if the president wants to know the total cost of running a single function and the chart of accounts is not departmentalized.

A more modern account structure is to organize accounts into ranges based on the type of account. For example:

1XXX	Assets
2XXX	Liabilities and equity
3XXX	Revenues
4XXX	Cost of sales—Purchases
5XXX	Wages
6XXX	Benefits
7XXX	Departmentalized expenses
8XXX	Nondepartmentalized expenses
9XXX	Nonoperating expenses

Like expenses should have the same base account number regardless of department. Each department, for example, might have the following expenses:

7000	Supplies and department expenses
7100	Repairs
7500	Training
7600	Travel and lodging
7700	Meals and entertainment

Most people-related department expenses can be posted directly by the payroll system. Payroll software would routinely be able to post all of these expenses by individual department:

5000	Regular pay
5100	Overtime pay
5200	Double-time pay
5300	Vacation pay
5400	Holiday pay
5500	Bonus pay
6000	Medical insurance
6100	FICA (Federal Insurance Contributions Act) expense
6200	FUTA expense (Federal Unemployment Tax Act)
6300	SUI (state unemployment insurance) expense
6400	Workers compensation
6500	Life and Disability insurance
6600	Pension

In these examples, the most commonly used expenses have been given account numbers with a single significant digit to make them easy to remember. Related expenses are listed in series to easily extract blocks of data. An inquiry on all accounts beginning with "5" would provide total company wages.

One implication of a structured chart of accounts is that even a one-location company with 100 employees may have 500 to 1,000 different account/department combinations. This quantity of accounts actually may be easier to manage than one quarter of that number using an unstructured numbering scheme because this method uses a logical combination of prefixes and suffixes to make up the account numbers. In the above illustration, if there were 10 departments (including the 00 default department), there would be 160 resulting account/department combinations. People who work with the account numbers regularly would have little to learn because the most prolific part of the structured chart of accounts, payroll and payroll-related benefits, is normally posted automatically from the payroll software and does not need to be learned. Even if it were, because "5" means Wages and "6" means Benefits, it is easy to remember the order within each series where each account segment falls. Accounts payable clerks have an easy time as well because a structured chart of accounts tends to have far fewer kinds of account bases, letting the account department combinations provide the detail.

Some financial managers make the mistake of preparing financial statements that are of little use because they contain too much detail. A key to effectively managing a structured chart of accounts is appropriate summarization of data so that it is relevant to each user. A good summarized income statement should fit onto a single page. A few pages of detail (which would still be at a fairly summarized level) would follow the summary page.

The use of a structured chart of accounts provides significant benefits beyond budgeting and responsibility reporting. A structured chart of accounts greatly enhances the organization's ability to do cost accounting using activity-based costing by providing a functional organization of costs. The time savings for cost accounting can be immense.

Account numbers should be logical and easy to remember. This reduces coding errors and data entry work. Avoid using more digits than necessary. If a company has 10 locations, a two-digit location code provides lots of room for growth. Most companies can comfortably use a four-digit account base. Account numbers can be easy to remember if successive digits are used to subdivide higher level categories.

For example, if "1" in the first digit means assets, the second digit might be used to further delineate asset categories:

10XX	for Cash
11XX	for Accounts Receivable
12XX	for Inventory
15XX	for Fixed Assets
16XX	for Accumulated Depreciation

Accounts that are not associated with a department should be avoided; for instance, cleaning supplies or office supplies. The maintenance department controls cleaning supplies and these supplies should be budgeted as an expense of that department. If someone in Accounting handles office supplies, the expense should be included in that department's budget. Alternately, some companies charge office supplies to each department or location according to actual usage. A commonly used method of assigning costs to a department is that expenses are assigned to an expense category for which the person authorizing the purchase is responsible.

Some organizations set up their computer systems to automatically apportion costs among departments or locations according to a specific measurement of that area's consumption of the resource. For instance, floor space costs such as rent and utilities may be automatically distributed according to the floor space used by each department. This helps categorize costs by function, which may later be further divided by activity. When costs are assigned using cost driver statistics, managers should be able to reduce their portion of assigned cost by giving back resources such as office space.

Structured methods also should be used within the balance sheet where appropriate. If a company has many locations, the location code in the balance sheet may be used to associate bank accounts, inventory, and fixed assets with various locations. The ability to extract asset and liability information by location will ease the preparation of tax returns for various states and municipalities.

Account numbers for prepaid, withholding, and accrued liabilities can be made easy to remember by combining balance sheet and income statement prefixes. Thus, if the format for withholding is 21xx (where xx is a sequence number), accrued liabilities is 22xx, and federal income tax expense is 9900, then 2199 could be "Withholding—Federal Income Taxes," and 2299 could be "Accrued Liability—Federal Income Tax." This method improves the ability to memorize account numbers.

Using Financial Accounting to Support Costing

Early cost accounting software essentially mechanized the processes that accountants already performed on green 13-column ledger sheets, categorizing costs as material, labor, and overhead. Some software would allow a separate overhead rate for machine usage and labor usage. Many inventory programs separated overhead into fixed or variable standard overhead cost categories. Such a separation was usually meaningless because the computer would than apply fixed overhead on a per-unit basis in the same manner as variable costs. Even in the twenty-first century, many software packages continue to use archaic conventions that are vestiges of these precomputerized times. Gary Cokins, Director of Industry Relations at ABC Technologies, notes that at many companies "the cost accounting system is a bunch of lies that we all agree to."[3]

A breakthrough in cost accounting came with the invention of the personal computer and the release of VisiCalc in 1979, the first electronic spreadsheet designed for a personal computer. This versatile, free-form calculating tool allowed accountants to do analysis that was previously too time consuming and impractical. Accountants were able to use VisiCalc to do common-sense analysis. If a company had high maintenance costs, an accountant could use machine repair department time reports to analyze which machines required the most maintenance and assign maintenance costs accordingly. The increased calculating power of computer spreadsheets made it practical to assign material handling costs to material and shipping costs to shipments, rather than to large pools of overhead. With all of this calculating ability, it became possible to analyze costs more accurately than ever before.

VisiCalc quickly became the hottest selling computer software package of all time, inviting competitors such as Framework, Multicalc, Multiplan, PeachCalc, and Lotus 1-2-3. The initial public offering (IPO) of Lotus Development Corporation in October 1983 raised $46,800,000, making it one of the largest start-up IPOs to date, giving it enough capital to quickly develop a feature-rich electronic spreadsheet that would compete with VisiCalc.[4] By 1985, VisiCalc had largely disappeared from North American businesses, leading one magazine to speculate, "Whatever Happened to VisiCalc?"[5] Meanwhile, Lotus 1-2-3 and other electronic spreadsheets were making their mark. The cost allocation methods that made sense in the 1920s became nonsense in the 1980s.

STATISTICS

Good cost accounting depends on having more than accumulations of costs. There is little basis for apportioning costs to activities, products, and customers if all of the information available is denominated in dollars. How much money was spent does little good without data to tell how it was spent.

The information that companies most commonly have available about their cost is how many units were produced and how many direct labor hours were required to produce that product. This is a good start, but it allows only limited information to be derived about product cost. Data about production and direct labor hours only provides information about direct costs. Costs that have been traditionally classified as indirect can be directly related to specific products or customers and can bear a direct relationship to business volume. To be able to understand product development costs, product launch costs, setup costs, and other indirect costs, more data are necessary than the dollar amounts consumed.

Direct labor may not even be the most significant wage cost for a company. Workers compensation insurance companies ordinarily base the rates that they charge on standard rates for various kinds of professions. Clerical staff has a low rate, tool and die makers have a higher rate, and metal stamping press operators have a higher rate still. Supervisory and support employees in a manufacturing plant typically are charged at the predominant rate in the plant for the production workers. One insurance company auditor was challenged by the company financial manager when he tried to charge the high metal stamping employee rate for all supervisory and manufacturing support employees at a company. After all, the financial manager pointed out, "We may produce metal stampings, but an analysis of our labor costs proves that the skilled trades people, like the tool and die makers, die setup, and machine maintenance personnel are our predominant wage categories. Direct labor for metal stamping equals only $2^1/2$% of our cost." The insurance auditor relented, and they agreed that supervisory personnel would be priced at a weighted-average workers compensation rate.

Statistics on direct labor often provide information on only the running costs and not the setup costs of a business's processes. If only running costs are collected, then there is no ability to differentiate the "good" long-running products from the short-running "dog" jobs with high setup costs. When direct labor personnel perform machine setup, the company should differentiate running time and setup time in its time-reporting process.

Companies can significantly improve their ability to analyze real costs by collecting data on significant indirect activities. This normally includes a measurement of the number of hours spent on tasks relating to various products and processes and a count of the number of times the task was performed. For example, if the company collected the number of hours spent by machine setup personnel, what products were set up on each machine, and the number of hours that were required to perform a setup, it would be able to identify the typical setup time for each product on a particular type of machine. These setup costs would be dependent on the kind of tooling to be set up and the kind of machine that the tooling would be used on, but would be completely independent of the number of units to be produced. If the company was bidding to produce a new product, it could examine similar products that were made using similar machines to determine a basis for its cost estimates.

Machine maintenance costs are likely to depend on many factors that have little to do with products. The most significant driver of machine maintenance time is likely to be the type of machine and the number of hours that the machine is operated. Companies using metal stamping presses know that two identical machines—one used for high-speed progressive dies, the other for slow-speed forming—will have very different maintenance costs. By analyzing machine maintenance costs, financial managers may be able to make accurate estimates of future costs on products that have never been made before.

Tool maintenance costs are likely to depend on the complexity of the tooling. The number of dimensions or critical dimensions might be useful in estimating product complexity for molded products. For a progressive stamping die, the number of stations in the die might provide a meaningful measure of complexity.

Sometimes only an expert can explain what has caused a costly product to be so costly. Hermann Kress earned a reputation for being one of the very best tool and die makers in Detroit. Born in Germany, Hermann apprenticed as a tool and die maker at a young age and became a master tool and die maker, one level above the journeyman training achieved by most tool and die makers in North America.

During the short-lived days of Total Quality Management (TQM) the financial vice president of the stamping company in which Hermann was part owner asked him why the tooling that made a part for the Ford Taurus was so costly to maintain. The finance people had figured that this particular part required over $100,000 a year in maintenance, more than double the cost of the next most expensive tool. Kress explained that the die was not made right. There were two holes that needed to be positioned correctly with respect to each other. The approach that the die builder had taken (before Hermann joined that company) was to punch the two holes at the same time and then bend the material at a right angle. If the material thickness were not exactly consistent, the orientation of the holes would change as a result. Each time the job was run, the die makers were spending a lot of time ensuring that the die was making good parts. Hermann explained, "What the die maker should have done was bend the metal and then punch the two holes." He pointed out that the die could not be modified because it was not long enough to add the extra station required. To eliminate the problem, another $100,000 would be needed to replace the die.

The design engineers had identified another change to the product that would save Ford a considerable amount of money when installing the product on its vehicles. Ford was willing to pay for a new tool in order to get this product improvement. Once other people in the company understood what caused that high maintenance cost, pushing through this product change became a high priority.

Statistics can provide insight into costs in many kinds of businesses. Services that are performed in the customer's home require drive time to the customer as well as time in the home performing the service. If a competitor charged a flat rate in a particular geographic area regardless of location, a company might be able to improve its profitability through a pricing structure that attracted nearby customers. By giving a preferable rate to nearby customers, who could be served at a lower cost, the company could improve profitability while allowing competitors to have the more costly customers who were located farther from the company's offices.

Retailers commonly have reams of data available from their retail scanning system regarding the sales and value added that is generated by their various products. If those data are analyzed along with the shelf space and stocking costs of those products, the retailer has the ability to improve profitability by culling products that do not pay for its stocking costs. The retailer also might improve profitability on some products by reducing the amount of shelf space used, raising price, or seeking price concessions from vendors.

If a company recognizes that it needs better cost information as a basis for its pricing, what kinds of information should it collect, and how should that information be used? The discussion of these topics begins in Chapter 6.

SUMMARY

The key points described in this chapter are listed below:

1. The term "cost" is not used uniformly between all companies. Cost may mean direct costs, gross margin costs, or full costs. In this book, the term *cost* refers to any cost (other than income taxes) regardless of where it appears on the company income statement.
2. Cost is important in pricing because most companies have revenues that are not substantially above their cost, leaving them with a profit margin that is less than 10% of revenue.
3. If a company plots its profitability by job as a percentage of revenue on a graph, the graph will not follow a normal statistical distribution. A few products may experience losses that represent a high percentage of their selling price, but no products will have a corresponding high percentage profit. Low volume products and complex products often have costs well above their price.
4. Competition usually prevents a company from earning a high profit as a percentage of sales on any product. High volume, however, may allow large profits to be earned on a product with a relatively low profit margin.

5. Cost accounting took many centuries to evolve, and its development was inhibited by the quality of the calculating tools available to accountants. The development of computers, particularly the introduction of personal computer spreadsheets in the early 1980s, led to rapid improvements in cost accounting techniques.

6. Many companies, particularly small and medium-sized companies, are using financial reporting techniques that have not fully evolved from manual accounting methods used before the development of computerized general ledger systems. Best practice today for organizing financial reporting systems is to use structured methods, including a structured chart of accounts where designing the financial reporting system begins with the company's organizational structure.

7. Good cost information requires more than an accumulation of dollarized accounting transactions. Operational information on the company's activities, both direct and indirect, is required to accurately make sense of the cost behavior for the company.

NOTES

1. Association of Chartered Accountants in the U.S. (ACAUS) *Intro to Accounting History* (*www.acaus.org/history/hsintro*, November 11, 2000).
2. William F. O'Brien, *The Controller as Operating Officer & Management Accountant* (Paoli, PA: Center for Professional Education, 2000).
3. Gary Cokins, "Are All of Your Customers Profitable?" (*www.bettermanagement.com*, December 9, 2000).
4. Dow Jones Newswires, October 6, 1983.
5. Walecia Konrad, "Whatever Happened to VisiCalc?" *Working Woman* (December 1985), p. 60.

6

ACTIVITY-BASED COSTING

Armed with solid cost data, management is able to structure a pricing strategy that encourages sales to the most profitable customers.

NEED FOR ACTIVITY-BASED COSTING

Professor Bala Balachandran, director of the Accounting Research Center at Northwestern University,[1] provides this example of how devastating the results of cost misallocation can be:

> You dine with three colleagues. Being health conscious, *you* skip cocktails and dessert and have a salad. The others have drinks and three courses. When the check arrives, the group divides the total by four and you get hit with $27. For a skimpy salad? Yep, that was the allocation plan.
>
> So on your next trip to Bala's Bistro you down a martini. It costs six bucks, but what the hell: you pay only $1.50 as your share. Why not a $6 cheesecake for dessert too?
>
> You really didn't want the martini, and the cheesecake condemns you to an extra half-hour on the treadmill, but that's what faulty allocation does to your thinking process.

Although this may seem like an extreme example, analysis of real companies shows that it is not uncommon for businesses to unwittingly sell a few of their products at half of their full real cost. Occasionally a product will be identified that is selling for one quarter of the full cost. When such products are identified, it is usually not difficult for everyone involved to understand why the product is so expensive. Unprofitable products lose money for common-sense reasons. These products are often complex, are sold in low volumes, require expensive specialized equipment, or have special administrative or other handling requirements.

Just like in Bala's Bistro, some products or customers are freeloaders, not paying their share of the bill. Like asking for "one check" in a restaurant, traditional cost allocations share all indirect costs among all products. When costs are arbitrarily allocated, the allocation obscures what a product or customer really costs. The result is effort wasted on products and customers that produce no profit. To make matters worse, profit that is earned on really profitable work is squandered on the freeloaders.

Activity-based costing (ABC) is a method of producing separate checks. It attracts to the table products and customers that can pay their own way, while identifying and preventing freeloaders from coming to the party. ABC can provide a competitive advantage to companies that understand and use its principles.

ORIGINS OF ACTIVITY-BASED COSTING

Activity-based costing was named and became a formal discipline in 1986 as a result of a project initiated by the Consortium for Advanced Manufacturing–International (CAM-I, pronounced with a long "I"). CAM-I is an association of large companies dedicated to the advancement of manufacturing technology. CAM-I's members include Boeing, General Electric, Kodak, Motorola, several U.S. government agencies, and most of the major accounting firms.

CAM-I put together a distinguished project team to improve cost accounting techniques. That team included, among others, Robert Kaplan from Harvard, Robin Cooper, now at the Claremont Graduate School, and James Brimson as Project Director. Each of these men became prolific writers on ABC subjects in the following years. The National Association of Accountants, now called the Institute of Management Accountants (IMA) worked closely with CAM-I on the ABC project. Although CAM-I has largely moved on to concentrate its efforts on other projects, the IMA continues to heavily promote ABC methods in their programs and publications. The IMA is the certifying body for the Certified Management Accountant (CMA) designation in the United States. CMA-Canada provides a certification of the same name in that country.

The collection of cost accounting techniques that became ABC in the late 1980s was not new or revolutionary. Activity-based costing largely consists of commonsense techniques developed by many financial managers to respond to the particular needs of their own companies. Most of these financial managers worked independently of each other, inventing methods that made sense in their own individual situations.

Although named by a group interested in manufacturing costing, ABC techniques also apply to service sector situations. The health-care industry in particular used certain ABC techniques long before 1986. Before health-care providers began paying hospitals based on diagnosis in the mid-1980s, they were paid through a cost reimbursement process. The step-down cost allocation analysis, a technique that was a major step toward the development of ABC, was a part of the healthcare cost reimbursement reports required by Medicare and Medicaid even before hospital financial managers had personal computer electronic spreadsheet tools to automate the arduous calculations. This analysis seemed like a bureaucratic nuisance in a not-for-profit cost-reimbursed environment. However, when financial managers began to replace arbitrary allocations with cost prorations based on a real evaluation of cost behavior, the step-down analysis led to the evolution of what is today known as ABC.

Activity-based costing is a common-sense method of assigning costs. There is no one "right" way of doing ABC. Each organization that uses ABC assigns costs in a manner that makes sense for the organization. The remainder of this chapter will discuss the concepts that make up ABC and the methods used to apply these concepts in the real world.

RESOURCES

Activity-based costing is a method of assigning the cost of resources to cost objects such as products, product lines, and customers. An organization's resources may include time, materials, floor space, equipment, technology and other things of value. Methods of assigning materials and direct labor costs to products are old, accurate, and well established. As a result, ABC concentrates on overhead costs that often have been arbitrarily allocated to cost objects in ways that related little to the factors that really caused costs.

Like other cost assignment methods, ABC uses financial information from the general ledger system as its primary source of cost data. Unlike traditional cost accounting, which normally uses highly aggregated cost information, ABC uses general ledger cost data in a less aggregated format. The highly regimented structure of a chart of accounts system that is organized around the business's organizational chart provides a good basis for the initial classification of resources under ABC. Although this functional classification of costs is not ideal for cost accounting purposes, a structured chart of accounts is vastly superior to the unstructured financial accounting methods used by many companies. (Structured financial accounting techniques are discussed in Chapter 5.) As ABC practices become better developed and better software and techniques become available, cost accounting considerations are more likely to influence the methods of how costs are captured in general ledger systems.

Although ABC uses the general ledger system as its primary source of cost information, good cost accounting practice sometimes does not coincide with the conventions of financial accounting. For example, generally accepted accounting principles specify that product development and launch costs are normally expensed as incurred. This convention is in apparent contradiction with financial accounting's *matching principle*. The matching principle specifies that costs are to be expensed in the same period as the corresponding revenues are recognized. Financial accountants also may recognize depreciation in ways that do not accurately reflect the way that the value of an asset is consumed. In these situations, ABC practitioners would attempt to recognize the economic reality of the circumstances.

ACTIVITIES

The term *activity* is used to describe the way that an organization expends its resources. Activities are what an organization does. Activities are often routine in nature, using a planned set of procedures that are performed on a repetitive basis. Some activities may be performed every time a product is made; other activities may be performed every time a batch of product is made; still others may be performed only prior to product launch. Some activities may be performed for reasons that have nothing to do with products. Activities may be customer related, facility related, or related to a number of other factors. Traditional cost allocation methods ignore this timing aspect of cost. This omission is a major reason for the distortions that may result from traditional methods of cost accounting.

The term *function* is used to describe groups of related activities. Functions often correspond to the departments defined by the company's organizational chart. Examples of functions would include sales, engineering, purchasing, manufacturing, or quality control. The logic of grouping similar activities together is that efficiencies may be gained by developing groups of people within the organization that specialize in performing a particular type of task. This specialization should allow those people to be more efficient than a generalist who performs many different functions.

Many organizations seem to have a problem getting the various parts of the business to work together effectively. A functional organizational structure creates the problem of integrating the various functions that the business performs into a smoothly operating whole. This situation often becomes most obvious when a task must be performed that does not fit nicely into the perceived responsibilities of any one functional area. This may result in all involved parties declaring, "It's not my job." Such problems may have to go "up the chain of command" to be resolved at a level where someone has joint authority over all warring functions.

PROCESSES

A *process* is defined as a group of activities that are linked together by the outputs that they exchange. The accepted best management practice today is for businesses to organize themselves according to their business processes. This trend has been heavily influenced by Harvard Professor Michael E. Porter's concept of the value chain.[2] According to Porter, there are nine basic activities that every organization performs—five primary activities and four support activities:

Primary Activities

1. Inbound logistics
2. Operations
3. Outbound logistics
4. Marketing and sales
5. Service

Support Activities

1. Firm infrastructure
2. Human resource management
3. Technology development
4. Procurement

Conceptually, the theory is intuitively appealing because businesses could organize around their business processes, seamlessly passing goods from receiving to operations to shipping to the customer. However, despite the acceptance of this theory, many companies have found the theory difficult to apply in the real world. For example, the operations function may require material-handling skills that duplicate those required by both inbound and outbound logistics. Particularly in a smaller organization, economics may not justify three separate work groups.

The difficulty in organizing businesses according to business processes often relates to the complexity of those processes themselves. It is quite common for one product to use one sequence of business activities while another product uses some of the same activities but not others and requires them in a different order. One activity may be a part of many different processes because an activity may be required to produce many different products. An activity may alternately be part of very few or only one process.

Sequencing activities into business processes provides the company with a good vehicle to examine and reduce costs. Companies that examine their business processes often find loops that can be straightened out, dead ends that can be eliminated, or activities that can be combined or eliminated to reduce costs. Because time is money, studying the sequencing of activities also may allow the company to increase the speed of throughput, thereby reducing the floor space, interest, and other inventory carrying costs.

WHY USE ACTIVITIES TO ASSIGN COST?

Activities are what an organization does. In most situations, people can easily identify the various activities that their company performs. Costs are easy to understand from an activity perspective. If the company must perform a process consisting of five activities in order to provide a service to a customer, then it is easy to understand that the price charged to the customer must be more than the cost of performing those activities if the company is to earn a profit.

Activities are actionable. It is easy to understand that if the company eliminates a non–value-added activity, the resources used to perform that activity can be redeployed and costs therefore can be reduced. It is also easy to understand that the amount charged to a client should exhibit a relationship to the cost of activities performed for that client. Furthermore, it is easy to understand that if a client wants the company to perform an extra nonstandard activity, the client should be charged more than a client that wants a standard product.

Using activities improves the accuracy of costs. Exhibit 6.1 provides a simplified diagram of the flow of costs in ABC. This exhibit shows that in ABC, the cost of resources is assigned to activities that in turn are assigned to cost objects such

Exhibit 6.1 Cost assignment using activity-based costing

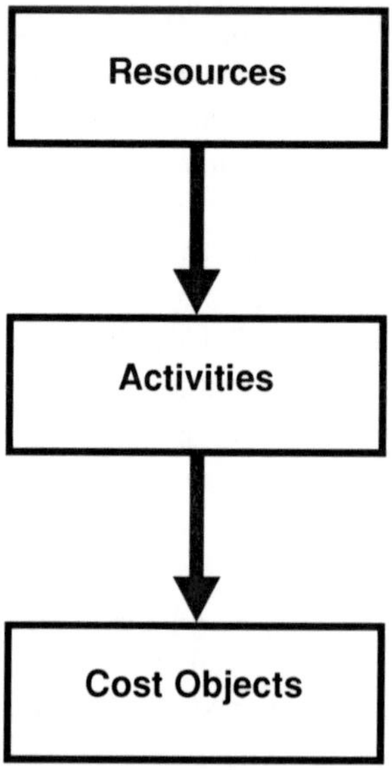

Note: Activity-based costing assigns costs in stages. Costs are consumed by activities and then activities are consumed by cost objects.

as products or customers. This exhibit also could be read in reverse. Cost objects cause activities to be performed, and performing activities causes resources to be consumed. In ABC, activities become the vital link between resources and cost objects.

A common cause for an unprofitable product is that a required activity was not considered at the time the price was established. When traditional costing methods are used for pricing, the omitted activity is often an "indirect" activity that is so time consuming that the estimator would have treated the activity as direct had the extent of the effort been considered at the time of quotation. Special packaging requirements often fall into this category. In examining its most unprofitable products, one company discovered that a customer required that the plastic parts that it purchased had to be packed in plastic bags filled with water to keep them hydrated. The company had never packaged any of its products in water before. Although the company considered this procedure a legitimate request, it was one that had not been specified by the customer's purchasing manager prior to quotation but had been added by the customer's quality control personnel after production had begun. Realizing that this extra activity created additional cost, the company then had a basis for discussions with the customer for a price increase.

Activities highlight the root causes of cost. Costs increase as the number of activities increase, and costs decrease as activities are eliminated. Some activities are very expensive to perform, while others cost very little. Sometimes several different methods are available for accomplishing a particular task. Understanding the activities required to satisfy a customer's needs substantially increases the likelihood that the company will be able to sell its services at a price that will produce a profit. A company that understands what causes cost is less likely to accept work that just provides a "contribution" to overhead costs.

The concept of a contribution margin almost disappears with ABC. When administrative activities are examined, for example, it is understood that almost none of them are truly fixed costs. Increasing the number of sales made increases the number of invoices that must be produced, the number of cash receipt transactions that must be entered, and the number of collection calls that must be made to customers. Although the addition of one new customer may not require hiring a new accounts receivable (AR) clerk, the addition of 10 customers together may require that additional personnel be added. While the addition of 10 small customers may require an additional AR clerk, adding the same amount of sales to an existing large customer may result in no additional clerical work at all. To an accounts receivable clerk, the number of transactions causes work, not the amount of those transactions. As a result, increasing an invoice quantity from 5,000 to 10,000 units may have no effect on the effort expended by the accounts receivable department.

Transaction volumes may mean little to the workload of the company Controller. Because the Controller's tasks largely relate to developing procedures, solving problems, and coaching the accounting staff, change means work to the Controller. To the Controller, work is usually lowest when the company is operating at a constant level of activity. Substantial changes in business activity, either up or down, will increase the amount of work that the Controller has to do.

ASSIGNING COSTS TO ACTIVITIES

Activity-based costing is a method of assigning costs. Every business accumulates costs through its financial reporting systems. Purchases are made and paid for through accounts payable, employees are paid through payroll, and information about these payments is posted to the company's general ledger system. In the general ledger, costs may be classified in many ways according to the company's account numbering scheme. Modern numbering schemes (i.e., those developed to take advantage of computerized sorting and summarizing capabilities) allow each expenditure to be categorized according to the type of expense (e.g., overtime pay versus training expenses) as well as to which business function the expense relates (e.g., quality control versus maintenance).

A result occurs when an activity is performed. There is a cause-and-effect relationship between performing the activity and achieving the result. Factors that cause costs to occur are called *cost drivers*. Cost drivers can normally be measured or at least estimated in some manner. Levels of activity are often measured in terms of the outputs that they create.

Transactions are used to measure the occurrence of an activity or frequency that it is performed. Transactions would include reporting production, a material receipt, a shipment, processing a time report or issuing an accounts payable check. The quantity measurement for an activity may be stated in time, number of units, or some other method of measurement. Transaction counts are often used as a measurement of the number of occurrences of a cost driver. Many such statistics are often readily available for use in cost accounting. Production reports may provide the number of cycles that a machine has made or reveal the amount of idle machine time available. Numbered shippers or invoices may reveal the number of sales transactions, and payroll data provide information about the number of hours worked.

ASSIGNING ACTIVITY COSTS TO COST OBJECTS

A *cost object* is anything to which costs have been assigned, such as an activity, customer, product, product line, or product family. In ABC the term *cost object* usually is used to mean the ultimate or final destination to which costs are assigned. In traditional costing systems, the final cost objects are usually products, but in

ABC, because costs are assigned according to what causes them, some costs are inevitably assigned to cost objects that are not products, such as customers.

Using ABC, the cost of a sales opportunity can be analyzed by identifying the activities that will be required to provide the specific product to the specific customer. Just as manufacturing companies use a *bill of materials* to accumulate the material content of a product, ABC uses a *bill of activities* to identify and quantify the activities that will be required to produce the product, service the customer, and make the sale.

Information about the costs to serve specific customers or categories of customers is quite valuable in pricing. Managers often intuitively understand that some customers are more expensive to service than others. Armed with solid cost data, management is able to structure a pricing strategy that encourages sales to the most profitable customers.

Traditional costing methods tell what the cost of a product would be if it were produced at an average volume, using average methods. ABC is able to provide reliable cost information in situations that are clearly not average. This information provides a powerful competitive weapon for companies in which diversity, not uniformity, describes the products that they sell, the processes that they use, or the sales volumes of their various products. The remainder of the chapter will provide insight into how this is possible.

HIERARCHY OF ACTIVITIES

One of the central concepts to ABC is that there are many different things that cause costs to be incurred. Costs do not "just happen." Costs are incurred for a specific reason. Not all activities are performed every day or with the same frequency. The nature of the activity determines the frequency that it is performed. Some costs are directly related to the number of units of the product that are produced. Some activities are performed every time enough units are accumulated to fill a box. Other costs, such as job setup, relate to the number of batches that are produced, which may be independent of the number of units that are made. Product launch costs occur only before a product is made for the first time and may be completely independent of either the number of batches or production volumes.

Some costs have nothing to do with products but have everything to do with having a customer. For example, setting up the customer in the computer, mailing catalogs to customers, or sending key customer contacts a small holiday present are costs that may have little to do with sales volume. Other costs may have nothing to do with either products or customers but may be facility-sustaining costs that are dependent on the number of locations or facilities that the company operates.

Although there are a dozen or more levels at which costs might be applied, some are commonly used:

- Unit level costs
- Batch level costs
- Product launch costs
- Product-sustaining costs
- Product line costs
- Distribution channel costs
- Customer level costs
- Facility-sustaining costs

Each company conceptualizes its own operations in its own way. There is not necessarily a "right" or "wrong" way to segregate an organization's activities. Each company should make a model that reflects the way that it observes cost to behave in its own real-world situation.

The concept of a hierarchy of activities is a major departure from the methods of traditional cost accounting. Traditional cost accounting examines only how a product consumes materials and direct labor, not how it consumes overhead. Traditional methods associate all overhead costs with labor hours. The total cost per direct labor hour is divided by the number of units produced to provide a cost of labor and overhead per unit of production.

Traditional allocation methods treat all costs as if only unit-level activities existed. By lumping all overhead costs together in a single pool, some products are assigned costs that have nothing to do with making that product, while other products that make heavy use of overhead resources get off easy. Because traditional methods treat all costs as unit costs, traditional methods provide a cost that is only relevant for an average product, produced at an average volume using typical processes for that business.

Traditional cost accounting produces one number to represent the cost of a product. This cost is supposed to be valid for a *relevant range* of business activity for the whole company, but is insensitive to even radical changes in volume for a single product. Accordingly, similar high-volume and low-volume products would look equally attractive on a per-unit basis because traditional methods are incapable of identifying the effect of volume on cost. Although traditional methods could produce a break-even point for the company as a whole, it cannot produce a break-even point for a product by itself because traditional cost accounting treats all costs as variable unit costs.

Traditional costs are valid for only a single level of business activity for the company. To the extent that business activity is higher or lower than the activity level that was used to calculate the burden rate, overhead is *overabsorbed* or *underabsorbed* by operations. Accordingly, if the company's business level was down due to a big decrease in the volume for a single product, the variance would be attributed to a change in general business activity, rather than an unprofitable production level on the product that caused the problem.

Many inventory control software packages use a standard costing method that separates both fixed costs and variable costs. Accountants who choose to break down their costs between these two categories might expect the package to provide a feature that would produce a unit cost that somehow treated the "fixed" cost as fixed and the "variable" cost as variable. For the most part, software that offers this feature treats all costs as variable, and the only real functionality behind this feature is that the software usually allows these two categories of overhead to be posted to different general ledger accounts.

Pricing is only one of the uses for ABC information. Activity-based costing can provide an excellent framework for cost-reduction efforts. ABC also can be an important budgeting tool that not only can improve budget accuracy but can also greatly reduce the amount of squabbles and political battles that often accompany the budget process.[3]

The planned use of ABC data will have a major effect on how much effort it takes to extract usable data. *Management Accounting* (now called *Strategic Finance*) magazine reported in 1998 that the average ABC project took 3.6 years in large companies and 2.3 years in small companies to reach the usage stage with ABC.[4] The demarcation line between large companies and small companies was defined as $100 million in sales. This appalling statistic is not consistent with the author's own experience and may not be true. The author's experiences in companies under $50 million in sales indicates that reasonably good ABC data can be derived in less than 12 weeks in a small company. Rough activity costs that are significantly better than traditional costing data may be developed in less than 10 days in some circumstances.

The wide difference in these numbers most likely relates to the definition of an activity. In much of the literature on ABC, the writers provide examples of activities such as issuing an accounts payable check or preparing a purchase order. In very few companies is the cost of performing these two particular activities material with respect to the total expenses of the organization.

The amount of work to implement ABC increases quickly as the number of activities that are considered increases. Many companies might have a hundred or more activities that have greater materiality than issuing an accounts payable check or preparing a purchase order. Still, accounts payable supervisors or purchasing managers would be interested in these statistics if they would help justify head counts during a budgeting or reengineering effort.

Such detail is not necessary for activity-based pricing. For pricing purposes, costs need to be understood well enough to quantify the cause–effect relationships that affect costs. For pricing, it is not necessary to identify the cost of each activity individually. If several activities have the same cost driver (i.e., they are caused by the same factor), then for pricing purposes these activities can be aggregated together in a *macroactivity*. Even rough, hastily prepared ABC data are likely to be significantly better than traditional cost accounting data for developing pricing, particularly if the product is far from average in any way.

ASSIGNING COSTS

Determining the cost of activities is a struggle for organizations large and small. Much of the ABC literature is critical of financial accounting systems for being organized to collect cost information at the function level instead of the activity level. One thing that many writers seem to miss is that many financial reporting systems, particularly in smaller companies, are not capable of providing costs at the functional level either.

Much of the ABC literature often suggests that ABC should be maintained as a second costing system for management decision-making purposes. This proposal has the potential to do significantly more to improve the profitability of the consulting firms that are advocating this approach than for the profitability of their clients. Businesses are not in business to produce cost reports or financial statements (unless the business is an accounting firm). As a discipline, ABC provides the potential of creating its own unwieldy bureaucracy dedicated to overanalyzing the costs of performing trivial activities that the organization performs. For ABC to be a value-added activity, the data collected must be relevant and material to the operation of the business.

At present, many companies maintain both a traditional costing system and ABC. The reason for this seems to be that thus far ABC efforts have concentrated on properly apportioning costs to activities. The tools available to reassemble activity-based costs to identify the full cost of a particular product to a particular customer are not yet as advanced or efficient. As a result, it is not uncommon to have a company use a computer spreadsheet to reassemble costs for pricing purposes or profitability analysis. The practice of maintaining two cost systems is likely to fade as ABC software matures.

When two cost systems are maintained, traditional costing is normally used for financial accounting purposes such as inventory valuation and recognizing cost of sales. ABC data are normally used for management decision making, such as quotation development or product profitability analysis. Companies that use ABC often develop hybridized overhead rates to be used in their traditional standard cost systems. Using activity-based techniques to assign some costs to direct activities while other costs are assigned using traditional allocation methods develops these hybridized rates. The standard cost system then usually treats all costs as variable.

Activity-based costing uses common-sense methods to assign costs to activities. The next few sections discuss common ways that costs may be assigned using ABC.

Floor Space Costs

Floor space costs may include rent, heat, lighting, cleaning, maintenance, and taxes on real estate. A common-sense method of apportioning floor space costs is to look at the space assigned to each of the activities that the company performs and distribute the costs accordingly. This is not hard to do. Obtaining a floor plan for the business, identifying the space occupied by each business function, and prorating costs accordingly may apportion floor space. Therefore, in a hospital, if radiology occupied 5% of the floor space and maternity occupied 10%, each would receive their proportional share of the building-related costs. What if the costs to build space for one department were not the same as another? Office space costs more to rent than warehouse space. In this case, floor space costs should be apportioned according to the activities that really caused the costs.

Equipment and Maintenance Costs

Some activities are very capital intensive. Rather than assign capital equipment costs as "overhead," a better way is to figure out what equipment is used by each activity and then recover the cost of the equipment over its useful life. In this manner, the costs of an expensive x-ray machine are recovered from the patients that were actually treated using that machine. Purchase costs are not the only costs that are associated with equipment. Maintenance costs should be specifically assigned to those pieces of equipment that require maintenance, and floor space costs should be reassigned from functional departments to the various activities, such as machine operations that the department performs. The cost of money is also an important consideration when considering equipment costs. This consideration is discussed later in this chapter under the section Interest and the Cost of Money.

Human Resources Administration Costs

Companies have human resources departments because they employ people. Some activities are people intensive and others are capital intensive. The costs of operating a human resources department is conventionally assigned to the various activities that a company performs according to the number of people associated with each activity. Some people-related costs may not specifically reside within the human resources department. For example, accounting may do payroll processing and training may be the responsibility of operations. Some kinds of positions require more human resources management effort than others. Computer programmers, engineers, and other kinds of skilled professionals often require significantly more recruiting effort and may require headhunter fees, whereas others do not. Costs should be assigned according to what causes costs in each organization.

Information Systems Costs

Many things cause information systems (IS) costs. A substantial portion of computer hardware costs is usually easy to assign because costs are represented by personal computers sitting on users' desks. Software costs may sometimes be specifically assigned to a particular business activity based on what the software does. Other IS costs may relate to the inherent complexity of the company's network or changes that are occurring within the business. Companies most often assign IS costs according to personal computers or other input/output devices on the computer system, but some companies apportion costs according to the amount of time that the IS department spends on user requests or other measures of computer usage.

Product Development Costs

Product development costs, sometimes also called launch costs, are costs incurred to design a product, develop prototypes, test the product, construct tooling, train sales people, prepare promotional materials, and get the product ready to be produced and sold in the expected full production volumes. A key characteristic of development costs is that they occur at the very beginning of the product life cycle.

Traditional accounting methods treat many kinds of product development costs as period costs. Although some development costs such as tooling are often capitalized, the prelaunch activities of sales, purchasing, quality control, IS, and accounting personnel are usually not. Indeed, the accounting policies at many companies collect costs associated with production but not costs associated with the launch or product discontinuation. Some companies may collect data associated with specific launch or development projects, but these project costs may include only technical personnel and not the many hours invested by sales or administrative personnel in product launch.

Development costs matter because many product costs are incurred only in development and have nothing to do with the production or service delivery process. This is particularly important because development costs are usually true fixed costs that are not related to production or sales volumes. Accordingly, development costs should be pulled out of the cost pools used to assign indirect costs to production running rates. When products have a significant fixed costs component, unit costs become highly dependent on the total number of units that will be sold over the product life cycle.

Development costs are usually found to be directly related to product complexity.

Information about these costs is often obtained by interviewing methods. Engineering personnel are often able to provide a menu of product features and the amount of engineering time necessary to develop each feature listed on the menu. From this list, development costs may be estimated based on initial product concept. These estimates may help kill an unprofitable product while it is still in the design stages or force a more cost-effective development process. When development costs for low-volume products are prohibitive, companies are sometimes able to find other ways of satisfying that market, such as modifying the design of a high-volume product to fill that niche. Although interviewing methods may be inexact, learning how to predict development and launch costs even in general terms is well worth the effort when these costs are significant.

Interest and the Cost of Money

Because financing equipment and accounts receivable normally cause interest costs, interest costs should be divided among the company's assets and accounts receivable. Although most companies plan for profit by marking up costs to provide a specific return on sales, there is a solid argument for planning profit from the perspective of a return on investment or a return on assets. Using this method, the company would associate its expected returns with the assets employed in producing the product. If this method is used, the activity rates should be broken up into their components to show how much of the rate was an actual cost and how much was planned profit. By showing the planned profit separately, management would then be able to choose to increase or decrease the planned profit based on the specific competitive situation.

ACCUMULATING ACTIVITY COSTS

Step-Down Analysis

A step-down analysis is a method whereby one category of cost is reassigned to other activities, functions, departments, or cost objects. This reassignment is normally performed successively for several different categories of cost, giving the numbers a stair-step look on a spreadsheet.

The step-down analysis technique has been used for a long time. Initially, it was used to apportion administrative costs to operating activities as a method of cost allocation. A step-down analysis was once required in the health-care industry in the United States for cost reimbursement under the Medicare and Medicaid programs. This analysis simply reassigned administrative costs to operating departments in proportion to the expenses that were charged directly to the department.

Although superior to previous allocation methods, when the step-down technique was applied in this manner, it was merely an alternate method of performing an arbitrary allocation.

Step-Down Analysis as a Method to Prorate Cost

An example of a traditional step-down analysis that arbitrarily allocates overhead costs to direct labor departments based on total expenses is shown in Exhibit 6.2. For simplicity, only four administrative departments and four operating departments are shown. This company has $5,530,000 of nonmaterial costs, including $1,280,000 in administrative costs that are to be assigned from the four overhead

Exhibit 6.2 Step-down analysis using traditional allocation methods

	Functional Costs Before Allocations	Step-Down Allocation of Overhead Costs				Functional Costs After Allocations
Rent and maintenance	250,000					
Information systems	750,000	35,511				
Accounts receivable	80,000	3,788	13,872			
Human resources	200,000	9,470	34,680	4,389		
Stamping—primary	2,000,000	94,697	346,804	43,892	116,960	2,602,353
Stamping—secondary	500,000	23,674	86,701	10,973	29,240	650,588
Welding	1,000,000	47,348	173,402	21,946	58,480	1,301,176
Assembly	750,000	35,511	130,052	16,460	43,860	975,882
	$5,530,000	$250,000	$785,511	$97,660	$248,539	$5,530,000

Note: This step-down analysis shows an allocation of overhead costs using the total cost of each business function as the allocation base. First, $250,000 of rent and maintenance cost is allocated to the other seven departments, then $785,511 of information systems cost ($750,000 of information systems department costs and $35,511 of costs allocated from rent and maintenance). Allocations continue in this manner until all costs are allocated.

departments to the four direct labor departments. The allocation base normally excludes material costs that are directly assigned to products.

In this example, $200,000 of human resources department costs were allocated to each department proportionately, based on the costs that were already directly assigned to each department through the general ledger system. Because the $750,000 in costs that were assigned to the IS department represents 14% of the company's cost base (excluding the $200,000 of human resources costs), IS will be assigned 14% of the human resources costs or $28,143. Information systems costs can be reassigned as well using the same technique. There are now $778,143 in IS costs that can be reassigned proportionately to the remaining departments. This process can be repeated until all costs are reassigned to direct labor departments.

Although the most common traditional method of cost allocation assumes that overhead costs are proportional to direct labor hours, the traditional step-down method of cost allocation assumes that overhead costs are proportional to total costs that have been incurred. The fault of both techniques is that they make assumptions about cost behavior that do not correspond with real world cost behavior.

Further Evolution in Cost Analysis

The step-down analysis was an important development in the field of cost accounting. Looking at a step-down analysis, the obvious question is, "Why do the assignments of cost have to be so arbitrary?" Human resource department costs obviously have some relationship with the number of people in the company, IS costs must have some relationship with the number of people who use computers, and building maintenance costs must have some relationship with the size of the building. A better assignment of costs could be achieved by determining rational, logical methods of assigning costs based on management's knowledge of what causes cost in the business.

Exhibit 6.3 analyzes the same costs that were used in Exhibit 6.2 from a completely different perspective. What if all rent and maintenance department costs were assigned according to the number of square feet occupied by each department? IS department costs could be assigned according to the number of personal computers owned by each department. Logically, human resources administration costs might be assigned according to the number of people who work in each department. Preparing invoices and collecting cash determines the amount of work of the accounts receivable department. Accordingly, the accounts receivable invoice itself should be the final cost object.

The major difference between the treatment of costs in Exhibits 6.2 and 6.3 is the existence of objective rational information that defines how costs should be distributed. Although the cost allocation performed in Exhibit 6.2 was arbitrary,

Exhibit 6.3 Step-down analysis using consumption data

	Sq Ft.	PCs	Head Counts
Rent and maintenance	450	4	4
Information systems	1,050	12	10
Human resources	400	1	4
Accounts receivable	350	3	3
Stamping—primary	15,000	3	30
Stamping—secondary	6,000	2	12
Welding	2,700	—	18
Assembly	2,400	1	16
	28,350	26	97

	Functional Costs Before Allocations	Proration of Overhead Costs			Functional Costs After Allocations
Rent and maintenance	200,000				
Information systems	750,000	7,526.9			
Human resources	250,000	2,867.4	75,753		
Accounts receivable	80,000	2,509.0	227,258	12,479	322,246
Stamping—primary	2,000,000	107,526.9	227,258	124,792	2,459,577
Stamping—secondary	500,000	43,010.8	151,505	49,917	744,433
Welding	1,000,000	19,354.8	—	74,875	1,094,230
Assembly	750,000	17,204.3	75,753	66,556	909,513
	$5,530,000	$200,000	$757,527	$328,620	$5,530,000

Note: This step-down analysis has used information about the usage of floor space, personal computers, and human resources administration to apportion the cost of three overhead functions to other activities. Note that the cost of processing accounts receivable has not been treated as overhead. This company will assign accounts receivable processing costs on a per-invoice basis.

there is a direct connection in Exhibit 6.3 between a department's use of a resource and the amount of cost that it is assigned.

In Exhibit 6.3 costs were assigned at multiple levels. Rent costs were assigned to IS, then IS costs were assigned to human resources. Activity-based costing is often diagrammed as being a three-level costing system, as shown in Exhibit 6.1. In the step-down analysis shown in Exhibit 6.3, costs were initially assigned to departments or functions. Most general ledger systems are set up to collect costs at the department or functional level.

FURTHER ANALYZING ACTIVITIES

One department may perform many different activities. As shown in Exhibit 6.4, accounting departments process accounts payable, accounts receivable, and payroll, and perform general accounting activities. Each of these major categories of activities is caused by different kinds of events. Accounts Payable costs relate to purchasing activities, whereas accounts receivable costs relate to making sales. Each of these major categories of activity could be further subdivided into more specific activities. For example, accounts receivable personnel set up customers, enter invoice line items, create invoices, and post cash receipts. Although in theory each business may perform hundreds of activities, in practice only a few dozen activities consume enough resources to be material by themselves. Activities that are immaterial by themselves are normally aggregated with related activities. An immaterial activity may be aggregated with another activity in the same department or an activity that is caused by the same cost driver. For example, some purchasing department costs and accounts payable costs may be combined as a single macroactivity.

Exhibit 6.4 Converting departmental costs to activity costs

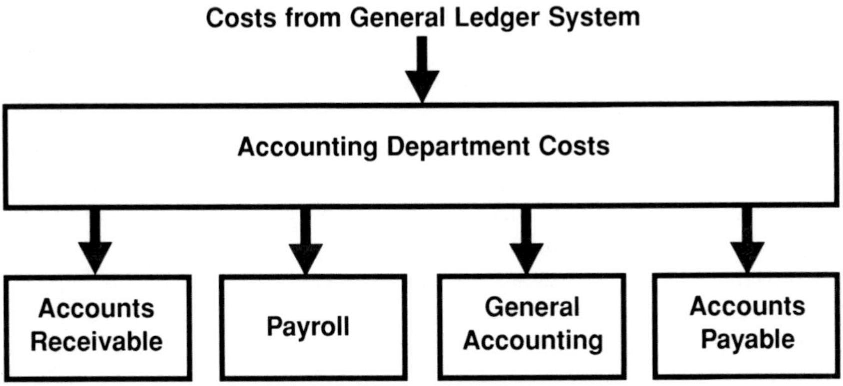

Note: Well-structured financial reporting systems assign costs that are accumulated from accounts payable and payroll to specific departments. Departmental costs may be separated into activity costs using data about the number of people working in each area, their salaries, or whatever information is available. When historical data are not available, the apportionment of costs is often based on estimates by the department head.

How would the costs of the accounting department be assigned to the four categories of activity in Exhibit 6.4? If the general ledger system is well organized, many of the costs related to the accounting department will have already been reassigned to that department. A well-designed financial reporting system collects all payroll- and benefit-related costs by department as well as anything that the department purchases through accounts payable. Some companies also apportion costs such as floor space or utilities to each department using factors established in their accounts payable or general ledger system. One obvious way to apportion Accounting costs among the department's four major activities would be to analyze the number of people assigned to each function. If the staff of each area had different salary levels, a more accurate way would be to look at the wage costs of each function. Rather than specifically study the benefit and other nonwage expenditures of each area, wages might be used as a surrogate measurement for those expenses.

Many companies do not have specific data available to measure resource consumption by many of their activities. For example, in a small accounting department, each of the employees may perform responsibilities in several different areas, crossing activity boundaries. In this case, the ABC team may apportion costs according to an educated guess. It will become clear from the following discussion on cost accounting that it is more important *how* costs are assigned than that they are assigned precisely.

ABC as a Closed-Loop System

All cost accounting methods are designed to be closed systems. In each of these systems, a total cost figure is apportioned to cost objects such as products, product lines, or customers using a method that is designed to assure that all costs are absorbed someplace. Therefore, any underassignment of cost in one area must be counterbalanced by an overassignment of cost in another. If the cost of a product is made up of only one factor, such as an hourly labor and overhead rate, that single factor may sometimes be grossly over or under the real cost of the product. More detailed methods of cost accumulation are more likely to be reasonably accurate. Because cost accounting systems are closed, the more factors that comprise the cost of an individual product, the more likely it is that the underassignment errors and the overassignment errors will be of similar magnitude.

Activity-based cost assignments resemble a network. Resources are assigned to activities that in turn may be prorated among other activities or be assigned to cost objects. For example, building maintenance costs might be assigned to IS and other departments according to square footage occupied. Information systems costs, including building maintenance costs, might be assigned to other departments, including the human resources department, based on the number of computers in the department. Human Resources costs that include the department's share of building maintenance and IS costs might be in turn assigned to the rest of the organization based on head count.

An example of a section of an ABC cost assignment network is shown in Exhibit 6.5. Here the cost assignment path for the accounting department shown in

Exhibit 6.5 ABC cost assignment network

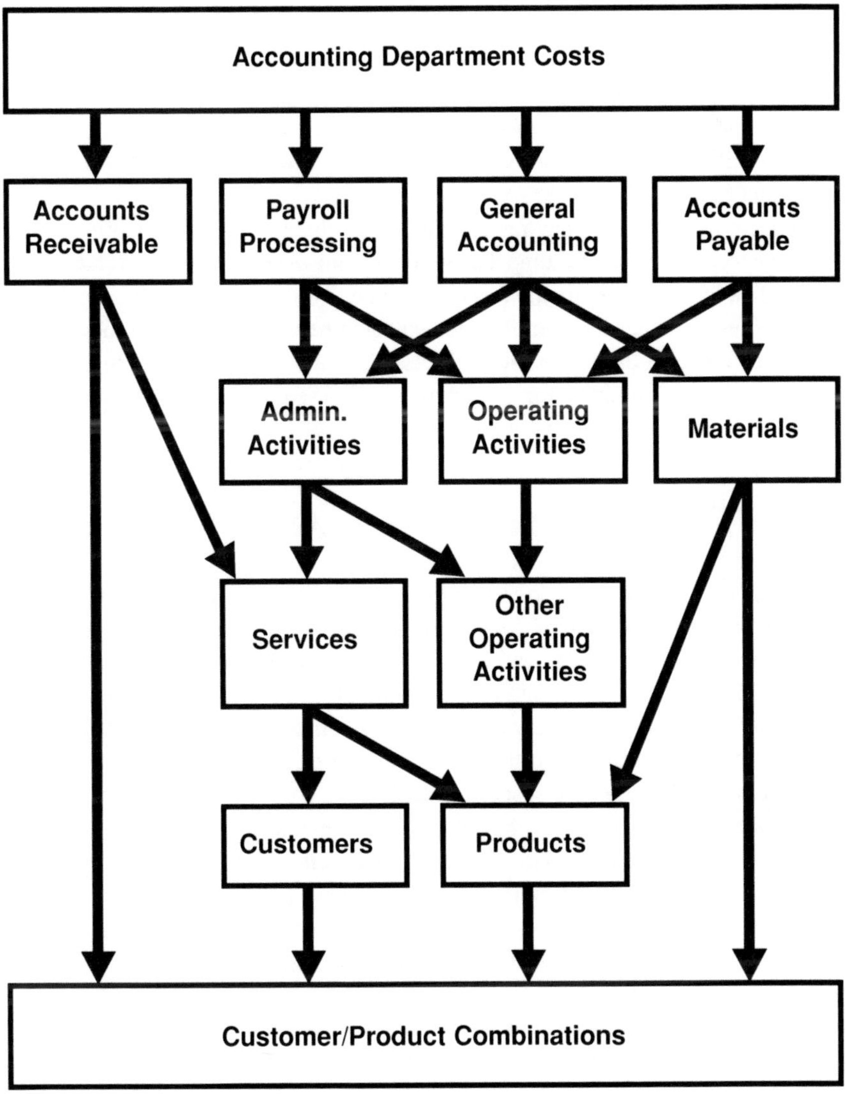

Note: Activity-based cost assignments resemble a network. Resources are assigned to activities that in turn may be prorated among other activities or assigned to cost objects.

Exhibit 6.4 has been further extended all the way to the final cost object. From this diagram it can be seen that some of the accounting department costs have been assigned to accounts payable. Accounts payable costs have been assigned to both materials and operating activities. The cost of the operating activities has been assigned to other operating activities, then to products and finally customer/product combinations. Because the number of cost assignments that occur can be enormous, the task is made much easier when it is performed using specialized ABC software.

Unlike a step-down analysis in which each cost assignment represents a different level in the cost assignment scheme, many allocations might exist on the same level using ABC. For example, when building maintenance, IS, and human resource costs are assigned, the costs of these departments may be prorated among all of the other departments, but not among each other, avoiding levels of cost assignment that have little meaning.

A customer expects to pay for some activities directly. At an accounting office, customers expect to pay for time that an accountant works on their tax return. They expect that the fee for preparing that tax return will cover the cost of having a voice mail system, but the customer does not expect to be billed every time they leave a message. The cost of support activities is supposed to be built into the primary activities that the organization performs. A cost assignment network apportions support activity costs to primary activities.

Other Thoughts on ABC

Although much of the ABC literature discusses assigning overhead costs relating to indirect activities, some of the biggest benefits of ABC techniques come from the assignment of operating overhead that relates to direct contact or touch activities. Traditional cost accounting examines direct labor or sometimes direct labor and benefits, but usually ignores the other costs that are directly associated with that activity. For example, traditional cost accounting treats depreciation, rent, and utilities as overhead, but the cost of a machine, the cost of the floor space, and the cost of the utilities that the machine uses obviously must be related to the activity that the machine performs. Not all machines cost the same amount of money. It may require a $10,000 investment to equip a worker who performs a welding operation but $1 million to equip a worker to perform some other task. The $10,000 machine may be relatively maintenance free, whereas the $1 million machine may require constant attention.

Activity-based costing becomes particularly important in capital-intensive businesses. High levels of automation may mean that the amount of skilled indirect labor required to maintain a machine might actually be more than the direct labor that tends the machine while it is running. Traditional cost allocation techniques can create huge distortions in these situations.

Many companies establish their prices without good cost information. A 1998 study by Kip R. Krumweide[5] revealed that 61% of service companies had adopted ABC compared with 45% of manufacturing companies. Combined, only 49% of all companies had adopted ABC. These statistics have interesting implications for pricing strategy. These data imply that more than 50% of all companies are operating with a significant handicap when planning for profit. This situation can provide a competitive advantage to their competitors who are armed with good costing data via ABC. The use of activity-based pricing is discussed in the next chapter.

SUMMARY

The key points discussed in this chapter are listed below:

1. Activity-based costing is a method of assigning costs according to the factors that cause costs. Activity-based costing can provide a competitive advantage to companies who use these methods.
2. Activity-based costing was named and became a formal discipline in 1986 as a result of a project initiated by the Consortium of Advanced Manufacturing–International (CAM-I) working in conjunction with the National Association of Accountants (NAA). The Institute of Management Accountants, the NAA's successor, remains heavily involved in promoting the use of ABC.
3. Activity-based costing techniques apply to all types of businesses in all industries.
4. Activity-based costing is a multistep method of assigning the cost of resources to activities and the cost of activities to cost objects, such as products, product lines, and customers.
5. Activities are what an organization does. It is easy for people to understand that performing activities consumes the resources of the organization. Businesses are usually organized functionally by department. One department may perform many different kinds of activities.
6. A process is defined as a group of activities that are linked together by the outputs that they exchange.
7. An important advance in the development of cost accounting occurred when accountants began to use the step-down technique to assign costs based on rational methods rather than arbitrary allocations.
8. A cost object is anything to which costs have been assigned. In ABC, the term *cost object* usually refers to a final cost object such as a product, product line, or customer.
9. Many levels of costs may exist in ABC. These include unit level costs, batch level costs, product development costs, product-sustaining costs, customer-

related costs, and facility-sustaining costs. These hierarchies of costs cause the costs per unit for a product to change as various factors relating to costs change. Volume is an example of a factor that has a big influence on the cost per unit for a product.

10. Activity-based costing software creates a closed-loop cost assignment network. The cost of resources is assigned to activities, which may in turn be assigned to other activities. Costs are assigned to cost objects according to how those cost objects require activities to be performed. All starting costs are assigned to cost objects.

11. About 50% of all companies in the United States use ABC in some form.

NOTES

1. As quoted by Srikuman S. Rau, "Overhead Can Kill You," *Forbes* (February 10, 1997), pp. 97–98.
2. Michael E. Porter, *Competitive Advantage* (New York: The Free Press, 1985), Chapter 2.
3. While a discussion of these uses of ABC is beyond the scope of this book, readers interested in these uses should read *Activity-Based Management for Service Industries, Government Entities, and Nonprofit Organizations* by James A. Brimson and John Antos or *Driving Value Using Activity-Based Budgeting* by James A. Brimson and John Antos with contributions by Jay Collins.
4. Kip R. Krumwiede, "ABC: Why It's Tried and How It Succeeds," *Management Accounting* (April 1998), p. 32.
5. Ibid.

7

ACTIVITY-BASED PRICING

ABP can improve a company's profitability relatively inexpensively and painlessly through the elimination of pricing mistakes.

ACTIVITY-BASED PRICING

Activity-based pricing (ABP) is a pricing method that uses knowledge about customer demand and knowledge about the costs of a specific selling situation to establish a price that will result in a specific planned profit. Market research can estimate the amount of product that will be sold at various prices. Activity-based costing allows the company to project costs corresponding to various sales volumes. When this information is combined, the company can project total revenue, expenses, and profit at any point on the customer demand curve. This process is called ABP.

Activity-based pricing is important because it marries volume-sensitive marketing data with volume-sensitive cost accounting to provide definitive answers about pricing. Market research data, when used alone, can project the price at which revenue is maximized, but not the price at which profit is maximized. Cost accounting data, when viewed without marketing data, tell how many units the company would have to sell at various prices to earn a profit, but provides no insight into how many units customers will buy. When both customer demand and cost are analyzed together, ABP can provide definitive answers about price. When activity-based costing data and customer demand data for many customers are combined, an analysis shows that in real-world situations profit is maximized at a price that is always higher than the price that maximizes revenues.

The techniques of ABP also can be used in competitive bid situations where customer demand usually consists of a single point. In a competitive bid, the buyer usually has specified that it will purchase a specific quantity of product and making a sale is an all-or-nothing proposition. For a competitively bid contract, ABP allows the seller to specifically project the profit that it will earn if it receives the contract at a particular price.

Because ABP uses activity-based costing to arrive at costs, the costs used are volume sensitive and can take into consideration the full costs that are unique to both the product and the customer. ABP prevents common pricing mistakes that many companies make, such as underpricing low-volume work, overpricing high-volume work, and losing bids for average work through introduction of "fudge factors."

Activity-based pricing provides a competitive advantage to companies that use it. This technique does not promise that a company using ABP will have big increases in sales. Many companies could quickly achieve large sales increases by simply lowering price. However, major price reductions are usually a formula for disastrous financial performance. ABP is a strategy for superior financial performance through superior financial knowledge. A company that uses ABP will often be able to win competitively bid contracts for desirable high-volume work when competing against companies using more traditional pricing methods. In addition, ABP will prevent companies from making mistakes such as underbidding undesirable "dog" jobs that may drag down their profits.

Activity-based pricing is a real-world technique that was developed by managers in real-world companies. Although specialized activity-based costing software such as Oros or Easy ABC[1] enhances the quality of ABP efforts, small companies using electronic spreadsheets can apply the technique with a modest amount of effort. ABP can improve a company's profitability relatively inexpensively and painlessly through the elimination of pricing mistakes.

OBJECTIVES OF ACTIVITY-BASED PRICING

The objectives of ABP are as follows:

- Establish price based on a solid knowledge of customer demand and product cost.
- Never unintentionally price a product at a loss.
- Know how much of price is profit.
- Generate a superior financial return through superior financial knowledge.

There are four commandments of ABP. They relate to required knowledge about both revenue and expenses. These commandments are:

1. Know thy product.
2. Know thy processes.

3. Know thy customers.
4. Know thy competitors.

This chapter will discuss the major factors used in ABP and serves as background for the discussion of the ABP models in Chapter 9.

RELATIONSHIP BETWEEN PRICE AND COST

Earning a profit is difficult. Not every company manages to be profitable. Even the largest and most successful companies do not necessarily earn a profit every year, and when they are profitable, the profit that they earn is usually not a large percentage of sales. The Standard & Poors 500 is an index that represents 500 of the largest publicly held companies in the United States. For a business to be able to grow large enough to be a part of the S&P 500 Index represents a certain level of achievement. It is interesting that the median profit as a percentage of revenue for these 500 very successful companies is 7.5% of sales.[2]

The S&P 500 represents a relatively profitable segment of the U.S. economy. The median profit in many industries is considerably lower. This can be observed just by looking at three industries that begin with the letter "A." The median profit margin for 34 publicly traded airlines is 2.4% of revenue. Profit margins average 1.9% for 103 apparel and accessories manufacturers and are 1.2% for 74 auto and truck parts suppliers. Profits for some industries are lower still.

The industries described above have very heavy competition. Their average selling price is only slightly above their cost. In most companies, total revenue is not far above full cost. Although most companies have relatively thin margins, not every company is in this situation. A few companies that have unique, proprietary products are able to price their products well above their cost. These privileged few include Microsoft, Intel, Merck, and other companies that have strong patent, trademark, or copyright protection for their products.

Most companies have profit margins that can be represented by a single digit percentage. Thin profits do not leave much margin for error. The 0.2% median profit for publicly traded grocery retailers implies that it takes $5 of sales just to make a penny of profit. This is why some people say, "To end up with a small fortune in business, start with a large one."

Pricing strategy must include not only an overall approach for the entire company, but an individualized approach for each product. Losses on one unprofitable product often offset the earnings on five or more profitable ones. ABP is particularly well suited for preventing big mistakes.

Suppose that a fictional business, Big John's Lumber Company, decided to establish all of its prices based on a markup of purchase cost. If Big John has good records for what it paid for the products that it sells and had basic accounting records, this would be an easy thing to do. Because Big John wants to use a markup method of pricing, it will probably use traditional allocation methods to determine its markup rates. One inevitable result will be that Big John's pricing will be different than its competition. Many factors would affect Big John's success or failure in this experiment.

One factor would be Big John's competitive position in the local lumber industry. The price move of a major competitor is more apt to motivate a reaction from competitors than the actions of a minor player. Competitor reaction will also depend on the visibility of the competitor's pricing structure. In the lumber business, each company can easily go into the other's store and learn its prices, so with a little effort, the competitor's pricing is easily known. If competitors adopted Big John's pricing structure, there likely would be no profit effect at all to the pricing change. However, if the competitors ignored Big John's shift in pricing, customer dynamics would begin to come into play.

When competitors have different prices, it is logical that a company would be more likely to sell products that are priced with a low profit margin than products that are priced with a high profit margin. Smart competitors will set their prices so that they receive an adequate profit. "Dumb" competitors, however, will unknowingly set their prices so that some products have uncompetitively high prices while other products are priced unprofitably low. Dumb competitors will win those sales that they unknowingly underprice with respect to their costs and their competitors.

When competitors have different prices, customers have the opportunity to price shop their purchases. When homeowners need a few little things for a weekend project, they may simply go to the store that is closest, but for larger purchases they are more likely to shop around. In the lumber business, certain products, such as 2 × 4's, are often purchased in large quantities. Other products, such as kitchen cabinets, are very expensive. Because both of these purchases involve a lot of money, customers are likely to compare prices.

Exhibit 7.1 shows the various possible outcomes of Big John's price adjustments from Big John's perspective. In Exhibit 7.1A, Big John and its competitors both have equally bad information about their costs because they each use arbitrary traditional allocation methods to distribute their overhead costs. Because all companies equally overprice and underprice their merchandise, no company's pricing methods provide a competitive advantage, and each company has a similar number of money-making and money-losing products. Because most companies tend to use traditional allocation methods in the same way, it is not unusual for several companies to overprice or underprice the same items as their competitors.

In Exhibit 7.1B, Big John's competitors have better cost information. This superior information does not necessarily mean that the competitor will get more sales, but those sales will be more profitable. When one company has better cost information, it is able to charge a slightly lower price for high profit margin items because it knows that it can do so and still make a profit. At the same time, better

Exhibit 7.1 Competition from Big John's perspective

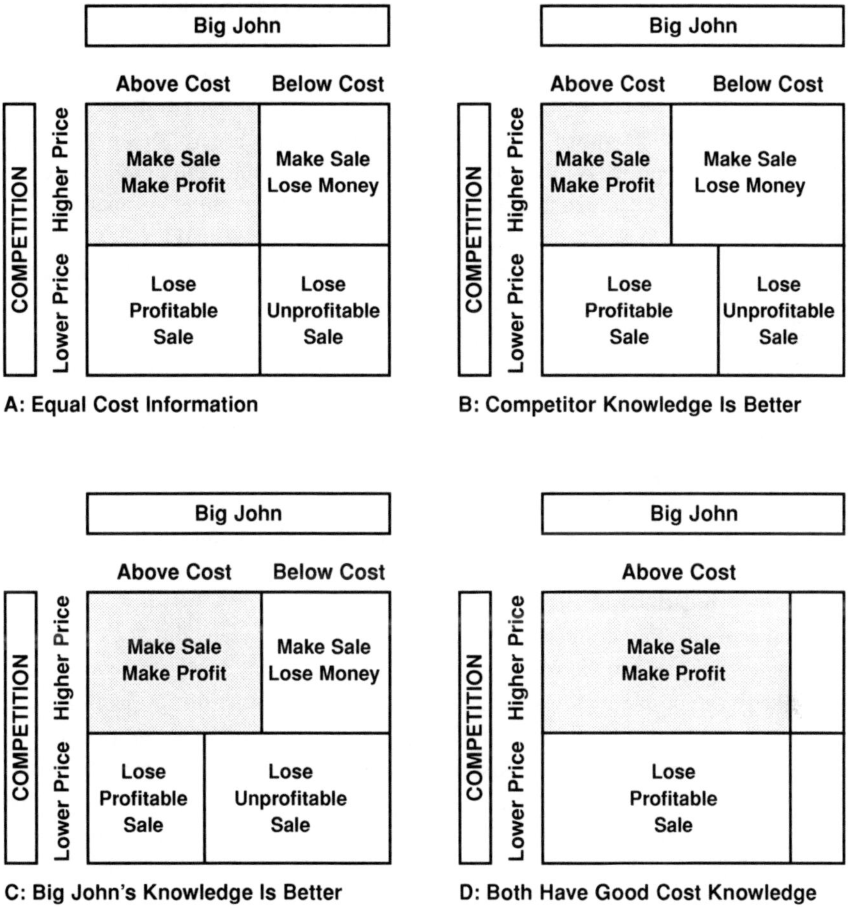

Note: A: Big John's Lumber has equally poor cost knowledge with its competitor, and neither has a competitive advantage. B: the competitor has better cost information, causing Big John to lose money. C: the situation is reversed and Big John has better information and a competitive advantage. D: both companies have very good cost information, avoiding making sales at a loss.

information allows a company to charge more money on products that would not otherwise be profitable. In effect, unprofitable sales are exchanged for profitable ones. Companies would rather keep the profitable sales to themselves and leave unprofitable sales to their competitors.

Exhibit 7.1C shows the same situation as Exhibit 7.1B, except that here Big John has the information advantage. The quality of Big John's information will determine what portion of its sales are made below full cost. This portion will be very small if its cost information is very good. Note that as long as these lumber companies are using traditional allocation methods to determine their cost, a significant portion of their sales will unknowingly be made at a loss.

Exhibit 7.1D shows a situation where both Big John and its competitors have very good information about their costs through the use of activity-based costing. Because they both have this knowledge, neither company will be willing to sell products that do not cover their full cost. If they are equally efficient, each company will receive an adequate return on investment. When either company sells a product at a loss, those products will tend to be carefully selected loss leaders used to attract customers into the store. When companies change to ABP techniques, prices on high-volume, fast-moving items will tend to go down while slow-moving items may significantly increase in price.

Some companies, when they repeatedly fail to meet their profit projections, stop using any cost information other than direct costs in their pricing process. Alternately, it is not uncommon for small company presidents who have lost faith in the cost information provided by accounting to develop their own quoting rate tables that use their own interpretation of overhead costs. For companies that make unique products to their customers' specifications, lack of good cost information combined with a lack of competitive pricing data becomes equivalent to setting price by throwing darts at a dartboard.

Bad cost information creates a fatal spiral. When a company that uses cost-plus pricing techniques fails to meet its planned profit margin, management will seek to remedy the problem. Knowing that it failed to meet its profit projections, one solution might be to raise price, often through the addition of fudge factors. Although raising price lowers the losses on products that were already badly underpriced, raising price will also make the company uncompetitive on products that had an adequate profit. The effect of using fudge factors is to lower sales through lower volumes.

USING COSTS IN PRICE DETERMINATION

Marketing people have long known how to estimate how many units of a product would be sold at various price points. Unfortunately, for a long time marketing's ability to accurately describe the behavior of the revenue side of the profit equation surpassed the ability of cost accounting to model the behavior of costs. Despite these shortcomings, cost accounting personnel still usually gave management a single number that represented cost and was able to convince everyone they knew what they were doing.

When management thinks that a single number that is independent of sales volume can represent the unit cost of a product, the related pricing decisions are often dead wrong. If a single number could accurately reflect unit costs at all volumes, there would be no rationale for volume discounts or economies of scale. Even for products that are produced in high volumes, the difference between high volume and really high volume can be very significant. In the real world, cost and sales volume are interrelated and unit cost decreases steadily as sales volume increases. In the real world, when dealing with many customers, maximizing revenue never maximizes profit. Profit is always maximized at a price that is higher than the price that generates maximum revenue.

Activity-based pricing provides the marketing and cost accounting departments with the ability to use their data to work cooperatively to arrive at definitive answers about price. Although no customer response curve or product cost curve will ever be absolutely correct, ABP provides an answer that is definitive for a given set of data.

Companies that do not use activity-based costing often establish prices for their products at relatively consistent contribution margin, gross margin, or profit margin based on whatever costing method they use. However, because these methods arbitrarily allocate large portions of the company's costs, the real profit margins for these products may be far from their planned profit margins. By objectively apportioning costs using activity-based costing based on the factors that cause cost, management can have a tool that will really allow them to plan for profitable sales.

RELATIONSHIP BETWEEN COST AND VOLUME

Pricing is a complicated subject because of the interactions between price and volume and between volume and cost. Because price affects sales volume when a company is dealing with many customers and sales volume affects cost, the full cost of a product can never be accurately stated in isolation without specifying a sales volume. Furthermore, because product profit is defined by price minus cost, pricing for profitability means that price and costs must be evaluated simultaneously.

There is a predictable relationship between cost and volume. As volume goes up, unit costs go down. Fixed costs cause this relationship. A *fixed cost* is defined as a cost that does not vary according to the number of units of product that are produced, as illustrated in Exhibit 7.2A. Fixed costs are not the same as *sunk costs*. Sunk costs are costs that have already been committed or spent. Fixed costs are often sunk costs, but not always. Variable costs can be sunk costs, too, such as when a company has already purchased enough material to produce 100,000 units.

There is a fixed cost associated with just about anything that a company can sell. A restaurant chain that wants to add a new product to the menu must invest time developing and testing the recipe and training the cooking staff regarding how to prepare the item. A wholesaler that wants to add a new product must seek and negotiate with suppliers, develop text and artwork for its catalog, figure out how

Exhibit 7.2 Types of costs

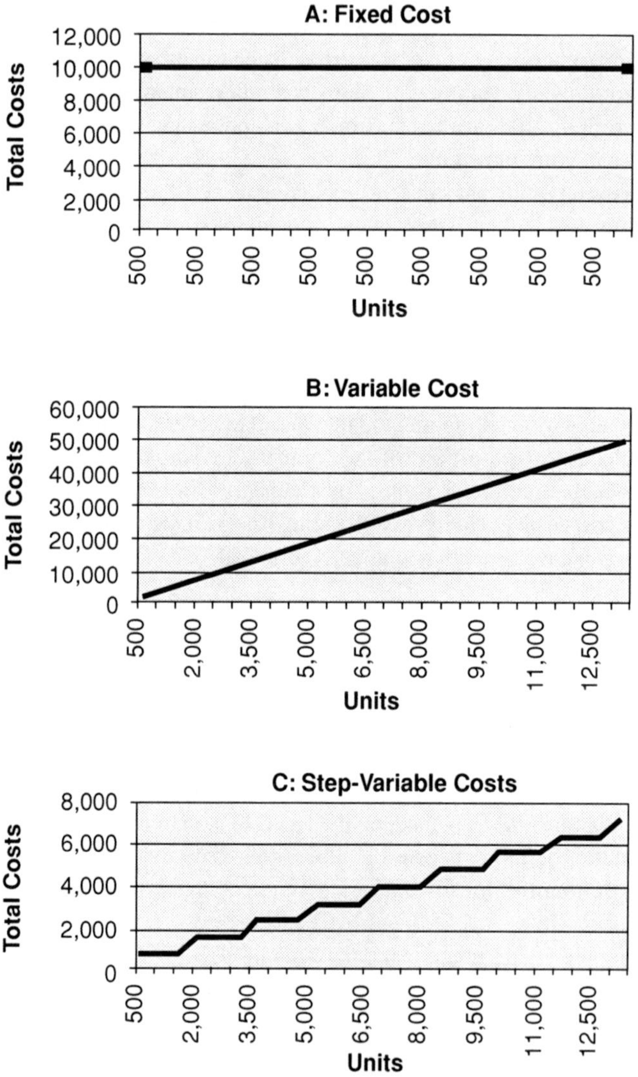

Note: Product costs normally include fixed costs that do not vary with volume, variable costs that increase directly with volume, and step-variable costs that increase in a stepwise fashion. These three types of costs represent three of the hierarchies of activity-based costing. When the costs are combined, the net result is a cost line that is fairly straight.

Exhibit 7.2 Types of costs (*continued*)

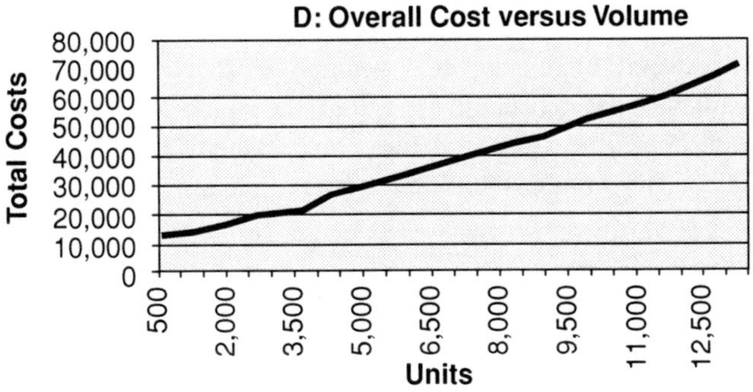

and where to stock the product, and enter product data into the computer. Physicians must learn a patient's medical history and set up charts before effective treatment can begin. Manufacturers must develop a product design, develop a target cost, analyze manufacturing feasibility, develop tooling, seek sources and competitive bids for materials, produce and test prototypes, develop manufacturing procedures, run and test production samples, develop packaging, and perform many other tasks before the product can be shipped to the customer. Fixed costs are very high for some products. It is very expensive to design a new automobile or to develop a pharmaceutical. Other products may have very low fixed costs.

Some costs vary in direct proportion to sales volume, as shown in Exhibit 7.2B. The materials and direct labor that are used to produce a product usually fall into this category. Traditional allocation methods normally treat all costs as variable costs, undermining efforts to analyze costs and profits at various sales volumes.

Large portions of overhead costs are normally step-variable, that is, they increase in discrete increments as shown in Exhibit 7.2C. These steps may involve adding an employee, a machine, increasing the number of batches that will be run, the number of shipments that will be made, or invoices that will be cut. Studies of management time in manufacturing companies often show that managers spend a lot of their time coordinating and planning the setup of production runs but spend little time on managing production once the job is up and running. Many other types of overhead exhibit similar behavior. As a result, a very high volume process that never stops running or a product whose volume is so high that it is produced on a dedicated machine may have very low overhead costs.

When all three of these types of costs are combined, a graph of overall costs is usually a little wavy, as shown in Exhibit 7.2D. As volumes increase, the effects of the step-variable costs become less pronounced, making the total cost/volume graph fairly smooth.

In the real world, of course, costs often defy a black-and-white, fixed or variable classification. A piece of machinery may represent a fixed investment to produce a particular product in quantities of up to a million units per year, but beyond a million units, an additional machine is required to produce any additional units. These step-variable costs may cause a graph of the unit cost/unit volume relationship to be a little bumpy, but in general, the cost of all products will produce a graph similar to the one shown in Exhibit 7.3.

COMBINING DEMAND AND COST DATA TO ARRIVE AT PRICE

Case Study: S'Mores

Suppose that a restaurant chain periodically introduces a new dessert special that is featured in each restaurant for 1 month. Looking for something warm and cozy for the winter months, the executive chef has decided that one of its February desserts would be s'mores, the traditional campfire concoction of the Girl Scouts. Girl Scouts make a s'more (short for "some more") by putting a hot campfire-toasted marshmallow and a piece of chocolate between two halves of a graham cracker. There would not be any recipe development time, but logistically the chef

Exhibit 7.3 Relationship between cost and volume

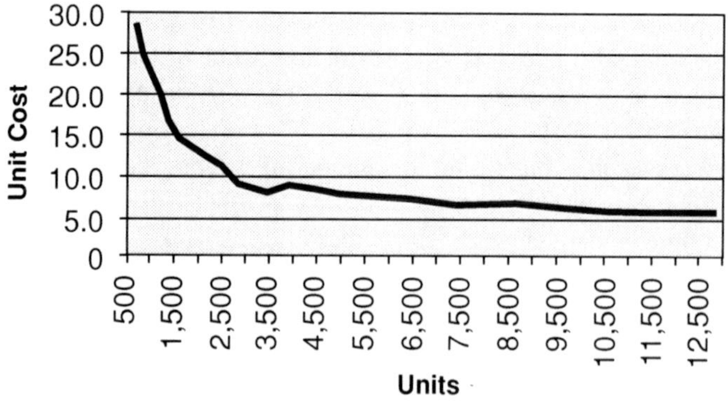

Note: Cost per unit may decrease dramatically as volume increases. As a result, product cost cannot be stated independently of sales volume. Because ABC recognizes heirarchies of costs that include fixed cost, variable costs, and step-variable costs, activity-based pricing can generate a cost curve that reflects this behavior. Traditional cost accounting, which uses only "average" costs, is unable to quantify this cost behavior. This graph is "lumpy" because of step-variable costs.

would have to figure out how to safely put a flame or hot coals on the customer's table in a restaurant. A sterno flame might do the job, but miniature hibachis purchased through a restaurant supply catalog or Pier 1 Imports would have more ambiance. Marshmallows could be cooked on a stick such as a shish-kabob skewer, but any experienced Girl Scout knows that once a marshmallow gets hot, it will not rotate on a single-pronged skewer, cooking unevenly. Fondue forks would work much better to cook marshmallows in a restaurant setting. The required ingredients of marshmallows, graham crackers, and chocolate bars could be distributed from the central commissary or purchased locally at a restaurant supply company such as Gordon Food Service. The total investment for equipment could be conceivably under $100 per restaurant.

What would be the best price to charge? Desserts at the restaurant normally sell for $4 to $7, but s'mores would be meant as a fun dessert for two people. The restaurant's marketing people envisioned that the dessert might sell very well to adults who had not had a s'more cooked over a campfire in decades. They saw it as a novelty dessert that might be brought back briefly each year if it was a success. Marketing was reluctant to sell the dessert for too much because patrons would recognize that it was made from inexpensive ingredients. Using an upscale brand of chocolate could enhance the image of the dessert.

Marketing research could provide a customer price response curve showing the number of units that the restaurant could expect to sell at various prices. An example of a price response curve is shown in Exhibit 7.4. This analysis showed that revenue would be maximized at $6.50 per dessert. On a per-person basis, this would make s'mores priced less than any other dessert. Restaurant management vetoed

Exhibit 7.4 Customer demand for S'Mores

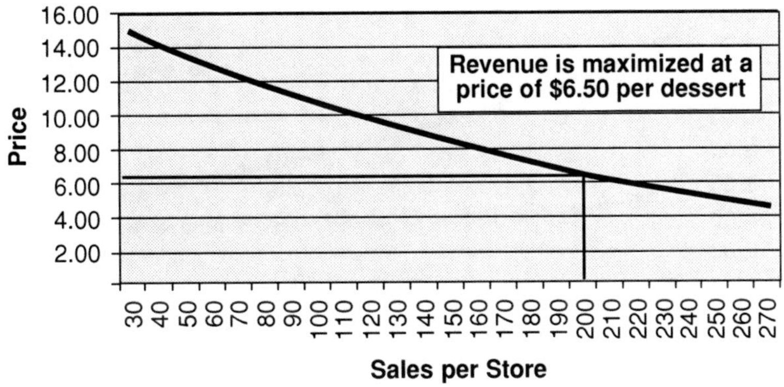

Note: Revenue is maximized at the point where the product of price times unit sales is maximized. This occurs at the point where the customer price elasticity equals 1.0.

this price, arguing a dessert meant for two people should be priced at least higher than the most expensive dessert for one. Besides, this was a special dessert that no other restaurant offered.

Accounting got involved next. One cost accountant argued that, based on the marketing data, $15 would provide a contribution margin of over $8 per dessert. "Whoa!" said the marketing vice president, "That's a lot to charge for four graham crackers, four marshmallows, and a couple of chocolate bars!" The ultra high price strategy was quickly dismissed when the accountant's cost curve was placed on the same graph as marketing's customer demand curve, as shown in Exhibit 7.5. That analysis revealed that the per-unit contribution margin should always be high for products that are sold in low volume.

The controller then suggested that total profit was more important than unit profit. Revenue at various volumes was calculated from marketing's customer response curve, and total costs were calculated from cost accounting's data. From these data total profits were easily calculated, as shown in Exhibit 7.6. This graph showed that although revenue would be maximized at $6.50 per unit, profits would be highest at $9 per dessert. This occurred because unit costs decreased faster than demand in this part of the graph.

"That's about where I thought the price should be," said the vice president of marketing, and a price of $9 was quickly decided upon. The dessert sold very well for the month that it was offered, with demand much stronger than the marketing department's numbers had anticipated. Restaurant patrons would see the little hibachi at someone else's table and want to get the same thing. As a result, restaurants often lost sales or had slow service as a result of not having enough equip-

Exhibit 7.5 Unit profit contribution and volume—S'Mores

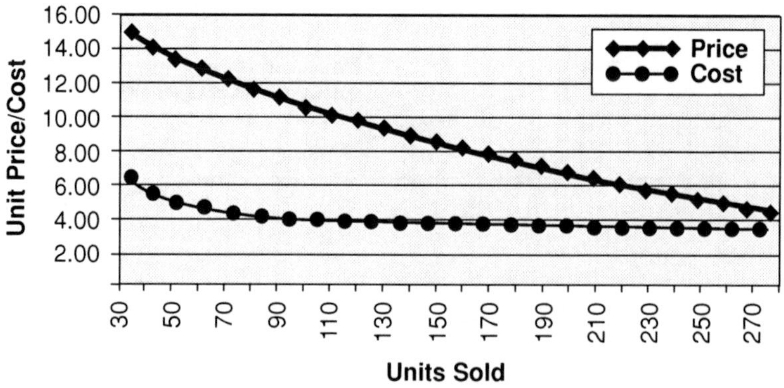

Note: Contribution margins for a product usually decrease as sales volumes increase. A high contribution margin does not assure a profit.

Exhibit 7.6 Revenue, cost, and profit

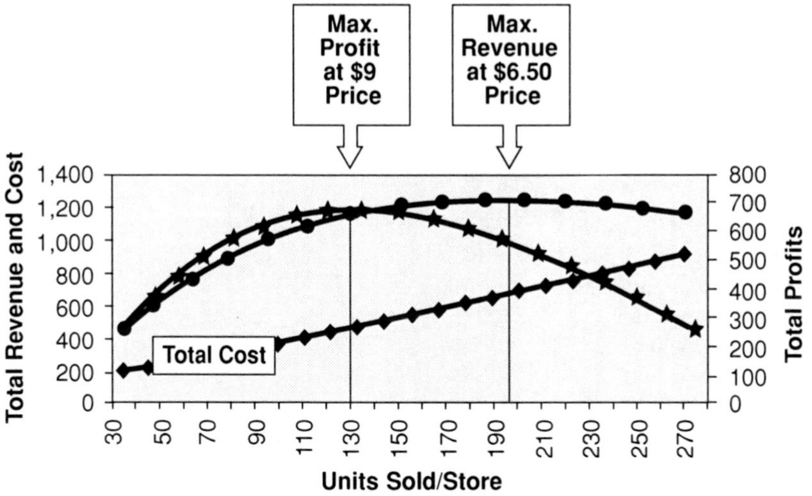

Note: Except for products with no variable cost, a situation not normally observed in the real world, profit is maximized at a price that is higher than the price that maximizes revenue. This occurs because an increase in price at the revenue maximization point has a much lower effect on revenue than it does on the variable portion of costs.

ment to go around. Restaurant managers found that patrons would order the dessert once for the novelty but not a second time. At the end of the 1-month rotation, the dessert was proclaimed a profitable success.

Using Activity-Based Costing in Pricing

In order to perform ABP, a company must be able to take the activity costs that have been derived through its activity-based costing efforts and recombine them based on the resources that a new product is expected to consume. Although some activity-based costing software packages will assist in this analysis, many companies continue to develop a separate pricing model using electronic spreadsheets that apply their activity-based costing data. Exhibit 7.7 shows how activity-based costing data might be used to determine price as shown for a fictional company, Washtenaw Products Corporation. This company has identified start-up cost differences for three different types of customers. Each type of product has its own characteristic launch cost, and Washtenaw has determined differences in setup and running costs for the three different types of processes that the company performs. The company has specified how many units the quoted product will use from this menu. The direct

Exhibit 7.7 ABP price development worksheet: Washtenaw Products Corporation

	Rates ($)	Estimated Units Used	Contract Cost ($)
Start-up costs			
Customer type A	1,250.00		—
Customer type B	900.00	1	900
Customer type C	750.00		—
Product launch costs			
Product type 10	5,500		—
Product type 50	1,600		—
Product type 600	3,700	1	3,700
Product type 700	4,200		—
Set-up costs (batches)			
Process A	150.00	26	3,900
Process B	75.00	13	975
Process C	25.00		—
Running costs (hours)			
Process A	125.00	416	52,000
Process B	60.00	104	6,240
Process C	45.00		—
Per shipment	20.00	52	1,040
Per box	1.50	208	312
	Subtotal		69,067
	Units to be produced	250,000	
	Direct materials	$3.58	
	Total material cost		$895,000
	Total cost		$964,067
	Commission	5.0%	48,203.35
	Planned profit	10%	101,227.04
	Planned revenue		$1,113,497
	Unit Price		$4.454

Note: This worksheet shows how a company might turn its activity-based costing information into a cost-based price. This worksheet shows fixed, customer-related, and product launch level costs, batch level costs for production, unit level running costs, and shipping costs per box and per shipment.

material content has been calculated elsewhere and was merely included as a line item in the total section of the worksheet. In this case, the company has determined a price at a level of 250,000 units. Should the number of units be increased, the company would lower its price in response to lower unit costs. If the number of units to be produced was lowered, higher unit costs would prompt a higher price.

Case Study: Plastic Injection Molding

One small plastic injection molding company with three partners has plants in Ohio and Tennessee.[3] The Ohio location produces hundreds of different products, whereas the Tennessee location makes four products that are very similar. Joe, the partner who runs the Tennessee plant, had done quoting corporation wide before the operation in Tennessee opened in 1998. Shortly thereafter, the Ohio plant implemented ABP. In 2001, Joe quoted a product for a customer that was to be produced in unusually high volumes—4 million units a year, far above the 250,000 units per year that was typical for the corporation. He used his old 1998 pricing model to come up with a quote of 5¢ a unit. When he learned that another company had bid 3¢, he reported to his partner Greg, in Ohio, that the competitor "bought" the work. Greg was not so sure that this was what really happened and ran the product specifications through the ABP model used by their Ohio plant. Had the Ohio plant's ABP model been used, Greg would have charged 2.8¢ and won the work. Knowing the real economics relating to high-volume products provides a competitive advantage.

ACTIVITY-BASED PRICING CONSIDERATIONS

Volume Discounts

Many businesses give discounts to their customers based on the volume of product that they purchase. Some companies define their discount based on the number of units of a particular product that are purchased, others provide a discount based on the value of all items purchased in one order, while still others consider the total amount of purchases that the customer buys for the whole year. A customer's buying pattern affects the cost to serve that customer. The way that a discount schedule is structured also may affect the manner in which a customer makes its purchases.

Suppose that a customer agrees to purchase 2,100 cases of copier paper from an office supply store. The paper is used relatively evenly throughout the business year and delivery is to be included in the price. This works out to 8 cases per day, 40 cases per week, and about 167 cases per month. Should all customers who purchase 2,000 cases a year be given the same price? There can be very different costs associated with customers that purchase similar volumes. A 4 × 4 foot wooden pallet will hold 10 cases of copy paper per layer. If the cases were stacked four high, 40 cases would fill a pallet. Because the office supply store purchases its copy paper on pallets, it would not even need to take the shrink-wrap off the pallet in order to deliver to a customer in pallet load quantities. The delivery truck could just back up to the customer's shipping dock and unload a week's worth of copy paper at one time. The office supply store might even be able to have the pallet drop-shipped directly from the manufacturer. This would be a very efficient and cost-effective way of delivering copy paper. Delivery could be even more efficient if the customer were willing to take a month's supply, four or five pallets, in one shipment.

What if the customer did not have a fork lift truck to unload a pallet? That would mean that there would be more unloading work requiring the delivery person to load cases of copier paper from the truck onto a handcart, pull four cases at a time into the building, and then restack them. This would be much more time consuming and costly. The customer also might ask that delivery be made every day instead of every week like its other "just-in-time" suppliers. Obviously, there are very different costs associated with these two different arrangements.

Activity-based costing can be used to identify the differences in the costs to serve various customers, categories of customers, or distribution channels. When these data are used in ABP, the company has the ability to seek out types of customers that are more profitable and charge customers differentially according to the cost to serve each customer group. Within each category of customers, ABP can distinguish between customers within each category according to other factors, such as the volume of product that they purchase. This relationship is shown conceptually in Exhibit 7.8.

The company could control these costs by building them into its pricing schedule. The price schedule might consist of a table giving one set of discounts based on material handling efficiencies and billing efficiencies and another set of discounts based on selling cost efficiencies to large customers. This method can be a big help in preventing a company from chasing situations where special requirements can make high-volume sales costly.

Making a Profit on Low-Volume Work

Because activity-based costing recognizes the real cost differences between high-volume products and low-volume products, ABP methods suggest much higher prices for low-volume products than traditional cost-based pricing methods. Although ABP provides a competitive advantage when seeking high-volume sales, most companies that use this technique do not get much low-volume work. This is

Exhibit 7.8 Cost differences for customers

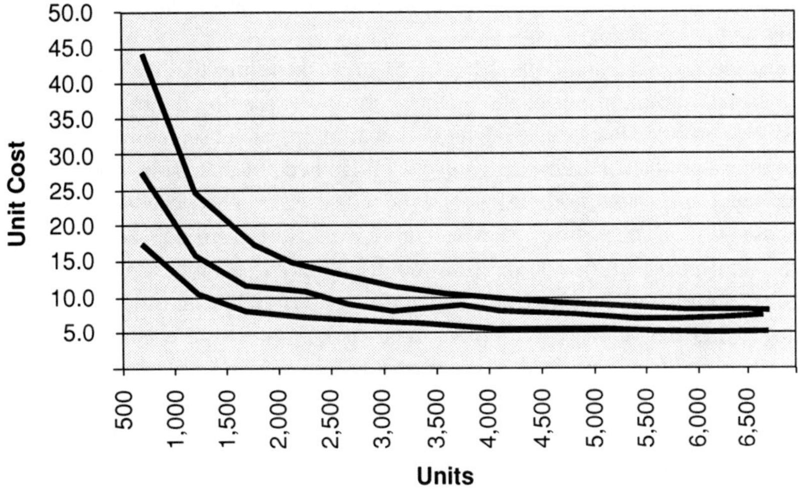

Note: Some costs have nothing to do with products and everything to do with customers. When different customers or classes of customers have different requirements, then the cost per unit to serve these customers may be very different.

because competitors that mistakenly bid below cost using traditional cost-based pricing methods outbid them.

Activity-based pricing changes the attitude of most companies toward low-volume work. Although many companies are wary of products that stray far from their average volume, companies that use ABP can be reasonably confident that any low-volume sale will not drag down their profits. The reason for this is that ABP, intelligently implemented, can appropriately differentiate between the cost of a unique one-of-a-kind product and a product that is produced in volumes of millions a year. When a company that uses ABP wins a low volume contract, it can be confident that this contract will add to, not drag down, their bottom line.

How Complexity Affects Costs

Work happens for a reason. Some things are easy to do and others are difficult. CPAs do not charge by the page for a tax return because some schedules are very easy and other schedules are very difficult. In preparing a shipment, it is very easy to pack a single case that contains 12 identical smaller boxes, but it is much more difficult if the stock picker has to take 12 different items of different shapes and sizes and package them together.

Everyone understands that it takes much more time to do something that is complex than something that is easy, yet many companies spend very little time studying how complexity causes work.

The screws, nuts, and bolts that hold together the things that we use every day are normally a minor part of the material cost purchased by the manufacturer to make that product. Is it really worth any time thinking about such tiny details when designing a product? Purchasing people would tell you that it hardly takes any extra time at all to purchase more fasteners if the type used on a new product is the same as those used on an existing one. Much more work is involved if an engineer wants to use a fastener that the company has not used before or if a new product design requires something unique. Hundreds of dollars of purchasing time can be spent trying to find and purchase a few thousand bolts. Complexity affects assembly time as well as quality rejects. If all of the screws required to assemble a product are all the same, it is very difficult for the assemblers to put the product together incorrectly. However, the chances of error grow exponentially as the number of different parts required increases. Some companies actually have to go to the trouble of color-coding their fasteners green, red, and gold to prevent mixing up similar items. Standardizing the fasteners in the first place could reduce these costs.

Some products may be complex because they require more coordination time. Customers with special requirements for shipping, billing, packaging, or delivery will be more costly just because they are different. A company that is willing and able to cater to these special needs should be able to receive a premium price for its services. A company that cannot differentiate "picky" customers from the general customer population is doomed to provide those extra services at no extra charge.

Predicting Product Complexity

In order to accurately predict costs, the company must understand what factors cause cost. By understanding these factors for current products, that knowledge can be used to predict the cost of something that has not been made before. Because work happens for a reason, the characteristics that cause cost are often well known even if they have never been quantified.

Once the conversation gets started, people are often very articulate about describing what causes them work. A few leading questions by a cost accountant will often lead an engineer to start enumerating how much time various product features take to design. If the company keeps engineering time reports, these estimates can be tested by using the engineers' estimates to see if they would have accurately predicted the time required to design products for projects that have already been completed.

Start-up and Coordination Activities

Similar questions asked of operations people will yield good results as well. Real cost savings may be discovered by getting design engineers, process engineers, purchasing, quality control, sales operations, and accounting together to talk about the causes of cost. The best time to initiate cost reductions is when products and processes are being designed.

In many industries, companies invest large amounts of money and effort before they are able to generate any revenue from a new product. Start-up and coordination activities may include market research to test the product concept, product design costs, and the design and development of prototypes, tooling, production processes, checking fixtures, procedures, and standards. Many of these costs are true fixed costs because they will only be done once and are completely independent of the product volumes that will eventually be sold.

Launch costs may exist for customers as well as products. Accounts receivable needs to set the customer up in the computer. Customer service may need to build a data base about the company's needs, and shipping may have to set up all of the customer's ship-to addresses and figure out the best way to send products to those locations. In some cases, management information systems may have to set up computer hook-ups with the customer so that orders and other information can flow smoothly back and forth.

These launch costs can be very small or very large depending on the product, customer, or industry. Launch costs generally fall into the category of true fixed costs. When companies using traditional cost accounting categorize launch costs as overhead, they create distortions that can substantially affect pricing decisions. In most cases, no company would ever take on a new product or customer if it knew that it would never recoup its launch costs, yet many companies do this unknowingly every day.

Launch costs can normally be attributed to specific product, process, or customer characteristics. Accordingly, a study of these characteristics can significantly improve a company's ability to predict their cost and, in turn, earn a profit.

Analyzing Selling Activities

What causes work in making sales? That answer may vary significantly from company to company, from customer to customer, and from product to product. Some customers are easy to serve. Their needs are always stated with plenty of advance notice, their requests are reasonable, they do not want to be lavishly entertained, and they get right to the point about what they want. These easy-to-serve customers are often loyal buyers who rarely price shop their vendor relationships. It is a pleasure to do business with these loyal buyers. Their accounts tend to be nicely profitable, and if modest price concessions were requested, they would be gladly granted.

Other customers are much more demanding. These customers are often price buyers who competitively bid every order that they place. It may take five or more quotations to get one job from these customers, and they often burn up a lot of selling time. Sometimes when signing the expense account checks for entertaining such customers, the controller mutters under her breath, "If we had any more customers like this, we'd be out of business."

Reality is that not all customers cost the same amount to serve. If a company could differentiate between the customers that were cheap to serve and those that were expensive, pricing could be adjusted accordingly. Larry Byrne, President of Ann Arbor Assembly Corporation (later part of Tower Automotive), made a practice of charging customers according to the demands that they placed on his company. When a customer's requirements were higher than usual, Larry would apply "factor J," which meant that the customer was quoted a higher price.

Companies rarely have good data about how they spend their sales efforts. Sometimes hard data are available when there are salespeople or groups of salespeople who are assigned to particular customers or channels of distribution. Cost accountants performing an activity-based costing analysis to apportion selling costs often use interview techniques. By assigning selling costs to specific customers, types of customers, or channels of distribution, the company can encourage sales for those efforts that most contribute to profitable sales.

Activity-based costing studies of how salaried salespeople spend their time often show that the amount of time that a salesperson spends to make a sale does not have much to do with the dollar value of the products sold. For example, it may take a similar amount of time to prepare a quotation for a $10,000 sale as a $100,000 sale. In this case, selling time could be considered a fixed cost. When such cost behavior is found, the company should either take steps to modify the behavior or to properly reflect those costs when it prepares its quotations.

When salespeople are paid a straight commission based on sales dollars, their emphasis is based on generating revenues. This emphasis is often in direct conflict with the company's objective of generating profits. Commissions may cause a salesperson to pursue an unprofitable large customer instead of several very profitable small ones. The next section will discuss how to structure compensation arrangements to motivate profit.

MOTIVATING PROFIT

Selling is not an easy job. There is a lot of competition for business. Purchasing Managers get many phone calls every week from people who want to sell products and services to their company. The calls are not limited to people in purchasing. Human Resource managers get sales calls from temporary help agencies, Controllers get calls from banks, accounting firms, and insurance agencies, and company presidents may hear from anybody in any kind of business. Even at home during dinner, consumers are sometimes bombarded by phone calls from people trying to pitch credit cards, replacement windows, long distance service, and donations to charity.

Any company that has been in business for any length of time has many established commercial relationships. It is efficient to deal with the same vendor transaction after transaction, month after month, year after year. The incumbent has a history with the customer. Packaging, delivery, and billing requirements are understood. Vendor and customer know each other's people and have developed a comfort level working with each other. When a company is happy with the product that it is getting from a vendor, it is often very difficult for a salesperson from another company to even get a brief visit with a person of buying authority to even leave a business card. Working in sales takes a certain personality type. Salespeople have to be persistent and must be able to accept rejection.

Students of organizational behavior have long known that how people are compensated and rewarded has a major impact on their behavior. This observation is true in sales. How a sales force is rewarded for its work is a major factor in how effective it is at selling profitable work. A look at the sales process from the salesperson's perspective will provide some insight into this situation.

There are a finite number of hours in a day, 24 to be exact. Salespeople cannot work all of them. Those hours that salespeople work are spent turning their time into earnings. Each company has its own compensation plan. Some salespeople are paid a salary, some receive a commission, while others receive some combination of a time-based wage and incentive pay. Most companies have some incentive provision built in to the way that they pay their salespeople in order to provide some motivation to do the difficult task of closing the sale.

A common way to pay incentive compensation has long been commission. If salespeople make a sale, then they receive a percentage of the selling price for having made the sale. For example, people who sell window treatments such as draperies, vertical blinds, and mini-blinds normally receive a commission that is 10% to 20% of the selling price, depending on the type of product that they sell. Manufacturers' representatives who sell industrial products negotiate unique contracts with each company they represent. A common contract would specify that the representative would receive 5% of sales for all sales up to some level, such as $2 million per year, with a declining percentage rate for each subsequent million.

For commissioned salespeople, there is a direct correlation between their performance and how much they get paid. If they sell more, they get paid more. This translates to a specific amount on each paycheck. Time is money, and salespeople want to spend their time with those prospects that are likely to yield the most commission for the time that is invested. When salespeople are paid a commission based on how much they sell, their personal objectives are clear and straightforward: Sell as much as possible.

When a salesperson is selling lots of product, does management care what or how it gets sold? Who is a better salesperson, someone who sells $10 million worth of product or someone who sells $5 million? Exhibit 7.9 shows sales data for Betty and Bob, the top two salespeople for ABC Corporation. Bob is a real star, selling $10 million of product last year. Betty is a good producer as well, though far behind Bob at only $5 million in sales. ABC sells its products to businesses, and a good customer might go through 10,000 or more units a year. ABC allows its salespeople to negotiate price with its customers up to a maximum discount of 25% on a list price of $10 per unit.

Bob is well paid for his efforts, earning $500,000 a year, while Betty is far behind, earning "only" $250,000. Everyone always knew that Bob got a lot of sales by discounting heavily, but because the company worked with a 30% gross margin, it was believed that his high level of sales made up a big portion of the company's profits. A study has shown that the product-related costs that the company sells are $7.75 per unit. This includes some corporate overhead costs that have been arbitrarily allocated on a per-unit basis.

Exhibit 7.9 Effects of simultaneously paying commissions based on sales and giving salespeople discretion over price

	Betty	Bob
Average price	$9.36	$8.20
Units sold	543,500	1,221,340
Sales	$5,087,160	$10,014,988
Cost of sales	(4,212,125)	(9,221,117)
Commission earned	(254,358)	(500,749)
Profit	$620,677	$293,122
Contribution to unassigned costs	12.2%	2.9%

Note: This exhibit shows the profitability of sales made by Betty and Bob, the two top salespeople for a company. The company has used activity-based costing to calculate the full cost of producing its products, excluding only a few administrative expenses and idle capacity that could not be rationally assigned to products or customers. Salespeople are paid a straight commission on sales. Bob is paid almost twice as much as Betty, but Betty has contributed more than twice as much to the company profit. Bob has discounted his sales much more heavily than Betty, illustrating why it is a bad idea to simultaneously pay a commission based on sales dollars and give salespeople discretion over price.

These data are very revealing. On average, Betty has given just a 6.4% discount off of list price, whereas Bob has given discounts averaging 18%. Betty's ability to sell at or near list price has made her sales very profitable, whereas Bob's heavy discounting has left his sales with very little margin. Betty's much smaller customer base has generated more than twice as much profit as Bob's.

The problem is a classic one. The company has allowed its salespeople to have discretion over price while compensating them based on how much they sold. The natural instinct of the salespeople is to make an "easy" sale in the most time-effective manner possible. That route is usually found by giving substantial price discounts.

Getting a top price is a more arduous process. To get a high price, the sales person will need to take the time to understand the customer's needs and communicate how the product will meet those needs better than a competitive product that may cost less. Getting top price may require twice the effort from the salesperson, who may only get a small incremental reward if working for a company that pays commission based on sales dollars.

In general, it is a bad idea to simultaneously compensate salespeople based on sales dollars or units sold and give them discretion over price. Straight sales-based commission compensation plans provide a strong incentive to sell products at the minimum allowable price to maximize commission earnings. Such a compensation system is directly contradictory to the corporate objective of making a profit.

If salespeople are to be compensated based on a commission system, they should either have no discretion to alter price or they should be paid not on sales, but on some measure of profit or value-added.

Automobile salespeople are compensated in a way that provides a high incentive to get as high a price as possible for each vehicle. A common pricing scheme would be to pay a salesperson a flat $100 per vehicle plus a percentage of the selling price to the extent that it was above the dealer invoice cost. Auto dealers are charged an invoice price by the auto manufacturer that does not represent the real price that the dealer will eventually pay. For example, a loaded 1999 Ford Windstar Van with a sticker price of $30,180 had an invoice price of $27,271.65. From that invoice price Ford subtracted out two categories of holdbacks from the dealer totaling $1,168. The dealer actually paid $26,103.65 for this vehicle. A *holdback* is a discount on the invoice price given to an automotive dealer by the manufacturer. Holdbacks are primarily determined by a dealer's sales volume.

Selling automobiles is a very competitive business. Sophisticated buyers are able to get information about dealer costs from *Consumer Reports* and other sources and obtain competitive bids for the purchase of an automobile over the Internet. Automotive dealers provide their salespeople with an incentive to make profitable sales by having the commission increase significantly as the selling price of a vehicle rises above dealer invoice cost. Exhibit 7.10 shows what commission would

Exhibit 7.10 Salesperson commission on a Ford Windstar

	Selling Price	Dealer Margin[1]	Commission	Commission % of Margin	Commission % of Sales	Commission % of $400 under Invoice
Dealer Invoice	$27,272	$1,169	$100	9%	0.4%	25%
	27,563	$1,460	173	12%	0.6%	25%
	27,854	$1,751	245	14%	0.9%	25%
	28,144	$2,041	318	16%	1.1%	25%
	28,435	$2,332	391	17%	1.4%	25%
	28,726	$2,623	463	18%	1.6%	25%
	29,017	$2,914	536	18%	1.8%	25%
	29,308	$3,205	609	19%	2.1%	25%
	29,598	$3,495	682	19%	2.3%	25%
	29,889	$3,786	754	20%	2.5%	25%
List Price	$30,180	$4,077	$827	20%	2.7%	25%

Note: Shown above is the commission scale on a Ford Windstar for a dealership that pays its sales people a commission equal to $100 plus 25% of the selling price over dealer invoice cost. The dealer really pays the manufacturer less than the dealer invoice price, here $26,103 on a $27,272 minivan. In effect, this commission plan really pays salespeople 25% of an amount that is $400 under dealer invoice with a $100 minimum. Vehicles are rarely sold for less than dealer invoice cost.

[1]Based on real dealer cost of $26,103

be for the Ford Windstar mentioned above under a commission formula where salespeople are paid $100 plus 25% of the selling price above dealer invoice cost. In effect, the dealership is paying its salespeople 25% of the selling price that is above an amount that is $400 under dealer invoice cost with a $100 minimum. (Car dealers rarely sell a vehicle for less than dealer invoice cost.) This commission method strongly aligns the motivations of the salesperson to earn a commission with the dealer's motivation to earn a profit.

Another way of controlling the margin at which products are sold is to provide salespeople with no discretion over price. This is often the case in retail stores. Such a policy is efficient in that it prevents consumption of salespeople's time. The store may allow some leeway to meet or beat a competitor's price, in effect allowing the salesperson to lower price in this limited situation.

In the final analysis, motivating profit requires an understanding of the behavior of the entire profit equation. The company must understand the interrelationships of price and volume as well as have a detailed understanding of the behavior of costs. Traditional cost accounting with its averaging techniques and arbitrary allocations is not adequate for this task. Only when costs are thoroughly understood via activity-based costing is good profit planning possible. This marriage of revenue and costing disciplines is ABP.

SUMMARY

The key points described in this chapter are listed below:

1. The objectives of ABP are:
   - Establish price based on a solid knowledge of customer demand and product cost.
   - Never unintentionally price a product at a loss.
   - Know how much of price is profit.
   - Generate a superior financial return through superior financial knowledge.
2. There are four commandments of ABP:
   a. Know thy product.
   b. Know thy processes.
   c. Know thy customers.
   d. Know thy competitors.
3. Activity-based pricing is a pricing method that uses knowledge about customer demand and knowledge about the costs of a particular selling situation to establish a price that will result in a specific planned profit.
4. Price influences the volume of product that will be sold. In general, as price increases, sales volume decreases. Sales volume affects product costs; therefore, costs can only be stated accurately for a specific number of units. ABP seeks to identify the appropriate price to charge for a product based on a specific situation.
5. Activity-based pricing provides a competitive advantage for companies that use it. ABP seeks to provide superior financial performance through superior financial knowledge.
6. Activity-based pricing will help companies that use it to win easy and high-volume jobs against companies that are using traditional pricing methods. It will also prevent companies from making mistakes on low-volume and complex work.
7. Most companies earn a profit that can be represented by a single digit percentage of sales. Because of these thin margins, it is very important that the relationship between price and cost be understood.

8. Costs are often categorized as fixed, variable, and step-variable. Most products have costs that fall into all three categories. Because of fixed costs and step-variable costs, unit costs decrease as sales volume increases.

9. Costs may be customer related as well as product related. Accordingly, different prices may be appropriate for different customers or categories of customers.

10. In the real world, when selling a product that will be purchased by many customers, the price that maximizes profit is higher than the price that maximizes revenue.

11. Companies should never simultaneously pay a commission based on sales dollars and allow their salespeople to have discretion over price.

NOTES

1. Oros and Easy ABC are trademarks of ABC Technologies, Inc.
2. The source for all industry profitability data in this chapter is Schwab Signature Research, *www.Schwab.Com* (January 9, 2001).
3. The names and places for this company have been changed.

8

ACTIVITY-BASED PRICING MODELS

Many companies who use activity-based pricing have reported that the most valuable use of their models is that it tells them which jobs to walk away from.

Robert A. Erickson, Michigan Manufacturing Technology Council

DETERMINING PRICE

If a company's objective is to make a profit, then logically the company will not want to sell individual products at a loss. As logical as this seems, many companies unintentionally sell 20% or more of their products at a price that is less than full product cost. These products drain company profitability. If a company's objective is to never unintentionally sell a product at a loss, then it is imperative to have a good understanding of cost behavior. To make profitable sales, a company must understand not just material costs and direct manufacturing costs, but all costs, because administrative and manufacturing overhead costs can be specifically product or customer related.

To many companies, "cost" refers to something less than full cost. Thinking of cost in terms of direct cost or gross margin cost is a dangerous habit to get into, because the company begins to think of anything above these partial costs as profit. Profit is achieved only when revenues exceed full cost. Selling price minus anything less than full cost is merely contribution margin. To make a profit, price must be greater than full cost. Anything less is a loss.

Sometimes there are strategic reasons for selling a product at a loss. Some companies are willing to make an initial sale at a loss to a potentially important new customer to "get their foot in the door." At other times a company may sell a highly visible product as a "loss leader" to entice the customer into the store to buy other products. Although the company may be willing to occasionally sell an individual product at a loss, the company certainly does not want to sell a substantial portion of its products at a loss or to sell any product at a loss unintentionally. In most cases, when a company takes on a new product or customer, there is an implicit intention that the additional revenues from the new business volume will be greater than the additional expenses, thereby generating a profit.

This book does not advocate that price be established based on a markup of costs. This book advocates that companies understand their cost in order to manage profits. To do an effective job at pricing, the company also needs to understand customer demand and the nature of competition for the product. Cost-plus pricing can leave money on the table by charging less than the customer is willing to pay and less than the competitive situation demands. Cost-plus pricing also can mean that the company has invested in a product that it cannot sell because of a lack of understanding of market considerations.

Management must determine its own strategy and policy regarding profits. In practice, although management often establishes a single profitability goal for all products, higher profits are more likely to result when flexibility allows different profitability goals for different situations. For example, the company may seek a 10% pretax profit when a sale is competitively bid, but seek 15% when there is no competition. That same company may be willing to accept zero profit or to sell at a loss to make the first sale to a new customer.

In companies where salespeople lack good cost data, or have access to only direct or gross margin costs, they often unknowingly argue for pricing that would generate a loss. The situation changes dramatically when salespeople are armed with good cost information. When salespeople have access to good cost data, they rarely argue to sell a product below full cost. In fact, when activity-based costing is available, salespeople frequently argue that the company can get a higher price than represented by the company's standard cost-plus markup formulas. One test to determine if a company's pricing/cost structure is doing its job is to ask the following question:

> If the company always quotes products at a minimum profit of 10%, when the books are closed at the end of the fiscal year, is the company making at least a 10% profit?

If not, then there is a problem with the company's pricing structure.

Understanding Pricing Models

A common method of establishing price is a pricing model. A pricing model is a representation of how the company plans to set its prices according to company policy. Pricing models are not new. No doubt merchants and tradesmen have always had their own particular methods to determine their asking price, perhaps longer than there have been formal systems of writing and arithmetic. As calculating tools improved, more sophisticated pricing methods became possible, but pricing methods often lagged far behind best practice at all but only a few companies. For example, many companies developed computerized pricing models, but few companies developed activity-based pricing models that recognized the hierarchical nature of their costs. Those companies that took advantage of activity-based pricing techniques gained an advantage that often left their competitors puzzled.

Methods of determining price differ greatly depending on the competitive position of the seller. A company that has a product that will be sold to many customers will approach pricing much differently than a company that is competitively bidding to make a sale to a single customer. A company that has a unique product will approach pricing differently than a company whose product is generic. Each company should tailor its pricing policies to correspond to its own competitive situation.

Many companies experimented with personal computer pricing models in the 1980s. The experiences of one company were perhaps typical of the evolution in pricing models that occurred during that era:

> Until the mid-1980s, Jim Lozelle, President of Edgewood Tool & Manufacturing Company, had personally prepared all of the company's quotes using a standard paper form that he had developed. Contrary to what the name of his company might imply, Edgewood was primarily a metal stamping company. Making tooling was only a small portion of the business. Lozelle's rationale for personally preparing the quotes was that when something out of the ordinary came along, he wanted to make sure that the costs associated with those unusual products were properly recognized and that the product was priced appropriately.
>
> Lozelle used a quoting rate of $70 per hour for all production processes that was developed using traditional cost accounting methods. The $70 rate was several years old, developed by the company's former Controller. Lozelle's method of pricing was to calculate the cost of materials, add labor, and then throw in a few "fudge factors" to ensure that the company made a profit. In fact, the quotation worksheet that Edgewood used during this era had no place for profit. Profit came only from the fudge factors. Lozelle's new Controller expressed some concern with the quoting rate and quoting methods. He thought that the company was vastly undercharging for some things that they did and overcharging for others. The Controller prepared a new analysis of what the company's new rates should be based on what he called a "rational" method of cost allocation. Among the things that the Controller did were to assign equipment depreciation cost to each work center according to the value of the ma-

chine and to assign building cost according to the amount of floor space that each machine used. Lozelle thought that this method of cost allocation made good common sense, so he began to use the new rates.

The Controller's next suggestion was to put the quotation worksheet on the electronic spreadsheet that the company was using, a piece of software called Framework IV, developed by Ashton-Tate. Framework was a software product that was highly regarded by computer publications but never received widespread use. Innovative for the mid-1980s, Framework allowed multiple frames to exist within the same workbook. These frames could consist of spreadsheets, graphs, or word-processing documents that could be organized hierarchically. When Borland acquired Ashton-Tate, Framework was retired in favor of Borland's competing Quattro-Pro spreadsheet package. Canada's Corel Corporation in turn later purchased Borland.

Executives of the mid-1980s rarely used computers, even if they had them in their offices. Lozelle looked at the spreadsheet model, listened to the Controller explain the methodology, and said, "I understand how this works and I agree with the way that you did it. Now that we have it on a computer, I don't need to do the quotes myself."

Edgewood's pricing model got progressively more sophisticated, adopting volume-sensitive and complexity-sensitive activity-based pricing techniques. Their pricing model was converted to Microsoft Excel by the early 1990s and included many features that were quite sophisticated for that time.

Activity-based pricing methodology recognizes that true cost cannot be stated as a single number that is independent of sales volume. In the real world, costs have many causes, and sales volume has an important influence on unit costs. For a new product, some costs are fixed and independent of volume, whereas other costs are variable and directly related to the number of units produced. Some costs relate to the number of batches produced, whereas other costs relate to the number of units that are shipped in a box.

Activity-based costing software such as Oros or Easy ABC[1] provides the ability to identify the cost of each activity that the organization defines. Activity-based costing is a closed system, so that after costs are decomposed into activities, they can be reassembled to provide the cost of each product from an activity-based viewpoint. According to Gary Cokins, Director of Industry Relations at ABC Technologies, 99% of the usage of the product cost buildup capabilities of activity-based costing software is for "cost autopsies" of existing products rather than to estimate the cost of future products.[2] Cokins says that most companies have their own ways of thinking about price and even if they are equipped with an activity-based costing software package, pricing tends to be done using a separate electronic spreadsheet pricing model. The activity-based costing software provides a crucial advantage, however, in the generation of the rate table used by the pricing model. Because activity-based costing software can provide very good data about costs, the rates that it generates become the backbone of activity-based pricing.

BUILDING AN ACTIVITY-BASED PRICING MODEL

An activity-based pricing model is a computer model that is developed to help management determine the "true" or "real" cost of a product. Activity-based pricing models are distinguished from traditional pricing models in that they include an analysis of the full cost of the product from an activity-based costing vantage point. Such models recognize the hierarchical nature of product costs that translate differences in unit costs for different sales volumes. If marketing determines the number of units that the company will sell at various prices, an activity-based pricing model will allow the company to take each of those prices and determine how much profit will be achieved at each level. In effect, the company is able to generate the cost curve for the product. This allows comparison with the demand curve (also known as the price response curve), which allows profitability to be maximized.

When there is a single customer for a product, such as when a company competitively bids to make a unique product, use of an activity-based pricing model requires a slightly different process. How much the customer is willing to pay will be secondary to the issue of how much the company's competitors are likely to charge based on their own cost structures. When competitors use unsophisticated pricing methods, the price that they quote using markup methods may be significantly above or significantly below the competitor's true costs. In these situations, an activity-based costing model can identify those products that the company should avoid because their costs may not generate the required profit margin. According to Robert A. Erickson, Program Manager for Costing Systems at the Michigan Manufacturing Technology Council, "Many companies who use activity-based pricing have reported that the most valuable use of their models is that it tells them which jobs to walk away from."[3]

Small and medium-sized companies often lack the benefit of specialized activity-based costing software. As a result, they often extract information from their general ledger system and then combine that cost information with data and management's knowledge of their company's cost behavior to arrive at activity costs to use in a pricing model of their own construction. The difference between small and big companies is that large companies have the advantage of ABC software to crunch their data, whereas smaller companies use electronic spreadsheets and other less sophisticated means.

Many companies, even very small companies, may make pricing decisions for hundreds of products each year. If the company is in an industry where pricing is competitively bid, only a portion of the bids will be accepted. The more competitors that exist, the fewer bids the company will actually win. Winning competitive bids is the lifeblood for many companies. The basic strategy of competitive bidding is to establish a price that is low enough to have a good chance of winning the bid, but high enough that the work will earn a profit once the bid is won.

This section will discuss how to construct an activity-based pricing model that allows the user to predict the profit that a company will have for a product at any selected volume. This method provides management with a powerful tool for marketing and cost accounting personnel to compare their data and discuss the interrelationships between price, volume, and cost. By allowing cost to be calculated at any sales volume, an activity-based pricing model allows management to compare the product cost curve with the customer demand curve and identify the price at which profits are maximized. Rather than maximizing revenue, the company now has the ability to maximize profits by understanding the price–profit relationship.

Pricing models are normally developed using a personal computer spreadsheet such as Excel, Lotus, or Quattro Pro.[4] The free-form flexibility of these tools allows a company to inexpensively create a model that is tailored to its own specific situation and the information that the company has available. When a pricing model is first developed, it is often very rudimentary. As new situations are encountered, management will often enhance the model, adding new features, making flexibility important. Pricing models may be particularly susceptible to changes and enhancements in their first few years of "live" use when the company is still gaining experience with the technique. It is not uncommon for a new pricing model to be developed in a hurry in order to develop pricing for a new project or an unusual new kind of product. The model is often refined later with better data for generalized use.

Activity-based pricing models are usually divided into several different parts:

- Rate table or bill of activities
- Pricing worksheet
- Quote letter

The model also may include a translator to convert the quote into the customer's preferred format or other parts tailored to the company's own situation. The translator may be part of the quote letter, may replace the quote letter, or may be a part of the quote letter.

Rate Tables

Rate tables that specify the cost of the various activities that the company performs drive pricing models. Another name for this rate table would be a bill of activities.

The rates are derived from the company's activity-based costing data and recognize the same hierarchies of cost that activity-based costing has identified. Companies that use activity-based costing data only for pricing normally have a much shorter bill of activities than companies that use it for cost reduction. Materiality is the key reason for this difference. Pareto's Law says that 20% of the items in a population will make up 80% of the value. In companies, 20% of the activities will make up 80% of the costs. Because 80% of all activities do not account for many dollars, costs that are immaterial by themselves are likely to be lumped together with other costs that have the same cost driver. For example, the cost of the accounting clerk that prepares payroll is probably not material to the company's total cost. However, the reason that the company has a payroll clerk is because there are employees, and the more employees the company has, the more work there is for the payroll clerk. Because the cost of the human resources department would have a similar cost driver as the payroll clerk, these costs are likely to be aggregated together.

Rate tables are divided up according to the kinds of things for which a company charges. This list of rates may change dramatically when changing from traditional estimating methods to activity-based pricing. Because traditional cost accounting does not recognize hierarchies of cost, all overhead costs are assigned on the basis of hours worked. Hours worked are in turn assigned on the basis of the number of units that are produced in 1 hour. The result is that traditional cost accounting assigned all costs based on the number of units of output. Although a traditional rate table will have only costs per labor or machine hours worked, an activity-based pricing rate table disassociates any overhead costs from labor or machine working hours that is not associated with them. In most companies, a significant portion of costs have no direct relationship to the number of hours that a production machine runs, but traditional costing systems assume a direct relationship. For example, there normally is no direct relationship between the cost of running an engineering department and a direct labor hour. As a result, activity-based pricing will use a lower machine running rate, but will assign the portion of cost corresponding to engineering based on other factors such as an estimate of the amount of design and process engineering time that will be used for a particular product/customer combination. Other examples of factors that have no direct relationship to labor hours are the number of machine set-ups, the number of shipments, or the complexity of product launch. An example of a rate table for a small plastic injection molding company is shown in Exhibit 8.1.

In a service environment, an accounting firm might develop a table that includes four or more levels of employees: junior, senior, manager, or partner. Each of these levels might have a different rate depending on whether the employee was performing accounting, audit, tax, or consulting work. Even for the same employee, the type of work that the person performs would affect costs because liability insurance is much higher for audit work than for a write-up or review engagement.

Exhibit 8.1 Rate table example

Rate Code	Workcenter Description	Total Rate	Excess Depr
0	Regrinding	37.10	0.00
10	Labor—molding	20.50	0.00
15	Labor—assembly	27.50	0.00
25	Pad printing	8.50	0.99
100	100-ton press	12.45	2.30
150	150-ton press	17.50	2.50
200	200-ton press	20.00	3.25
250	250-ton press	22.50	3.50
350	350-ton press	25.00	3.75
300	100-ton vertical press	35.00	3.50
500	Material handling	2.25	per tote
600	Annealing	1.75	per hour
700	Layouts	3.25	per dimension
800	Engineering coordination	$2,325	per tool
Build	Launch costs	$5,850	
Debug	Launch costs	$2,925	
Transfer	Launch costs	$0	
	AR carrying cost	1.3%	
	Cost per invoice	$9.60	

Scrap History

FC	Functional—critical	7%
FN	Functional—non-critical	5%
FV	Functional—visual	23%
NC	Nonfunctional—critical	16%
NN	Nonfunctional—noncritical	19%
NV	Nonfunctional—visual	18%

Easy/Medium/Hard Table		Setup Costs	Trials
E	Easy	135.00	3
H	Hard	285.00	9
M	Medium	185.00	6

Packaging Costs

Part #	Description	Desc 2	
PK1023	Medium premiere box	13 × 9.75 × 10	$0.03
PK1026	Medium chipboard	12.75 × 9.5 × .024	$0.03
PK1290	Medium premiere foam	White	$0.25
PK1351	Blue JC returnable tub	Blue	$0.30
PK1367	Large poly bag	24 × 20	$0.14
PK1386	Assembly foam	22 × 13 × 1/32	$0.01

Packaging Costs			
Part #	Description	Desc 2	
PK1394	Clear sealing tape	Clear	$0.99
PK1396	Case-clear confiner	30 × 60	$0.05
PK152	Tasket bag	36 × 36 × .002	$0.22
PK174	Medium zip lock	10 × 12 × .004	$0.09
PK232	Premiere box (small)	12 × 12 × 6	$0.44
PK239	Foam packaging	9.5 × 1/32 × 12.75	$0.01
PK243	Premiere box (large)	19.88 × 13 × 10	$0.53
PK246	Large chipboard	19.375 × 12.25	$0.06
PK316	Small polybag	5 × 10 × .0015	$0.01
PK318	Small chipboard	11 7/8 × 11 7/8	$0.03
PK364	Medium polybags	12 × 12 × .001	$0.02
PK380	Box pad lid	11.5 × 42.5	$0.25
PK382	Assem. partitions	5.44 × 12.38 × 43.8	$0.30
PK383	Small zip lock bag	5 × 8 × .004	$0.03
PK599	Large zip lock bag	13 × 18 × .004	$0.15
PK730	JC bag (X-LG)	12 × 24 × .003	$0.08
ZZZ	Invalid Part Number		

Note: This rate table is used in the pricing model of Premiere Plastic Products, Inc., a plastic injection molding company.

A manufacturing company often has many different categories of rates and factors, which might include rates for the following:

- Material and outside processing costs
  - Standard costs for commonly used materials
  - Standard cost for common outside processing
  - Material movement
  - Cost of storage or warehousing
- People
  - Cost per man-hour for direct labor categories
  - Cost per man-hour for other labor categories
- Processes or machines
  - Running costs
  - Setup costs
- Launch activities
  - Coordination cost per new job
  - Inspection cost per dimension

- Packaging
  - Material cost per box
  - Handling cost per box
  - Tare weights (the standard weight of an empty container)
- Process yield standards
  - Expected scrap rates by process
  - Destructive testing standards by process
- Commission rates

Material and Processing Costs

Many different techniques are used in manufacturing companies to estimate the amount of material that will be used to make a product. Some materials are sold by length, some by area, some by volume, and some by weight. The recipe to make a manufactured product normally consists of a list of the required materials, called the *bill of materials*, and a list of the processes that will be used, called the *routing*. Not all industries use these generic terms. For example, companies that make food commonly use the terms *recipe* and *ingredients list*.

In the foundry business, scrap iron, steel, aluminum, or other metals are melted down and poured into a mold. The mold consists of one or more cavities that will form the part as well as a downspout into which the hot metal is poured and runners that connect the downspout to the parts. Once the castings have solidified, they will be separated from the runners and downspout, collectively called *sprue*. Although a foundry may waste *effort* by making bad products, there is no appreciable waste of *material*. Sprue as well as any defective castings may be remelted to make a different product. Once a single copy of the product has been created, the amount of material used by the product can be calculated by simply weighing it. Calculation of the amount of material used can also be done by any computer-aided design software that has solid three-dimensional modeling capability. Once the volume is known, the weight of material used is easily calculated by multiplying the volume times the material density. (Steel has a density of 0.2833 pounds per cubic inch).

Plastic products are molded in a process that has many similarities to a metal foundry. Plastics are made up of long chains of carbon atoms with repeating sections called polymers. Many plastics (called thermoplastics) may be melted more than one time and reused. This is accomplished by grinding up the sprue and defective parts (collectively called offal) then melting them again. As plastic is melted in the molding process, the heat breaks and shortens some of these polymer chains. Shorter molecules make plastic more brittle, changing the properties of the material as it is repeatedly melted and cooled. Limitations are necessary on the number of times that a plastic molder can remelt material to prevent the plastic from becoming too brittle. In practice, controlling the portion of used material (called regrind) that may be used in the production mix prevents the proportion of relatively short-chained polymers from getting too high. For example, product specifications may limit the production mix to 30% regrind material.

As a practical matter then, the amount of material consumed to make one unit is dependent on the amount of regrind allowed and the relationship of the weight of the sprue to the weight of the parts. It is common for the plastic manufacturing process to generate more offal than may be reused in the production process. When this occurs, the material consumed must include the excess yield loss as part of the cost of the product. Some types of used plastics may have a scrap value, thus recovering a small portion of the original cost.

The steel, aluminum, and other materials used in the metal stamping industry are commonly sold in coils or bars of specific width and thickness but often of varying length. This material is often sold by weight without regard to dimension. Only in a few rare instances is the offal from a metal stamping process reusable by the same company to manufacture a different product. Except in the case of a few unusual materials, all offal from a metal stamping process is saleable as scrap. This material may be remelted by a foundry to produce castings or by a steel minimill to make steel bars or coils. Because most manufacturing offal of metal is recycled, steel is the most recycled major raw material in North America. In large quantities, steel scrap typically brings about 20% of the per pound cost of coil steel.

Purchasing and material handling costs should be associated with the products whose production processes require these efforts. These "overhead" costs should not be added to the costs of manufacturing processes. Likewise, purchasing and material handling costs should not arbitrarily be applied to materials based on a flat markup on cost. It is likely to be much easier to purchase $1 million in steel ordered $25,000 at a time, than to purchase $1 million in fasteners ordered $1,000 at a time. Most companies will likely find that the number of orders is the primary cost driver of purchasing department costs. Products that have more components in their bill of materials should consume more purchasing department costs than those products that have only a few components. It is difficult to make generalizations about material handling costs which must be studied on a company-by-company basis. In practice, many companies divide the kinds of things that they purchase into relatively homogeneous categories, and apply purchasing or material handling costs on a per-unit basis using a rate different for each category.

Process Rates

The bulk of costs for manufacturing companies normally revolve around their major manufacturing processes. In some companies, staffing for each manufacturing process is standard and unchanging. Some companies establish their rate tables so that the cost of one person is always included in the process costs because there will never be less than one person performing the process, only more. If exactly one person always staffs a type of machine, then there is little motivation to have separate rates for the person and the machine. However, in some companies staffing may vary from situation to situation. When this is the case, it is advisable to have separate rates for the person and the machine. A compromise between the two methods is also possible. If an additional person were required, that person is often added as a separate line item in the pricing model.

Exhibit 8.2 shows yet another approach. Here the company has included two separate rate codes (5 and 2000) for a "person without machine" for each of two plants within this division. It also has associated one direct labor person with each operation. Rather than add on additional people for those processes that commonly have more than one person, it has simply built the rate table so that there are rates for a machine at several different staffing levels. Here the cost for rate code 1202 (transfer press—2 people) was obtained by simply adding together the costs for rate code 1201 (transfer press—1 person) and rate code 5 (person without machine).

This pricing model has another interesting feature shown for rate code 2999 (assembly cell). This company uses cellular manufacturing, a technique where workers move from work station to work station depending on production demands. This particular pricing model allows the estimator to configure and calculate an hourly running cost for an entire manufacturing cell in a separate worksheet. The rate table, then, pulls a cost from the cell worksheet, making it available for the pricing worksheet. Ordinarily, when a company has several similar machines, those machines are grouped together into a single *work center* and a single rate will be developed for those interchangeable machines.

Manufacturing rate tables should have separate setup rates and running rates. Although some companies use the same hourly rate for setup and running costs, an examination of the underlying activities often reveals that the hourly cost of performing a setup and running the machine are not quite the same. Although a machine occupies the same amount of floor space in each situation, the energy consumption costs may be very different. Maintenance is normally associated with the wear that occurs from running a machine, not the idle time associated with setup. A machine may require a highly skilled and highly paid setup person, but afterward may be tended by a less skilled worker. In many companies, both workers will be involved in the setup. For these reasons, it is common to develop both setup rates and running rates for a process.

The significance of separating running time with setup is that running time is a variable cost that will be directly associated with the number of units produced. Setup costs are associated with the number of batches of the product that are produced. Another way to look at the differences is that setup costs are generally fixed for each batch (e.g., the machine takes 2 hours to set up, whereas the length of the

Exhibit 8.2 Example of a componentized rate

Rate Code	Work Center Description	Total Rate	Direct Labor	Direct Fringes	Indirect Labor	Maint. & Repair	Utilities	Indirect Mat'ls	Insur.	Interest	Maint. Mat'l	Floor Space	SG&A
0	No operation	0.00	0.00	0.00	0.00	0.00	0.00	0.00	0.00	0.00	0.00	0.00	0.00
5	Person without machine	30.00	9.75	3.51	0.20	3.00	2.30	3.14	0.10	0.05	0.24	0.05	6.54
10	Simple welder	45.00	9.75	3.51	0.41	11.62	2.55	3.24	0.14	1.17	3.55	0.07	7.13
15	Simple welder w/nut feed	50.00	9.75	3.51	1.59	12.63	2.60	3.52	0.15	1.30	3.54	0.08	7.98
20	Dedicated press welders	55.00	9.75	3.51	2.25	14.05	2.80	3.92	0.20	1.74	4.26	0.10	9.07
25	Robotic welder	70.00	9.75	3.51	3.25	13.91	3.15	3.88	0.82	6.95	4.74	0.42	11.06
50	Secondary press	50.00	10.35	3.62	0.40	10.00	2.37	4.30	0.61	5.21	3.09	0.31	8.07
100	100-ton press	85.00	13.05	4.44	5.25	14.50	5.50	4.75	1.25	13.25	1.25	0.72	17.04
200	200-ton press	120.00	13.40	4.56	12.45	26.72	8.81	6.06	1.63	13.89	2.35	0.83	21.25
400	400-ton press	175.00	13.75	4.68	23.68	38.91	8.89	9.77	1.65	16.57	3.96	0.84	27.53
600	600-ton press	220.00	14.10	4.79	36.12	46.45	10.15	12.97	2.63	22.36	5.53	1.34	32.27
1201	Transfer press—1 person	360.00	14.45	4.91	47.10	59.07	18.98	17.65	7.50	53.82	8.91	3.83	44.85
1202	Transfer press—2 person	390.00	24.20	8.42	47.30	62.07	21.28	20.79	7.60	53.87	9.15	3.88	51.39
1203	Transfer press—3 person	420.00	33.95	11.93	47.50	65.07	23.58	23.93	7.70	53.92	9.39	3.93	57.93
1999	Stamping crew	140.56	0.75	2.00	9.64	11.00	6.25	0.00	10.92	100.00	0.00	0.00	0.00
2000	BC man without machine	25.00	8.78	2.20	1.25	0.00	0.25	3.25	0.25	0.00	5.27	1.00	2.25
2010	Single-headed riveter	35.00	8.78	2.20	1.25	2.75	1.50	4.00	0.50	0.50	5.52	4.00	3.00
2021	Rotary multiriveter—1 person	75.00	8.78	2.20	1.25	16.25	2.75	8.75	0.75	1.75	7.10	10.00	5.00
2022	Rotary multiriveter—2 person	100.00	17.55	4.39	1.50	16.50	2.75	16.75	0.75	2.00	9.64	11.00	6.25
2023	Rotary multiriveter—3 person	125.00	26.33	6.58	1.75	16.75	2.75	22.00	0.75	2.25	15.17	11.50	7.75
2100	press w/rotary table	55.00	8.78	2.20	1.25	16.50	3.00	4.00	1.00	1.75	6.46	4.00	2.25
2200	Rotary MIG welder	60.00	10.80	2.70	2.00	13.50	3.75	5.00	1.50	1.50	8.03	2.00	5.25
2400	Springer	30.00	8.78	2.20	1.25	1.25	1.50	2.50	0.50	0.50	3.63	3.00	3.00
2999	Assembly cell	140.56	0.75	2.00	9.64	11.00	6.25	0.00	10.92	100.00	0.00	0.00	0.00

Note: This rate table has subdivided each activity-derived rate into its component expense categories using traditional accounting classifications to allow the company to translate its cost into the format required by the customer's traditional mentality quotation form.

production run will vary with the quantity of product being produced). The amount of set-up cost that is assigned to each unit is therefore dependent on the number of units per batch. Although batches of low-volume products may be produced only once a quarter or once a year, high-volume products may involve even fewer batches because production for high-volume products may never be shut down. It is very cost effective to produce a manufactured product in dedicated machinery that runs all or most of the time. As a result, it is important to recognize efficiencies or inefficiencies relating to batch size so that the company can be cost competitive on what manufacturing people think of as the "good" products and get paid for the extra work on the "dog" jobs.

People

A particular problem when determining the cost of people is deciding which costs should be associated with the people and which should be associated with the processes that the people are performing. Supervisory costs provide a good example. Does setting up a machine, running the machine, or supervising the people that run the machine create supervisory work? In many companies, 50% or more of supervisory costs are found to be associated with setting up processes, not running them. These setup costs include scheduling, planning machine changeover, and trouble shooting startup of a new task. Once production is up and running smoothly, there may be little difference in the amount of supervisory work consumed by 8 running hours or 80 running hours because the supervisory work occurred at setup. For this reason it is not uncommon to see a company apportion 50% of supervisory cost to process setup, 20% to new product launch, and only 30% of supervisory time to process running cost and people.

Packaging, Material Handling, and Shipping Costs

Packaging, material handling, and shipping costs often receive little attention at the time of pricing. In some businesses these categories may be a significant part of cost, particularly for low-cost products. These costs merit special attention because they tend to depend not on how many units of the product the company produces, but how many units are shipped in each box. Many companies that have a traditional standard costing system put packaging costs in overhead, because they cannot have more than one standard cost per part. But what if they sell the same product in bulk to an original equipment manufacturer and individually package it as an aftermarket part? Packaging costs can vary significantly in these two situations and should be identified.

The following is an example of where material handling costs really matter.

Worthington Manufacturing Company[5] is a plastic injection molding company whose customers produce assembled electrical systems for the automotive industry. One of their major customers provides Worthington with returnable containers in which to ship their products. These containers come in several sizes and are designed to hold no more than 4 hours worth of product consumption by the customer in order to minimize the storage space requirements in the customer's assembly operation. Because of this 4-hour requirement, in some cases a very small part might be shipped in a very small container that was well under half full. Worthington has analyzed the cost of performing its various material handling operations and has calculated that it costs $3.95 to do the inspections, prepare the bar code labels, and handle the inventory control related to each container that it ships, regardless of size. If a part with 2 cents of manufacturing cost is shipped with 400 units in a returnable container, the material handling costs would be 49% of manufacturing cost. In this example, there is an obvious opportunity to reduce cost by offering the customer a choice of receiving the product packaged as requested or of purchasing the product at a lower price in a larger returnable container.

Launch Activities

Launch activities are things that a company must do before it produces and sells even the first unit of a new product. An example would be the advanced quality planning process that automotive suppliers must establish prior to production of any part. Launch costs are a common type of product level costs. It would be hard to come up with an example of a product for which there was not some type of up-front cost associated with its launch. When an accounting firm takes on a new audit client, the client's procedures and internal controls must be documented and "permanent" files must be created. In order to add a new cable television client, the cable service provider must run wiring into the neighborhood and into the customer's home. For a manufacturing company, there are issues of product design, prototype development, market testing, tooling development, packaging development, and myriad other things that must be done before the company can sell its first unit.

Each company has its own unique set of required launch activities to introduce a new product. These activities sometimes cover several years and require a significant investment. Even within a single company, one product may require a significantly different launch effort than another. Product complexity may be a cost driver of launch activity. Intuitively, it makes sense that it should be more expensive to bring a complex product to market than an easy one, but how should complexity be measured? It is usually worth the effort to study what drives launch activity costs.

One large publicly traded automotive parts manufacturer interviewed all of the people that were involved in product launch. From these interviews, product attributes were identified that caused cost and a value was assigned to each attribute. Engineering costs made up the biggest portion of the launch costs at this company, and the engineer's estimates were tested against actual time reports from earlier products that the engineers had designed. This company assigned launch costs according to the schedule shown in Exhibit 8.3.

Launch costs generally fall under the category of period costs for financial accounting purposes. Not only are these costs expensed as they are incurred, but they are often expensed long before these efforts generate any revenue. The real economics behind launch costs is that they provide a benefit over the entire life of the product by enabling the product to exist in the first place.

Launch costs are significant because they represent true fixed costs. Because launch costs are incurred at the beginning of a product's life cycle, the eventual number of units that will be sold will not affect the total amount that was spent. This cost behavior can have a big effect on overall profits, because these fixed costs must somehow be recovered over the life of the product.

There are several different strategies for recovering launch costs. In the simplest case, a company might choose to recover launch costs evenly over the entire estimated life of the product. If the company from Exhibit 8.3 expected to sell 750,000 units over the life of the product, that would mean that the company should attempt to collect $0.0385 per unit in launch costs. This strategy would most likely be used in a very competitive situation where the seller did not expect to see any change in price in real dollars over the product life.

Other strategies recover launch costs unevenly over the life of the product. In a situation where the ultimate number of units to be sold is uncertain, the company

Exhibit 8.3 Table of estimated launch costs by product attribute

	Cost Per	Cost for Simple Hinge	
Description of Attribute	Attribute	Count	Cost
Each new product	$1,525	1	$1,525
Each stamping in product	4,925	2	9,850
Inside operation	1,750	3	5,250
Other details	1,750	2	3,500
Moving parts	4,375	2	8,750
			$28,875

Note: In this example, a metal stamping company has estimated the launch cost of a simple hinge consisting of two stampings connected by a rivet.

might attempt to disproportionately collect launch costs in the early years. This strategy is common with automotive parts suppliers, who are often asked to commit to a pricing schedule where the price of the product is reduced each year. For a program that is expected to last 5 years, launch costs might be apportioned so that they represented 8% of price in year 1, 6% of price in year 2, 4% in year 3, 2% in year 4, and 0% in year 5. In this manner, the customer would receive a 2% annual price reduction, and the company would reduce the risk that there would be unrecoverable launch costs if the program were cancelled after only 4 years.

Sales of innovative new products are often capacity constrained. The consumer electronics industry provides many examples. When a new product is introduced, the developer of the product may have little idea of how well the product will be accepted, how many units will be sold, or how long the technology will remain leading edge. For every successful long-lived product like the Sony Walkman, there are products like eight-track tapes and Beta-format video tapes that either sell well but do not last or never sell well at all. In view of these possibilities, management is often conservative in the development of production facilities.

If the volume that the company is able to produce is only enough to satisfy the high-end demand, then the company may choose to sell its product at a high-end price, in effect recovering product launch costs on an accelerated basis using a market-skimming strategy. If the market supports a high-end price, collecting development costs early on may be a good idea. Because price is one of the things that signals value to customers, starting the price off high also may help support good pricing in the future.

Process Yield

Scrap does not just happen. When a process produces a bad product, there is a reason for the error. Sometimes the reason is related to the process; sometimes the reason is related to the product or materials used to make the product. For example, buyers expect the surface of many products to be blemish free. An irregularity in the texture or color of the product would not be acceptable, and the defective unit then must be scrapped or sold as a "second." Not all products are that way. Carpenters expect that some pieces of lumber will be better than others and that not all nail heads are perfect. For some products the primary concern is functionality; for other products, cosmetics play an equal or greater role.

Many manufacturing processes require destructive testing as part of the standard quality control procedure. A company may have to tear apart 1 out of every 100 products made in order to confirm that the welds holding the product together are of adequate strength. Because of these considerations, a pricing model might include a table of rates that provides data regarding process yield. The table might say that expected scrap was 1% for one type of product, yet 5% for another.

Componentized Rates

From a general ledger perspective, pricing model rates may be made up of many different kinds of costs. The cost of running a machine includes depreciation, maintenance, rent, utilities, and many other kinds of expenses. If the company's customer requires that a quotation provide a detailed breakdown of costs in a particular format, a componentized rate table will help in this task. An example of a componentized rate table for a metal stamping company is shown in Exhibit 8.2. Here the running rate for a 200-ton press is $120 per hour. Of this $120 per hour, maintenance and repair make up $26.72 of that cost. If this machine produces 1,600 units per hour, at a machine running cost of $.075 each, the company would also be able to calculate that $0.0167 of that cost is attributed to maintenance and repair. By extending all of the parts of the $120 rate in this manner, the company will be able to translate its activity-based way of thinking about costs into the traditional world of its customer's purchasing agents.

MANUFACTURING PRICING WORKSHEETS

Exhibit 8.4 shows a pricing worksheet used by Gale Manufacturing Co. Although the name and a few details have been changed to disguise the identity of the company, this is an actual pricing worksheet used by a large, publicly traded automotive supplier. The original quotation from which this was taken also had room for more line items and was made to fit on legal size paper.

Some of the more interesting features of this model are as follows:

- Number of images
- Volume
- Product complexity
- Material cost
- Production run time
- Production setup
- Packaging
- Other features
- Selling costs
- Profit

Exhibit 8.4 Metal stamping company quoting model—Gale Manufacturing

Quotation Summary					
Part #	Description	# of Images	Print Level Date	Prepared by	Preparation Date
G39B-99999-AA	CLAMP	1	9/9/99	JRJ	13-Mar-00

Volume each side	2000	2001	2002	2003		Prodn. Yrs.
Annual volume in in 1,000's"	99	102	102	102		9.00
	2004	2005	2006	2007	Dynamic Details	Avg. Vol. (000)
	102	0	0	0	1	99.0

Blank Weight Computation						
Part #	Material Type	Gauge	Progression	Width	# Out	Gross Weight
G39B-99999-AA	HRLC	0.0900	9.9990	9.9990	1	2.54919
						2.54919

Material Pricing Information						
Part #	Operation	$/lb.	Qty. Req'd.	Handling	Extended Cost	
G39B-99999-AA	PROG	0.9900	2.54919	4.5%	2.63726	
0						
0						
			Material subtotal		2.63726	87.2%

Workcenter Utilization						
Part #	Operation	Pieces/Hr.	Rate Code	Rate	Extended Cost	
G39B-99999-AA	Blank	1600	200	120.00	0.07500	
				0.00	0.00000	
				0.00	0.00000	
				0.00	0.00000	
Setup costs					0.01955	
Launch costs				0.00	0.01215	
			Labor subtotal		0.10670	3.5%

Other Details						
Part #	Description	$/Each	Qty. Each	Handling	Extend. Cost	
0	0	0.0000	0.000	0.0%		
Engineering amort.		0.0000	1.000		0.00000	
Destructive testing						
Packaging		$18.00	2,000	0.0%	0.00900	
			Other subtotal		0.00900	0.3%

Comments:

Total costs		2.75297	91.0%
Profit	10.00%	0.26394	8.7%
Subtotal		3.01691	99.7%
Sales cost		0.00787	0.3%
Selling price		3.02477	100.0%

Approvals					
Initials					
Date					

Note: This is the activity-based pricing worksheet used by Gale Manufacturing Company, a large automotive parts manufacturer.

Number of Images

It is common in the automotive industry that a vehicle will require parts to be made in mirror-image pairs, one for the left side of the vehicle and one for the right. These parts are often made simultaneously in the same production operation. This factor tells the computer that the production will be, in effect, doubled because the volumes of two similar parts must be considered.

This problem with multiple versions of a product affects many industries. In the garment industry, it is common for one basic style to be made in multiple colors, sizes, and fabrics. There will be design costs for the overall design plus costs of making patterns for each size alternative for the garment. Interestingly, garment production costs can differ significantly for fabrics that are solids and patterns. Quality construction using a patterned fabric calls for the pattern to be matched where two pieces of material meet.

In plastic injection molding, the same mold may make a family of different but related parts that are each components for the same end item. Cost considerations of family molds can become very complicated because a high scrap rate on one part can cause unbalanced production. Plastic molding companies may also produce parts that are identical except for color. A product may have one or more high volume popular colors and other colors that make up only a small portion of production. Because the machine must be purged of one color before another color may be produced, there may be a very different real cost associated with different colors of products that are otherwise identical.

Volume

Production volume is important because it influences unit costs. Fixed costs and step-variable costs decrease per unit as production volumes increase. In the second section of Exhibit 8.4, it can be seen that Gale Manufacturing Co. has collected projected sales volumes by year. Many companies' forms ask for the total number of units that are expected to be produced or ask for the number of production years and the average volume. Collecting sales volume by year instead of by number of units would help the company to introduce a method of recovering launch costs unevenly over the life of the product.

Product Complexity

An unusual entry for dynamic details seen in the volume section may seem out of place. *Dynamic details* is the term that Gale's engineers use to describe one of the things that causes complexity in the type of products that it makes. To Gale, a dynamic detail is a spring or a moving part. Purchasing, quality control, and production control at this company have all defined what causes launch-level work for them as well. This model takes key attributes from the quote to estimate the complexity of launching its products.

The quotation model for Premiere Plastic Products, Inc. (Exhibit 8.5) provides another look at a company that estimates launch costs based on product complexity. Premiere is a medium-sized, two-location plastic injection molding company whose major launch activities include performing numerous sample layouts (measuring product samples and comparing them to the engineering specifications). This company found that layout work was dependent on the number of dimensions that a product had, the number of critical dimensions (important close tolerance dimensions), and the number of cavities per mold (because each part that the mold produced must meet the same specifications). Premier determined a cost to check each dimension and make corrections based on a typical error rate. Because the layout for a single mold could involve checking hundreds of parts, quality control, engineering, and tooling could spend several weeks getting sample approval. Although the cost to measure a single dimension was very low, Premiere sometimes expends a significant amount of money during the launch phase of a product's life cycle compared with other product-related costs.

As a matter of policy, both Gale and Premiere attempt to recapture launch costs up front by billing for it through the cost of the tooling rather than through the cost of the product. In the lower right-hand pricing section of Premiere's quotation model is a box for the amount of billable launch costs. No launch costs are included in the product price for this particular quote because the launch costs that the model calculated will be billed as part of the tooling.

Material Cost

Gale Manufacturing breaks their material cost calculation into two parts. The gross weight of the part is calculated in the third section of the worksheet that Gale has labeled "blank weight computation." Because metal stamping companies think in terms of flat, rectangular sections of steel, this model calculates the volume of the part and then multiplies it by the density of steel at 0.2833 pounds per cubic inches. Gale follows a common practice in the metal stamping industry of calculating material cost based on the gross weight of the product rather than including a scrap credit. This is a significant departure from normal activity-based costing theory and practice. If the gross weight of a product were 2 pounds and the material cost $0.25 per pound, then this model would conclude that the material cost was $0.50 plus a 4.5% handling markup. If the net weight were 1 pound and $0.05 per pound could be recovered by selling the material trimmed from around the part, then the "true" costs using activity-based costing would be 5 cents less or $0.45 plus the 5.0% handling markup on the lower amount.

Exhibit 8.5 Plastic injection molding company quoting model—Premiere Plastic Products

Quotation Worksheet

Customer	Buyer				Cust. Inq. #	Quote #	Reason for Revision	
Johnson Controls	Kazu Wantanabe					50644 A	Original Quote	
Customer Part #	Rev #	Description			Program	Estimator	Prep. Date	Ave Volume
50644	B	Terminal				Larry Lindowski		900,000
Setup/mold maint (E,M,H)			Part Type	Launch Type		Print Level Date	1st Ship Date	Production yrs
$500	H	FV	Functions-Visl	Transfer			6/1/2001	2.0

Layout							
Trials (E,M,H)	# of Trials	Pcs/Cavity	Dimensions	# of Cavities	Critical Dim.	Samples	Cost
H	9	1	100	4	7	30	$6,073.20

Material Usage	Part Weight (g)	# of Cavities	Runner Wt (g)	Shot Wt (g)	Scrap %	Mat'l Usage (g)
	20.0	4	10.0	90.0	5.0%	24.19

Material Spec	Import?	Custom?	PPP Mat'l #	Cost/KG	Mix	Regrind %		Batch Cost
Valox 420-5453 Brown	N	Y		$5.50	100	Allowed	Available	$481.25
	Y	Y				30%	13%	100.00KG

Purchased Part #	Description	Qty Used	Cost Each	Scrap %	Ext'd cost
		1.0	0.5000	5.0%	0.5250
				5.0%	0.0000
			Total Purchased Parts		0.5250

Production Specifications	Target Machine	Cycle Time (Seconds)	Effective Cycle Time	Set-up Freq (Weeks)	Run Characteristics		
					Run Quantity	Kgs/Run	Duration (Hrs.)
100 Ton Vert. Press	300	63	66.3	2	36,000	762	166

Labor	Rate Code	Rate	% Usage	Pcs/Hour	Cost/Part	Economic Level
Labor—molding	10	$20.50	100%		0.0944	Jun-99
Labor—assembly	15	$27.50			0.0000	Jun-98
				Total Labor Cost	0.0944	

Packaging					
Description	**Pack Type**	**Cost Each**	**Qty/Container**	**$/Container**	
Premiere returnable gray tub	PK1382	$0.0000	1	$0.0000	
			0	$0.0000	
			0	$0.0000	
		Total container cost		$0.0000	Shipments
		Parts/container		50	Per Month
		Cost/part		$0.0000	20

Internal Comments

Customers Comments
Quote valid 60 days from quote date

Approval	
Name	**Date**

Pricing				
Launch	Billable	6,073	0.0000	0.0%
Material			0.1185	9.3%
Purchased parts			0.5250	
Regrind			0.0090	0.7%
Setup			0.0139	1.1$
Machine			0.1612	12.7%
Labor			0.0944	7.4%
Material handling			0.0650	5.1%
Packaging			0.0000	0.0
Invoicing & AR carrying cost			0.0179	1.9%
Annual cost downs		2.50%	0.0247	85.0%
Total cost			1.0810	
Sales commission		5.00%	0.0636	
Profit		10.00%	0.1272	10.0%
Total price			1.2718	100.0%

Note: This activity-based pricing model is used by Premiere Plastic Products, Inc., a small plastic injection molding company.

For Premiere Plastic Products, the nature of plastic injection molding makes its Material Usage section very different from the one used by Gale. This model provides no tool for estimating product gross weight, but does provide assistance in calculating the weight of the shot of hot plastic that the machine will inject into the mold for each cycle. Note that the quotation specifically asks for an expected scrap rate. If the scrap rate that is entered is less than the historic scrap rate for the part type listed in the quotation header, an error message will be displayed. Two different materials are often mixed to make plastic parts. One is often a neutral-colored basic material, whereas the other is a concentrated coloring. The second material line allows Premiere to include quantities of colored concentrate when it is required for a part.

The sprue and runners that connect the part in the mold may sometimes be reused in the process. Unlike Gale, Premiere provides a credit for any material value that can be recovered from the production process. Exhibit 8.3 shows a part that is allowed 30% regrind. However, the model has calculated that due to the relationship between the weight of the sprue and runners compared with the weight of the parts, only 13% of the material used in the process is available to be reused. Therefore, the model gives credit for the amount of regrind that is actually generated. If this company had a different product that used the same material, it would be possible that excess material from the other product would be available to produce this part.

Gale Manufacturing uses many purchased parts in its products and therefore has developed a method of adding handling costs to those component parts that it purchases. Premiere deals with very few purchased parts and has included these costs elsewhere.

Production Run Time

Gale's quote model has labeled the section that calculates the cost of production processes "work center utilization." Premiere has used the term "production specifications." Gale's work center utilization rate table combines the cost of people and machines because people hours and machine hours are normally the same. Premiere's rate table completely separates people and machines because machines are not normally attended by a person 100% of the time. The percentage of a production operator's time that is expected to be devoted to tending the machine is specified in the "% usage" field.

Gale determines the number of pieces that will be produced per hour based on the historical throughput of similar products. Accordingly, the "pieces/hr" shown on the quotation worksheet has a provision for downtime already built into it. Premiere has not taken downtime into account in calculating its cycle time, but has taken downtime into account in calculating the hourly production rate. The effective cycle time is increased, however, for the effects of the scrapped parts specified in the material usage section.

Production Setup

Setup costs should be calculated separately from running costs because batch size usually differs significantly from product to product. If the cost to perform a setup is $100, then the cost per unit is $1 for a batch size of 100 units, $0.10 for a batch size of 1,000 units, and $0.01 for a batch size of 10,000 units.

Gale Manufacturing uses an economic order quantity (EOQ) calculation to determine how often a job will be set up. This calculation is not shown on the basic quotation worksheet. The estimator may view the number of annual setups that the quote has used, but the estimator would not normally manipulate the number of setups that is calculated. The company performs many different kinds of stamping and assembly operations. Because the first (primary) stamping operations all run at a rate in excess of 1,000 units per hour and all of the secondary operations run significantly slower, one day's worth of stamping production may take several weeks to go through the other manufacturing processes. As a result, the economic order quantity is geared to this primary operation.

The economic order quantity calculation balances the inventory carrying cost with the setup cost of the primary operation. Gale does not set up any primary operation more than once a week; thus, this upper limit on the number of annual setups is imbedded into the EOQ equation. The minimum number of setups that will be used by the quote is determined by their customers' fabrication release horizon. A fabrication release is a customer's authorization to produce a specific amount of products, normally specified in the form of a list showing expected requirements for a number of weeks in the future. Eight weeks' requirement is a typical fabrication release from their customers. Although Gale normally establishes the price of each job as if it would have a minimum of six setups per year, the company may choose to run low-volume products less often. The added setup cost included in the quote is viewed as payment for the obsolescence risk of running production beyond the fabrication release.

The order quantity parameters used by Premiere are visible in the production specifications portion of Exhibit 8.5. Although it is not shown in these specifications, Premiere has scheduling guidelines that specify a minimum run duration of 8 hours. Its high volume jobs are usually set up every 2 weeks. Its plant runs around the clock 7 days a week for approximately 350 days a year; thus, the 166-hour run duration shown on the quotation worksheet is equal to just under 7 days of production.

Packaging

Packaging costs are product specific. The cost per unit of packaging ordinarily has nothing to do with production volume but everything to do with the way the product is packaged and number of pieces in a box.

Premiere uses many different kinds of packaging. Many of their products are sold in returnable containers. Some of their products are layered in boxes or packed in plastic bags within the box. As a result, the company provides a special section to calculate the cost of the various materials that make up one box. Gale is far less sophisticated in its packaging quotation. Using only three kinds of boxes, Gale charges a fixed rate for each box that includes both the material cost as well as the cost of box assembly.

One useful feature that does not appear in either of these quotes is a calculation of how much a full container is going to weigh. To minimize back injuries, some companies calculate the weight of a full box in their quotation models. A good strategy is to optimize box weight so that a full container either weighs less than 40 pounds so that it çan easily lifted by a person or weighs so much that no one would attempt to pick it up without proper material handling equipment.

Other Features

Because many of Gale's products require welding operations, there is an interesting destructive testing feature in their model. Running down the right side of the worksheet, just off the printed portion visible in the example, is a column where the estimator can specify any line of cost that will be subject to a yield loss through destructive testing or other process limitations. Destructive testing costs are added when the estimator specifies the percentage of loss that will occur. This result of calculation is shown in the "other details" section of Exhibit 8.4.

Gale also includes a line for "engineering amortization." Under a complicated arrangement with one of its customers, Gale is reimbursed for the design engineering work that it performs. Billable engineering costs are excluded from the cost base used to derive the rate table, but engineering may be specifically added into product cost on this line.

Selling Costs

Although at first glance Gale would appear to be charging selling costs as a markup on all other costs, something different is really going on here. After all, what sales representative would be happy with compensation that was a mere three-tenths of a percent of selling costs, as shown on this quotation worksheet? A study of the cost behavior of Gale's salaried sales force showed that the company's selling costs were largely a fixed amount for each job. Accordingly, Gale calculates the bulk of its selling costs as part of its launch cost calculation. The selling costs that are shown separately near the bottom of the quote are only the small amount of incentive pay that each salesperson receives. Interestingly, that incentive is calculated based on value-added (revenue less purchased parts and materials) instead of sales dollars.

Premiere uses some commissioned outside sales representatives, whereas other customers are house accounts handled by the owners. The commission rate for outside salespeople declines from 5% based on sales volume. Premiere also charges the same selling costs on jobs that are sold by the owners. It could be argued that the company should make a better study of how costs are expended on these house accounts. However, most of its selling costs are devoted to the overall customer relationship, not any individual product. These sustaining costs, therefore, have been arbitrarily assigned.

Profit

Gale and Premiere both operate in very competitive, cost-conscious industries. Although both are seeking a profit that represents a 10% markup on pretax costs, both companies adjust their profitability depending on the competitive situation. Gale has a policy that they will not sell a product below cost, but will sometimes quote at a 0% markup to get new work.

Premiere also adjusts its profit percentage but also has established some costs that they are willing to give up to make a sale in a competitive bid situation. Premiere believes that its equipment has a 12-year useful life, but management wishes to recover the cost of this equipment in 6 years. The company also has a small amount of excess capacity. These costs are excluded from competitively bid quotes but are included when the company thinks that it has no competitor. The estimator can check a box that is not shown on this quote page to include or exclude these costs.

It is not enough to know the costs of existing products. For cost information to be truly useful, what causes the cost must be understood well enough that the lessons learned from existing products can be used to predict the cost of a product that the company has yet to produce. For each new product, there is often a new twist that makes the product a little different than anything the company has done before. Sometimes a new product is a lot different than anything the company has done before.

Determining profitability for current or past products is considerably easier than predicting profitability for future products. There may be sales reports, time reports, production reports, invoice registers, and other information that allow an accountant to piece together the profitability story. For an existing product, even if little cost data exist on paper, a person can observe the product being produced to gain a feel for its costs.

In these two models, profit has been added to each quote as a markup on cost. However, there are compelling reasons to consider basing the quoted profit on other factors. Many companies have huge sums of money invested in their equipment, facilities, and personnel. Some work that is performed for customers may engage equipment that is very expensive, and other work may involve little more than the time of an unskilled worker. If a company is cash rich, no interest cost may have been passed through to the pricing rate tables. In such a case, the company may seek what looks like an attractive return on sales that proves to be an inadequate return on investment. The opposite also may be true. A company may seek a return on sales that appears modest but that translates into a return on investment that is unreasonably high. In order to receive a satisfactory return on investment, yet not overprice low investment opportunities, companies should explore ways to plan for profitability not in terms of a return on sales but in terms of a return on investment.

PRICING MODELS IN OTHER INDUSTRIES

Retailing

Although retailers often use cost-based pricing methods, retailers usually examine only the purchased cost of the goods that they are selling, assuming that the "average" cost of floor space, shelving, stocking, and checkout are all the same as a percentage of purchase cost.

Restaurants consider themselves retailers, often referring to each location as a "store," yet in many ways the cost considerations of a restaurant are much like a manufacturing company. Most of the items that a restaurant serves consist of raw materials that need to be converted into a menu item before they are saleable to a customer. Restaurants purchase eggs, bacon, bread, industrial sized bags or cans of soup, whole pies by the dozen, hamburgers by the gross, and all of the other items that would be served in their restaurant. Each type of ingredient has a different type of storage requirement. Some items are stored in a freezer, other items are stored in a walk-in refrigerator, and still others may be stored at room temperature in a pantry. Refrigerator space is more expensive than pantry space. Preparation time varies widely from one food item to another. It takes more time to section a grapefruit than it does to ladle soup into a bowl. There are compelling reasons for retailers to make more detailed studies of their costs when determining price.

Retailers are often able to sell the same product to different customers at different prices through a number of different techniques. One of these is the frequent buyer program, now common with grocery retailers. A&P's Farmer Jack division offers a program where members receive discounts on certain items, in effect providing a lower price to regular customers. Members are provided with a small tag for their key chain that contains a bar code to identify them at checkout. Farmer Jack also provides Northwest Airlines frequent flyer miles, further cementing the relationship with regular customers. The Safeway Club programs at Safeway supermarkets provide similar features that may be used with either a card or the member's phone number. Acquiring new customers is an expensive proposition, and even substantial discounts for customer loyalty are often well justified.

Service Businesses

Service businesses have been slow adopters of activity-based costing techniques. Service businesses often develop their rate tables based strictly on a markup on direct costs. Rates for professional services, for example, are often established as 2.5 to 3.5 times the salary of the professional. Although accounting firms often sell their clients activity-based costing services, they rarely use it within their own firms. There are many obvious differences in costs between the various kinds of services that accounting firms provide. Tax people of all levels normally have office space or at least a cubicle that they can call their own, whereas auditors and consultants spend most of their time at their clients' locations. For this reason, auditors and consultants often have no permanently assigned space at their offices, receiving temporary space whenever they are not at a client. This practice is called *hoteling* within the accounting industry. Computer hardware is cheaper for tax people who have desktops rather than the laptop computers that auditors and consulting people use, but tax software is more expensive. Consultants rarely sell audit or tax work, although auditors often spend much of their sales efforts on consulting services.

Quotations for services are often prepared by establishing a work program listing the tasks to be performed. For example, a quotation to perform an audit or consulting work might be supported by a list of the hours required to perform each audit task, with a different billing rate for each type of personnel involved with the audit. When this method is used, project startup activities, such as documenting client procedures for the auditor's "permanent files," are usually enumerated and visible, allowing the person preparing the quote to see these fixed costs separate from the ongoing annual efforts. Indirect costs such as clerical support services also may be specifically enumerated, providing a more accurate estimation of costs.

Most businesses can improve their profitability by studying the relationship between price and cost. Understanding this relationship marks the difference between a "smart" competitor and a "dumb" competitor, and the companies that have used activity-based pricing have found that it has provided them with a competitive advantage.

SUMMARY

The key points described in this chapter are discussed below:

1. Activity-based pricing models use activity-based costing data to identify the cost of producing a product at any selected volume.
2. The activity-based pricing model is used in conjunction with customer demand data to determine the price at which the product can be sold most profitably.
3. The most common pricing strategy is *satisficing,* where companies seek to earn an adequate financial return. Companies in competitive bid situations may routinely use a cost-plus pricing technique for most of their pricing.
4. The rate tables used in activity-based pricing may come from specialized activity-based costing software or may be developed using other tools such as personal computer spreadsheets.
5. Most companies that use specialized activity-based costing software still develop their pricing using a personal computer spreadsheet.

NOTES

1. Oros and Easy ABC are registered trademarks of ABC Technologies, Inc.
2. Source: Phone interview with Gary Cokins, December 13, 2000.
3. Bob Erickson, Program Director–Costing Systems at the Michigan Manufacturing Technology Council. He provided his thoughts on a draft of this chapter.
4. Excel is a registered trademark of Microsoft Corporation, Lotus is a registered trademark of Lotus Development Corporation, and Quattro-Pro is a registered trademark of Corel Corporation.
5. The real name of this company has not been used.

9

INFLUENCE OF CAPACITY UTILIZATION

There is an *opportunity cost* that relates to excess capacity. By filling up capacity with marginal work, the company may not have available capacity when a better opportunity arises. In theory, the company should throw out the marginal product when a better opportunity comes along. In reality, this is not what companies do. In the real world, a company that has a mix of winners and losers will add capacity to accommodate a new winner rather than throw the loser out. In effect, the company is then adding new capacity to continue to make the marginal jobs at a loss.

INFLUENCE OF EFFICIENCY ON PRICE

Efficiency matters. Companies that have efficient operations are more cost effective than their average competitor and can deliver their products faster and at a lower price. A key measure of efficiency is capacity utilization. Companies that have a higher capacity utilization than their peers may use their cost advantage to gain market share through lower price or earn higher profits than the rest of the industry. Companies with inefficient operations are forced to pay for their inefficiency through lower profits or no profit at all.

Just as capacity utilization can affect price, pricing can have a major impact on capacity utilization. Variations in price may be used to allow companies to fill otherwise unused capacity or to earn premium prices at time of high demand. Using these two factors together can have a major influence on company profitability.

CAPACITY CONSIDERATIONS IN PRICING

Dictionaries define *capacity* as active power or productive ability. Capacity is measured differently from industry to industry. Indeed, different companies within an industry may measure their ability to produce their product from a different perspective. In a service business, capacity is likely to be measured in terms of available people or people hours. The ability of an accounting firm or law firm to do work for its clients is limited by the number of people that it employs. Many other factors may limit a service business's capacity as well. The firm may have the ability to hire accountants, but not the capacity to train the accountants that it hires. An accounting firm also may be limited by the amount of office space that it has to house people.

Similar constraints may affect companies in a distribution, retail, or manufacturing business. Manufacturing companies frequently think of their capacity in terms of floor space and machinery. A plant whose machinery operates 70% of the available business hours is said to run at 70% of capacity. A distribution company may measure its capacity in orders processed, and a retail company may measure its capacity in terms of the number of customers served or by the amount of display space.

One of the most influential writers about business capacity is Eliyahu M. Goldratt, a physicist specializing in fluid dynamics. When asked to help a relative with a business problem, Goldratt applied his fluid dynamics background to look at capacity with a perspective that was revolutionary for its time. Goldratt published these theories in the form of a novel, *The Goal*.[1] Although *The Goal* would not stand up against the literary standard of a Stephen King novel, it is a refreshingly readable business book that has sold some 2 million copies.

The Goal is the story of a plant manager, Alex, whose life is falling apart. His wife has left him to go back and live with her parents, and the plant that he manages is struggling to earn a profit while inventory clogs the plant floor. Jonah, a management consultant, coaches Alex through periodic phone calls. Eventually, Alex mends his marriage and the problems of his manufacturing plant.

The main business lesson of *The Goal* is that a process is constrained by the operation that has the most limited capacity. The slowest operation, called a *bottleneck* operation, will limit the output of the whole process. Another way of saying this is that a chain is only as strong as its weakest link. This is illustrated in Exhibit 9.1. In this six-operation process, Operation D moves at the slowest rate, producing only 200 units per hour. Increasing the efficiency of the other operations would not increase the efficiency of the process as a whole. If the company were able to increase the speed of Operation D to 400 units per hour by buying a second machine that would duplicate Operation D, then Operation B would be the new constraining operation, limiting system throughput to 250 units per hour.

Exhibit 9.1 Bottleneck operations limit process flow

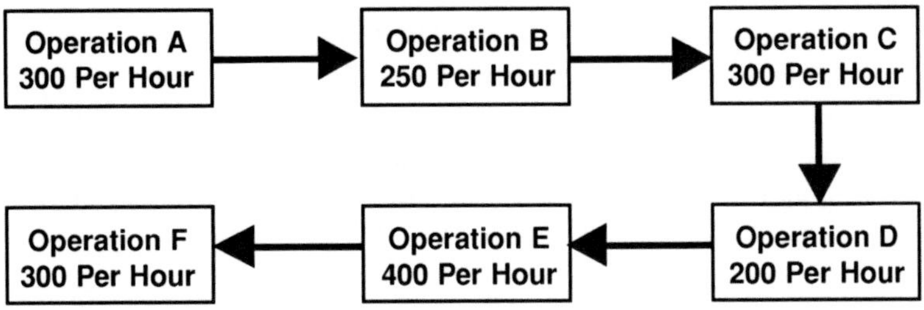

Note: This six-operation process is able to produce 200 units per hour. The capacity of Operation D, the slowest operation, limits the speed at which the process can operate.

The Goal introduced concepts that would later become the center of Goldratt's Theory of Constraints, a philosophy of managing process flow that was the subject of several later books.[2] One of Goldratt's unconventional ideas is that all overhead should be applied to the constraining operation of a process. Critics of the Theory of Constraints say that the resource usage in most companies is fairly well balanced and the constraining operation "travels." Sometimes one work center is overloaded, sometimes another. As a result, they say, the Theory of Constraints works well to describe the temporary condition when a bottleneck exists, but does not fit well into normal steady-state operations.

Capacity utilization is an important consideration in pricing. A company that is inefficient or is operating well below normal capacity for its industry cannot expect to recoup all of its costs and enjoy a normal profit. Pricing also can be used as a tool to increase profit through increased capacity utilization. By studying interrelationships of capacity, price, and demand, it may be possible to increase revenues, lower costs, and increase profits. This chapter will discuss some of the ways to make it happen.

SHORTAGE OF CAPACITY

Most businesses would like to have the problem of a shortage of capacity. When a company has a shortage of capacity, it usually means that sales have been good, often rapidly rising, perhaps catching even management off guard. Occasionally business advice columns will contain letters from entrepreneurs who have this problem. The letters often read something like this:

Dear Dr. Debit,

Two years ago I left corporate America to start my own management consulting firm. I do market research and for the last year I have had more work than I can possibly handle, sometimes working 60 or more hours a week. Despite all this, I am still not making as much money as I would like. I want to make more so that I can save some money for my children's education, but there are not any more hours in the day. What should I do?

Signed,

Overworked in Omaha

Most readers of this book will have no problem identifying a remedy for "Omaha's" problem. Demand for Omaha's market research is greater than the supply. There are two obvious solutions. Omaha could hire an associate who could do some of the research. This would be a form of adding capacity. This action might also improve overall business income by leveraging Omaha's talents. However, not everyone is cut out to be a boss. An alternate solution would be to raise price.

Although these two solutions are obvious when described on the scale of a one-person business, many business people only think of adding capacity when the same scenario is described on a larger scale. Runaway demand is often a sign that a company has badly underpriced its product. Too many small companies have had years where they have had huge increases in sales, only to find out that the new work that was added was more costly to produce than management had anticipated. For many companies, growth has actually meant going from being profitable to losing money faster than management ever dreamed.

Many companies are driven by growth. This seems to be particularly true when executive management does not own the company or when they come from a sales background. It is easy to understand why this might happen. When executive management does not own the company, such as when a company is publicly traded, a major factor in determining the size of executive compensation is a comparison of the salaries of similar executives at companies of the same size. It stands to reason that executives would want to grow their companies in order to be paid more. It is also easy to understand why companies that are run by executives with a sales background often have strong revenue growth. After all, "Sales is what I do."

Growing sales and growing profits is not necessarily the same thing. Although a nonowner company president may want to manage the largest company in the industry, most owners would rather have stock in the company that was the most profitable. There are strategic decisions to be made regarding the relationship between capacity and price. Managing these relationships well can lead to increased company profitability.

EXCESS CAPACITY

Businesses more often have excess capacity than not enough. A company may have excess capacity for many reasons. Seasonal businesses will often have capacity based on their annual peaks with their facilities operating at less than full capacity for a substantial portion of the year. Hotels in resort areas, for example, may be full "in season" but have so few customers out of season that they close for part of the year.

The normal ebbs and flows of businesses may create excess capacity as projects and contracts are completed. In good times, automotive manufacturers run their plants on a steady schedule but close down for 2 weeks each summer and another week or more at Christmas. Inevitably, their suppliers have excess capacity because of these schedules. As a result, they may observe holiday shutdowns as well or use the slow period to catch up.

The ability of a company to produce output depends on the capabilities of many different resources. These may include people, equipment, floor space, and other resources that are required to produce a product. Rarely is a company's capacity completely balanced. A company may have enough floor space to produce $20 million a year in sales, but only enough equipment to produce $15 million. There is enough management talent to produce $17 million in sales, but only enough production workers to handle the current workload of $10 million. In this example, production labor is the constraining resource at the company. At present, this company only has the real capacity to produce $10 million of product, but in a few months they could be producing at a $15 million level.

How should the existence of excess capacity affect pricing decisions? Obviously there is a cost corresponding to excess capacity. The company must still pay rent on empty floor space. The bank still wants monthly payments on idle equipment, and people still need to be paid even if there is not enough to do. If a company has excess capacity, should the cost of that excess capacity be included in the costs used to determine price?

HOW EXCESS CAPACITY SHOULD INFLUENCE PRICE

Many activity-based costing experts advocate segregating the cost of excess capacity so that its cost can be isolated and brought to management's attention. Using this method, total available capacity is often measured in terms of 24 hours a day, 7 days a week, 365 days a year (24/7/365). They then suggest that the cost of excess capacity may be added back into the cost of products as long as the company is still competitive after doing so.

This method may produce a huge difference between the theoretical capacity of the company and the amount of capacity the company is actually using. This can be observed in Exhibit 9.2. In this example, the cost per machine-hour has been calculated by taking $20,000 in fixed machine related costs and dividing it by the number of hours in four different operations schedules. In column 1, hourly costs are shown for a round-the-clock schedule, column 2 shows costs for an efficient business that operates its facility 24 hours a day, 250 days a year, and columns 3 and 4 show the numbers for companies that work 16 hours a day and 8 hours a day, respectively. The range of $2.28 to $14.29 per hour represents a large difference in hourly machine-related costs.

Scheduling can provide a competitive advantage. A company that operates around the clock, particularly in a manufacturing setting, may have significantly lower fixed costs than a company that operates only one or two shifts. Industry surveys often include data about the business calendars common in the industry. Companies that obtain and review these data will have a better understanding of their competitive situation.

A major factor in deciding how to treat capacity costs is whether the excess capacity is "normal." Most companies, particularly those that perform many value-added processes, are never at or near capacity on most of those processes. In many industries, 70% capacity utilization for machinery is considered normal and 80% capacity utilization is considered good. A company that can operate at 90% of capacity would have a cost advantage over a company that operates at 70% to 80%.

There are several unfavorable consequences of operating at or near capacity. First, the company may not be able to take advantage of new sales opportunities. If the lead time between winning a bid and producing a product is less than the lead time to add capacity, the company may only be able to sell additional work if excess capacity already exists. Second, running near capacity reduces the company's ability to react to unplanned spikes in demand or workload. Such a spike is often caused by a problem with the quality of the product that was produced.

Exhibit 9.2 Effect of capacity utilization on cost: fixed cost/unit

	Hours			
	All Available Hours	Schedule for this Business	Normal Manufacturer	Single Shift Operation
Machine-related costs	$20,000	$20,000	$20,000	$20,000
Days/year	365	250	250	250
Hours/day	24	24	16	8
Percentage available	100%	100%	70%	70%
Available hours	8,760	6,000	2,800	1,400
Cost/hour	$2.28	$3.33	$7.14	$14.29

Note: To the extent that costs are fixed, cost per hour decreases dramatically as capacity utilization increases.

Although a quality rejection by the customer is damaging to the vendor's reputation, a quality rejection that the company cannot quickly remedy is far worse.

Some kinds of companies run their operations continuously. Public utilities run on a 24/7/365 schedule. Utilities present an interesting capacity utilization problem because their demand is cyclical throughout a single day. Because demand for electricity is greatest during the day and evening hours, utility companies may give industrial customers a lower electrical rate for the nighttime hours. Foundries often take advantage of this price break by running their energy-intensive melting operations in the wee hours of the morning, when electricity rates are lowest. Some retailers come close to operating a 24/7/365 schedule, often closing only for Thanksgiving, Christmas, and New Year's Day. Like utilities, retailers have cyclical demands on their capacity within the day and within the year.

In manufacturing, plastic injection molding machinery takes several hours to get warmed up after it has cooled down. For this reason, some plastic injection molding companies run their equipment around the clock for months at a time, stopping individual machines only for tooling changes and an occasional holiday weekend. Although a plastic injection molder may get many running hours during a normal week, these companies ordinarily have some machines that are idle, representing excess capacity. Most businesses do not operate around the clock. Industry traditions, customer demands, employee desires, and other factors all influence business schedules.

It could be argued that machinery-related costs are not independent of the number of running hours and that costs such as maintenance and the decline in value of a machine are directly related to running hours. Exhibit 9.3 shows an alternate

Exhibit 9.3 Effect of capacity utilization on cost: total unit cost

	Hours			
	All Available Hours	Schedule for this Business	Normal Manufacturer	Single Shift Operation
Machine-related costs	$28,514	$24,571	$20,000	$18,000
Days/year	365	250	250	250
Hours/day	24	24	16	8
Percentage available	100%	100%	70%	70%
Available hours	8,760	6,000	2,800	1,400
Cost/hour	$3.26	$4.10	$7.14	$12.86

Note: Even when the cost structure for a work center contains a mix of fixed and variable costs, cost per hour can still decrease dramatically as capacity utilization in increased.

view of the cost per hour of machinery where 20% of the machinery cost is directly related to the number of hours run. Although the gap in the various cost scenarios has narrowed, there is still a considerable range of possible hourly capacity costs for the same piece of equipment.

Each management team must decide what capacity level is appropriate to use for the costs that support pricing decisions. It might be argued that some excess capacity has been purchased in order to be able to accept additional work in the future. The cost of this capacity, it would follow, does not relate to current work, but to future work that has not yet been obtained. Following this argument, the cost of all extra capacity should be assigned to the work that will actually fill the excess capacity, not the current work that happens to use the same machine. Proponents of this approach would point out that if the cost of excess capacity is included in the quoted price, when new work is won to fill the capacity, then the company is collecting money corresponding to that capacity twice. The correct strategy can only be determined with respect to competitors. Because most companies attempt to recover the cost of normal excess capacity, the decision to recover these costs as a component of price should not provide a competitive disadvantage.

Goldratt's Theory of Constraints has been applied to the pricing strategy. It has been argued that because capital equipment represents a sunk cost, a company should be willing to accept any new work for any price that exceeds variable costs. Because the company will have incremental revenues that are larger than incremental spending, the company will be better off and it should take any marginal work available.

There are several different counterarguments to this approach. The first is that, in the long run, there are no costs that are truly fixed. Although in the long term, buildings and equipment can be sold and people can be laid off, it is usually not practical to sell part of a building, part of a machine, or to lay off part of a person. Capacity, therefore, can be thought of as being added in steps. One additional job may not require the company to purchase a new machine or add an addition to the building. However, one job, added to 20 more just like it, would likely cause the need for additional capacity. Although one new job will not *cause* capacity to be added, it will *contribute* to the need for additional capacity.

A second argument for not accepting work at a marginal price relates to human nature. There is an *opportunity cost* that relates to excess capacity. By filling up capacity with marginal work, the company may not have available capacity when a better opportunity arises. In theory, the company should throw out the marginal product when a better opportunity comes along. In reality, this is not what companies do. In the real world, a company that has a mix of winners and losers will add capacity to accommodate a new winner rather than throw the loser out. In effect, the company is then adding new capacity to continue to make the marginal jobs at a loss. Accordingly, a company that lacks the discipline to get rid of unprofitable jobs or if customer relationships do not allow the company to unilaterally discontinue a money-losing product, then the company should not accept work at a marginal price.

Seasonal businesses such as resorts in northern climates present an interesting pricing problem. Many northern resorts are designed to accommodate skiers in the winter and golfers in the summer. Some resorts, such as those around the Great Lakes, may have a very short ski season, with the bulk of ski business running less than 3 months from Christmas Day to roughly St. Patrick's Day in mid-March. Golf begins when the weather gets warm enough, perhaps a month later, but golf will primarily be a weekend pastime until Memorial Day, when people begin to come for vacations. The weekday golf business will slow again after Labor Day, but the weekend business will continue until after the leaves fall in late October. By Thanksgiving, there may be snow enough to ski, but most people will wait until after Christmas to get into a skiing frame of mind.

Effectively setting price for a seasonal business involves having a good understanding of demand. A golf and ski resort must consider strategies for making each sport profitable as well as an overall strategy for the business as a whole. There are many choices of ski resorts within easy driving distances of major metropolitan areas in the Midwest such as Chicago, Detroit, Milwaukee, and Minneapolis. These resorts cater to customers who ski primarily on weekends and during holiday periods. Demand is highest between the day after Christmas and New Year's Day. If New Year's Day falls late in the week, such as on a Thursday or Friday, the peak holiday period will get a few days' extension. The weekend after New Year's Day is usually a relatively quiet weekend because most die-hard skiers have skied during Christmas week. After that, each weekend will be very busy until mid-March. Presidents' Day weekend and Martin Luther King's Birthday weekend will be particularly busy because many people head to the slopes to take advantage of long weekends.

Midwestern resorts tend to have less acreage and a smaller total vertical drop than western resorts. Because the resorts are smaller, a family might rotate their ski weekends among three or four different resorts for variety. Each ski resort has its own distinctive personality that is established by the terrain, lift equipment, and lodge and dining accommodations. The differences in resorts can be huge. Some resorts may have a dozen or more chair lifts, whereas others are serviced by only one or two chair lifts, supplemented by budget lift equipment such as T-bars and rope tows. There is a corresponding wide price difference from resort to resort.

It is common for ski resorts to charge different rates according to the calendar. Ski resorts get a premium price for lodging because it is close and convenient to the slopes. Skiing is a strenuous sport, and not all members of the family may want to ski the same number of hours. Having accommodations near the slopes allows teenagers to ski all day and into the evening while their parents are soaking their aching muscles while sipping a glass of white wine in the hot tub. Being within walking distance from the slopes has its advantages.

Many resorts have three or four different rates for hotels and lift tickets. The following types of rates often exist, listed in descending order by price:

- Holiday rate
- Regular weekend rate
- Off-peak weekend rate
- Weekday rates

Exhibit 9.4 shows the price of lift tickets for Boyne Mountain in Boyne City, Michigan.

Although many skiers are affluent, price still matters. Even when done cheaply, a 2-day ski weekend for a family of four may exceed $750. Because skiing can be a big-ticket item, people planning a ski weekend often comparison shop. The cost of lift tickets is frequently published in ski magazines and in the travel sections of Sunday newspapers or can readily be obtained on-line. Lower prices are available if a package of lifts and lodging are purchased together. Package deals also may include breakfast or other meals. A family can make their ski trip more affordable through the selection of the date that they ski or the resort that they visit. If the pricing of lodging at the resort is very expensive, many families will choose to stay at a less expensive hotel away from the slopes at a lower rate.

Intelligent pricing can help a resort increase their profit. Setting a very high price over holiday weekends can maximize revenue at peak times when the lifts and the

Exhibit 9.4 Differential pricing for a ski resort: 2000/2001 ski lift ticket rates (Boyne Mountain, Boyne City, Michigan)

Age Category	Holiday	Weekend	Weekday	Early/Late Season
Adult (Age 20+)	$43.00	$41.00	$35.00	$35.00
Teen (13–19)	$39.00	$38.00	$33.00	$33.00
Junior (9–12)	$30.00	$29.00	$24.00	$24.00
Senior (65+)	$30.00	$29.00	$24.00	$24.00
Child (8 and under)	$—	$—	$—	$—

Notes: Holiday rates in effect: Dec 26, 2000–Jan. 1, 2001; Jan 13–14, 2001 (MLK weekend); Feb. 18–19, 2001 (Presidents' Weekend); March 17–18, 2001 (St. Patrick's Day)

Early season: before December 26, 2000

Late season: after March 21, 2001

Ski resorts use price as a means of getting better utilization of their capacity. Lower rates at off-peak times encourage people to ski when the resort is underutilized.

Source: Used with permission of Boyne Mountain Resort, Boyne City, MI. www.boyne.com (January 15, 2001).

accommodations are at capacity. Some skiers will select slow periods for their ski trip if there is a lower rate available. The weekend before Christmas, the first weekend after school resumes after New Year's Day and the last two weekends in March fall into this category. Because some high schools have nontraditional schedules that include a week-long mid-winter break, low priced mid-week ski packages will attract families whose budgets would not allow flying to New England or the Rocky Mountains. By providing people with an incentive to come at off-peak times, resorts are able to get paid for their fixed investment at times when it otherwise would be idle or underutilized.

Other types of businesses may use pricing as part of their strategy to balance their capacity utilization:

> Gary's Barber Shop in a small midwestern town is always busy on Saturday morning. Gary operates an old-fashioned Main Street type of barbershop. On the wall are pictures of local athletes who have gone off to play football in college as well as other pictures that reveal that Gary also roots for the Detroit Tigers and the Michigan Wolverines. He has three chairs and there are at least two barbers working on most days. He is a friendly, outgoing type, and even if one of the other barbers is cutting your hair, Gary is part of the overall experience. Gary charges $12 for a haircut, and his prices are the same every day of the week. He doesn't take appointments, and on Saturdays the wait may be in excess of an hour. There is no excess capacity at Gary's on Saturdays. His Saturday crowd is a cross-section of the local community: businessmen, teachers, farmers, schoolboys, and retirees.
>
> Not everyone waits the hour for his turn. Often patrons walk in, look at the crowd and nod, "I'll come back." Most of them do, but it may be several days or a week later, reducing the number of haircuts that Gary will give this head in a year. A few will go to the unisex haircutting salon in the shopping plaza near the freeway, but most of them will be back because they like their barber.
>
> Gary is undoubtedly not maximizing his revenue. To his businessman clients, time is money, particularly their precious free time on Saturday morning. This group may not have an opportunity to get a haircut during the week and would gladly pay, say, $15 to reduce their wait on Saturday morning. Students and teachers might alter their schedules to receive a lower price. Because school gets out at 3:00, there is no reason for them to pay a premium for a Saturday morning time slot. For the retirees, the day of the week that they get their haircut does not matter much. This budget-conscious group would gladly come during off-peak times to get a discount. By altering his price schedule, Gary could level out the capacity utilization in his establishment, improving his profitability.

Restaurants often have acute peaks and valleys in their capacity utilization, having a busy lunchtime crowd but little business again until after 5 p.m. Crowds may vary depending on the night of the week as well, with long lines on Friday and Saturday night but few guests on Sunday, Monday, or Tuesday. It would not be cost effective for a restaurant to build enough capacity to meet their peak demand for two or three seatings on Friday and Saturday nights. Hence, it is common to experience an hour or more wait for a table at some restaurants on weekends. Instead, they plan the size of their restaurant based on a compromise between their peak needs and their normal requirements. Restaurants can strengthen their off-peak business through price incentives during those times. "Early-bird" specials aimed at senior citizens may be used to attract dinner customers during the slow, late afternoon hours. Discount coupons good only on weekdays may encourage patrons to come on an otherwise slow night. Done right, differentiation based on when the customer buys can have a significant positive impact on profitability.

A company whose excess capacity is normal should strongly consider including the cost of this capacity in its pricing. This cost should be included in the cost of the corresponding activity rather than be assigned arbitrarily. To the extent that excess capacity is above what is common for an industry, it should usually be excluded from the costs used to evaluate pricing. When a company has some sales that are competitively bid and others that are not competitively bid, excess capacity costs may be excluded for price calculation in one situation and included in the other.

If capacity utilization is below industry norms, it will usually not be price competitive to include these costs when determining price. One exception would be in situations where the customer receives a benefit from keeping capacity underutilized, such as when productive capacity must be left idle to meet a customer's response time requirements.

SUMMARY

The key points discussed in this chapter are listed below:

1. The word *capacity* means productive ability. A company's capacity to produce its products is limited by the human resources, floor space, machinery, and other resources that it has available.
2. Most companies include the cost of excess capacity that is normal for the industry in the costs used in pricing decisions. These costs should be assigned to the related activities, not to general overhead.
3. Seasonal or cyclical businesses often charge a lower rate during off-peak times to provide an incentive for customers to buy when demand is lower, thereby utilizing capacity that would be otherwise idle.

NOTES

1. Jeff Cox and Eliyahu M. Goldratt, *The Goal: A Process of Ongoing Improvement* (Great Barrington, MA: North River Press, 1st ed. 1985, 2d ed. 1992).
2. Eliyahu M. Goldratt, *Theory of Constraints* (Great Barrington, MA: North River Press, 1987).

10

TARGET PRICING

Together, disciplines of target pricing, value engineering, and activity-based costing can help assure that planned profitability becomes actual profitability.

PRICE POINTS

Many categories of products have a well-established market price. When diners go to a restaurant, they have an expectation that the prices on the menu will be about the same as the prices at similar restaurants that they have been to before. Someone purchasing jeans from an apparel catalog has an expectation that the pants will be in a particular price range. If the garment was not available at the expected $29.50 price from L.L. Bean, the customer might look further in Land's End or Victoria's Secret. The customer for an economy car would expect the price of that vehicle to be closer to $15,000 than $45,000. Customers have at least a general expectation and sometimes a specific expectation of the price that they will pay for a large portion of the things that they buy.

Prices for many classes of products are conventionally set at price points that are at or near "nice round numbers." For example, $99, $99.50, $99.95, $99.99, and $100 are all common price points for products selling in that general price range. The next closest price points would likely be about 10% higher or 10% lower, at $110 or $89. It would be unusual to see another product that was priced in between these ranges, such as at $96 or $103.

High-end items are often priced at whole dollars to signify value. Products that are sold based on price are more often sold with 95- or 99-cent price suffixes. Catalog retailers L.L. Bean, Land's End, and Victoria's Secret all conventionally set their regular prices at whole dollars. However, the close-out and sale catalogs of all three companies feature odd-cent pricing. L.L. Bean prefers 95-cent suffixes, and Land's End prefers 50 cents. Victoria's Secret is inconsistent in its sale pricing, using whole dollars, 50-cent, 99-cent, and sometimes an unusual 2-cent suffix, depending on the section of its catalog. This inconsistency may reflect a difference in responsibility for pricing that is separated by product line.

PLANNING PROFIT

Price point conventions drive much of pricing strategy, profit planning, and the design process for products. A company cannot establish its pricing based on a markup on cost if its business is not a cost-effective producer. A major prerequisite for an effective pricing strategy is having products that have the features that customers want that can be profitably sold at prices that meet customers' expectations. This is the task of *target pricing*. In target pricing, a target price is determined early in the product development process.

The process of developing the target price may be as simple as surveying the market to learn the price point at which similar products sell. For some products, developing the target price can be a complicated affair. Because most businesses compete using a differentiation strategy, their products and services may not have directly comparable competition in their market. When a product does more than one thing, the task of target pricing often involves an analysis of the various product functions and the cost of providing each one. This discipline is called value engineering.

Value engineering is the term used to describe a structured examination of the product features that provide value to the customer in order to be able to design and produce a product within the constraints of a target cost. Value engineering techniques are often used for complicated products such as an automobile. An automobile represents different things to different people. To most customers, an automobile is more than transportation. It is a living space for people while they travel. Features such as cup holders, storage space, a sound system, and styling all have value to customers. Smart manufacturers study the value of these various features to the customer and use those values to guide their spending on development of the product design. Spending money to provide customers with a product feature does not make sense if the customer is not willing to pay enough to cover the cost of the feature. Automobile buyers, for example, almost universally say that they want the vehicle they buy to be environmentally friendly. However, when asked how much they would be willing to pay to have superior, rather than average, emissions ratings, market researchers know that customers are not willing to pay very much for a "clean" car.

Without the use of target costing, the use of price points makes it impossible, even in theory, for a company to have consistent profitability across all of its product lines. In a cost-plus world, if a company has full cost for a product of $94 where

$10 pricing multiples ending with $9 is the norm, then management has a choice of making the price $99 or $109. The profit could then be 5.3% or 15.9% of sales with no alternatives in between. In a target cost environment, price planning and cost planning are done up front. In this situation, the company's thinking would likely be:

- The product should be positioned at $99.
- The required target profit is $9.90.
- Therefore, the target cost is $89.10.

The requirements to earn a profit in a target-pricing environment become obvious upon analysis. Given the target price, the company also must determine a target profit, which makes the target cost easy to calculate. Thus,

Target cost = target price – target profit

This relationship is illustrated in Exhibit 10.1.

This discipline is sometimes referred to as target pricing and sometimes as target costing. It could also have conceivably been called target *profiting*. Robin Cooper defines this body of practice in *When Lean Enterprises Collide*[1]:

Exhibit 10.1 Determining target cost

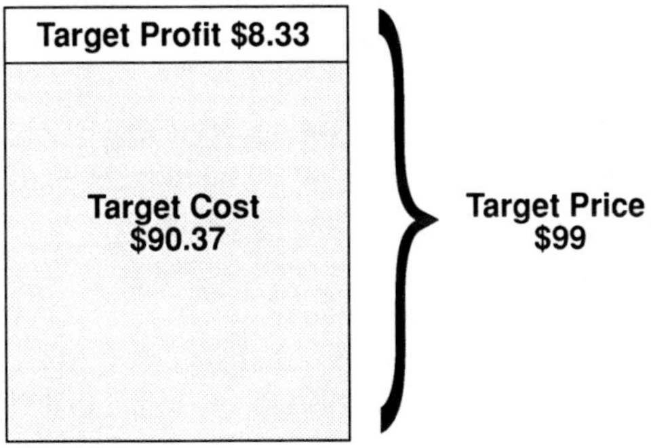

Note: With target pricing, the price of the product is determined at the time that the product concept is developed. The target profit is initially determined based on the target price but may be further refined based on a return on investment analysis. Target price – target profit = target cost.

> Target costing is a structured approach to determining the cost at which a proposed product with specified functionality and quality must be produced in order to generate the desired level of profitability at the product's anticipated selling price.

Allowable cost is another term that is sometimes used instead of target cost.

The target-pricing/target-costing methodology, which originated in Japan, is different than the conventional Western approach. Traditional Western practice has been that price and cost determine profit. Accordingly, profit was whatever was leftover after price and cost was determined. In a target-costing environment, price and profit are a given. The task that remains is to determine how to design a product that can be made within the constraints of the target cost.

An alternate Western method is *cost plus*. When a cost-plus method is used, the cost of providing the product is determined and profit is added to the cost to determine price. This process may be appropriate in situations for new products that lack an established market price or where unique products are being produced and directly comparable products do not exist.

In practice, the target profit is normally determined based on a percentage of sales. Theoretically, a return on investment (ROI) approach would provide better assurance that stockholders' objectives would be met. To use ROI to determine the target profit would require a far more complicated analysis that would include identifying the assets and liabilities associated with a product. This analysis would not be cost justified in many situations. In practice, many corporations determine the overall profit that they need to meet their overall ROI objectives, which can be stated as a percentage of projected sales. This profit percentage can then be used as a rule of thumb that is applied to all products. When a significant amount of money is involved, particularly when there are significant differences in the capital structures necessary to make various products, the target profit should be analyzed from an ROI perspective.

Cooper's research in Japan suggests that the target costing process leads to lower costs by targeting a specified low cost than the Western practice of directing costs to be kept to an unspecified minimum.[2] This observation is consistent with our knowledge of human behavior. To say to a person "Do your very best" is not as effective as setting a specific, challenging goal.

In *First, Break All the Rules,* Marcus Buckingham and Curt Coffman describe a project in which the Gallup Organization worked with Allied Breweries to develop an incentive system for bartenders in pubs. Customers like to be recognized and called by name, and a program was developed called the One Hundred Club. Any Allied Breweries bartender who could remember the names and favorite drinks of 100 patrons would receive a button and a cash bonus. The program was designed so that the recognition and bonuses increased for each 100 patrons that the bartender learned. The Five Hundred Club was envisioned as the top level of recognition that few bartenders would ever achieve. When bartenders began reaching the Five Hundred Club level, higher levels of recognition were repeatedly devised. The 500-patron benchmark was completely demolished by a bartender in northern England in 1990 who learned the names and favorite drinks of 3,000 patrons.[3] Had a specific objective of 500 patrons never been set, Allied Breweries might have never learned its people's true capabilities.

The target price may come from a number of sources. The price may be based on the current price for similar products in the market. That price may be adjusted upward for inflation, downward based on management's expectation of productivity improvements, or otherwise adjusted up or down for the addition or subtraction of features from the current model. In many industries there has been a constant downward trend in cost, offset by a constant increasing trend in functionality.

Once the target cost is calculated for a product, the target cost may be apportioned among the various components of that product as shown is Exhibit 10.2. For example, the cost of an automobile might be divided so that there was a target cost for the engine, wheels, seating, transmission, exterior sheet metal, and various other major parts of the vehicle. The target cost for each feature is determined by the value that it provides the customer. This relationship is shown in Exhibit 10.3. If a feature provides less value than its cost, the feature may be eliminated or reengineered to use a less costly design. The target cost for each of these major subsystems would then be further subdivided so that there might even be a target cost for the lug nuts that hold the wheels on the vehicle.

Companies that use target costing have a general rule that "the target cost must never be exceeded." It is the discipline of this rule that makes target costing effective. There is some flexibility as to how the target cost can be achieved. As costs

Exhibit 10.2 Target price of major product features

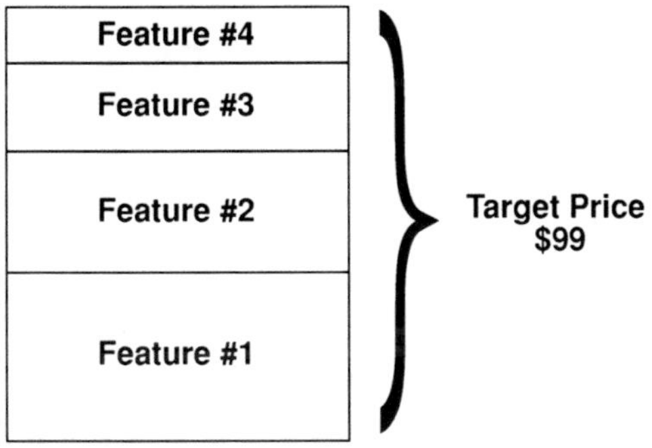

Note: For complicated products, the target price may be analyzed in terms of the value that each feature brings to the customer.

Exhibit 10.3 Determining the target cost of product features

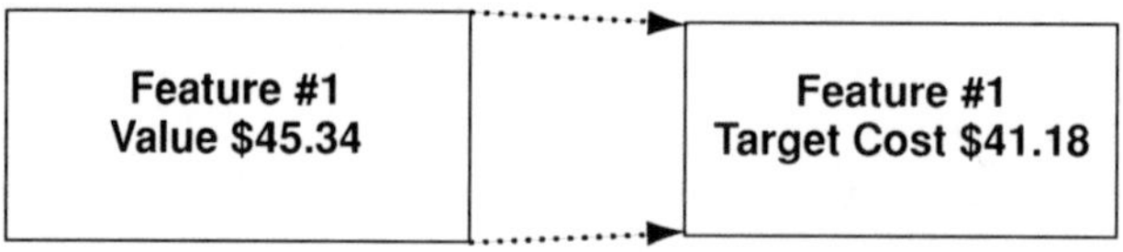

Note: The target cost for each feature is determined by the value that it provides the customer. If a feature provides less value than its cost, the feature may be eliminated or reengineered to utilize a less costly design.

are analyzed for the various components that will go into a product, it is possible that some of those components will cost less than estimated. To the extent that this happens, a manager may allow one component to go over target if there is an offsetting savings elsewhere for an item that is part of the manager's responsibility, as shown in Exhibit 10.4. It is also possible for the design of a product to be renegotiated so that cost and functionality are changed. For example, the target cost may be increased if additional functionality is added. Conversely, the company may eliminate features and reduce the target cost if the company is not able to provide a particular feature within the constraints of the target costing parameters.

TARGET COSTS FOR COMPONENTS

Some product features may have their own separate target price and target profit. This is common when there are options that may be added onto a base product, such as a towing package on a minivan or a service contract on an appliance. Such

Exhibit 10.4 Making trade-offs in target cost

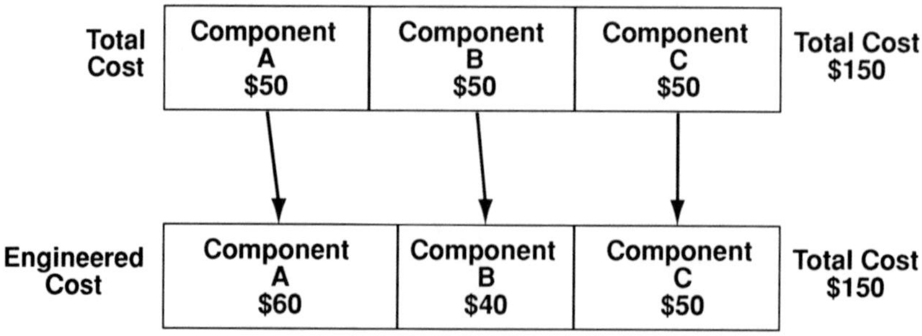

Note: When one component cannot be produced for the target cost, management may apply cost savings from one product component to another component as long as the overall target cost is met.

options are frequently sold at much higher profit margins than the base product. In some cases the company may sell the base product at no profit at all to attract customers where there is a high probability that the customer will also buy the high–profit margin option.

When the target cost of a product is broken down into the product's various components, a major implication of this process is that some of the components of costs will be purchased from outside vendors. It is common that the various components of manufactured products are actually produced by many companies. Today, for example, automobile manufacturers produce very few of the parts that go into an automobile. The business of an automobile manufacturing plant is to put together major subassemblies made by their suppliers. Dashboards come into an assembly plant with the lights and electronics already installed, seats are a complete product that just need to be bolted to the floor, wiring harnesses just need to be snapped together. Target-costing methodology provides purchasing personnel with guidelines that define acceptable costs for the various components that must be purchased.

Today many companies provide their vendors with target costs as part of the process of seeking bids. It is the author's experience that when a customer provides a target cost to a vendor, the purchasing agent is often not truthful about the real target cost, or the cost accounting people at the customer company are not competent estimators.

Purchasing people are sometimes less than honest and forthright with their vendors. It is not uncommon for a purchasing manager to provide a target cost to a vendor that is barely above the direct material cost of a product. Such behavior is counterproductive. It sends the message to the vendor that the customer is not willing to pay enough to allow the customer to earn a profit. A vendor that has alternate sales opportunities would be wise to seek to sell products to different customers. If confronted with this situation, an alternative would be to respond to the purchasing manager that the company is unable to provide the product within the buyer's target cost. Another alternative is to invest the time to provide a quotation that is above the target price. If there are few bidders, this strategy sometimes results in a sale.

Buyers of industrial goods may be particularly vulnerable if they force concessions out of their suppliers that are too onerous. An auto assembly line may generate $1 million an hour in revenue. It is possible for that entire revenue stream to come to a sudden halt for lack of a one-of-a-kind part made by a bankrupt supplier. If the supply of such a product were interrupted, the person who gave the contract to that vendor would feel the weight of the world on his or her shoulders. Although the dollars involved may not be as large, businesses of all sizes have large financial exposures if they lose the services of a key supplier. A small company that loses the source of a key component of its product may be out of business or at least unable to make sales for some period of time.

The company cultures of some businesses seem to prevent them from getting competent people. This seems to be particularly true when multinational companies send people from their headquarters country to manage or "shadow" their employees in another country. When this occurs, the nationals of the local country perceive that there is little opportunity for advancement, leading to a difficulty attracting and retaining competent personnel. This problem is not restricted to one particular national culture. German and Japanese companies have often done very poorly at managing their American subsidiaries, and American companies have often poorly managed their subsidiaries all over the world. Ford Motor Company has had better success with its acquisitions of Volvo, Jaguar, and Mazda than other companies have done with their acquisitions, in part because of their method of managing international operations. Ford, a truly international company, normally has managers run operations in their own countries. Neither of Ford's past two presidents, Alex Trotman and Jacques Nasser, has been an American.

Sometimes the cost accounting personnel assigned to assist purchasing agents are simply lacking the data, experience, and perspective necessary to provide the vendor with a realistic target cost. For whatever reason, the target costs that purchasing personnel provide their vendors are often not realistic. Target costs are sometimes unrealistically low, but they are also sometimes unnecessarily high.

In some situations, the customer will specify that the initial quote be for a particular period of time but that pricing concessions are expected over the life of the contract. Such an understanding can help promote cooperation and trust between the customer and vendor while still complying with the customer's desire for continuous price improvements. Astute vendors build these expected price decreases into their pricing models. Establishing understanding about possible future pricing concessions up front can actually lower the customer's cost. When the threat of a future price concession is undefined and unquantified, managers will tend to add in an allowance for future price concessions anyhow. In the absence of a firm understanding, estimators tend to try to err on the high side.

CONTROLLING COSTS

Planning costs in the design phase of development is vital for cost control. Product design determines the amount of material and purchased parts that go into the product. Product design also strongly influences process design. Together, product design and process design determine the type of equipment that will be required, the cost of tooling, and the amount of labor, maintenance, and support that will be needed to make the product. It has been estimated that 85% to 95% of costs becomes uncontrollable once the product design and process design are finalized. Gary Cokins, Director of Industry Relations at ABC Technologies, frequently notes to his professional society audiences, "Once design is completed, the only thing that operations people can do is minimize the unfavorable variances."[4]

A prospective evaluation of product costs is vital to profit planning. In many businesses, management has close to zero influence over product price by the time actual costs are known. When work is won through a competitive bid, many contracts provide no opportunity to change price except in the case of a change in specifications. This makes it imperative that the team that analyzes the design and target cost has a thorough understanding of what generates cost.

Activity-based costing is an indispensable tool in target pricing and value engineering efforts. Because activity-based costing seeks to identify and quantify the cause–effect relationships involved with cost, it is well suited as a tool that will allow management to predict the outcomes of future costing situations based on past experiences. When a new product is introduced, many if not all of the processes that will be used are usually the same or similar to situations already familiar to the company. If the company knows the causes and costs of their various launch activities, the cost of a machine setup, machine running costs, shipping and handling costs, and the various other costs that the organization performs, it is possible to prospectively calculate the costs of a future product. This can be done in a manner that is similar to ordering items out of a supply catalog—"We'll need two of these, three of those, and 100,000 pounds of that red stuff . . ."

Ordinary cost accounting will not do for target costing and value engineering. Ordinary allocation methods can only identify "average" costs. In the real world, where a profit of 7% of revenues is good, even a 7% variation from average can mean the difference between winning a contract and losing it or between enjoying a profit or suffering a loss. Together, the disciplines of target pricing, value engineering, and activity-based costing can help ensure that planned profitability becomes actual profitability.

SUMMARY

The key points discussed in this chapter are listed below:

1. A target price is a planned price for a future product. Target prices are usually based on the existing prices for similar products in the market. The target price may be adjusted up for inflation, down for expected productivity gains, or up or down for changes in features or functionality.
2. The target profit is determined based on the target price. ROI techniques also may be used to refine the target profit.
3. Target cost is the dependent variable.

Target cost = target price – target profit

4. Value engineering analyzes the value that the customer receives from the various features of the product. The target price, target profit, and target cost may be componentized so that the various product features are analyzed separately.
5. The target cost is conventionally divided among the various components that make up the product. Some portions of the target cost may be for components that are made by outside vendors.
6. Target costing has important strategic implications in that it provides management with a greater control over profit by moving profit planning earlier in the product development cycle.
7. The use of activity-based costing is an important part of the target costing/value engineering process. Because cost analyses in activity-based costing are based on knowledge of the factors that generate cost, it is an excellent tool for predicting future costs.

NOTES

1. Robin Cooper, *When Lean Enterprises Collide* (Boston: Harvard Business School Press, 1995), p.135.
2. Ibid., p.137.
3. Marcus Buckingham and Curt Coffman, *First, Break All the Rules* (New York: Simon & Schuster, 1999), p.187.
4. Source: Phone interview with Gary Cokins, December 13, 2000.

11

PRICE NEGOTIATIONS

Preparation helps get the best deal in negotiation.

SHOULD PRICE BE NEGOTIATED?

American consumers are not accustomed to negotiating the price of the things they buy. Clothing, groceries, gasoline, movie tickets, and most of the things that are for sale to consumers in the U.S. economy are offered at a set price. Although Americans often "shop around" for a deal, price negotiations are largely restricted to a few big-ticket items such as homes and automobiles.

No one is born a great negotiator. Negotiation must be learned. Individuals can substantially increase their negotiation abilities through reading, seminars, or practice. This chapter is designed to provide the reader with a basic understanding of price negotiations. These few pages are far from exhaustive. Anyone who will be regularly involved in price negotiations will want to investigate some of the other resources mentioned in this chapter.

In some parts of the world, price negotiations are an art form. When American tourists make the short trip from San Diego, California, to Tijuana, Mexico, part of the overall experience is bartering for leather goods, rugs, and pictures of Elvis painted on velvet. Savvy tourists know that the posted price is often considerably more than the vendor is willing to accept, and negotiating purchases can be an entertaining experience. Although some business people view price negotiations as fun, others see it as a stressful and loathsome task. Some people are very good at negotiations, whereas others too often come out of it feeling like a victim. Studies have shown that poor negotiators can substantially improve the outcome of their negotiations with training and preparation.

The Internet has become an important tool in price negotiations. Consumer-oriented sites such as ebay.com have created auction sites for a variety of goods.

Priceline.com allows consumers to "name their own price" for airline tickets and other goods, while skilled professionals bid for projects on guru.com or freelance.com. Corporate purchasing sites with auction-like bidding features are becoming more common. Although most corporations have done no more than dabble with on-line buying, the Internet has the potential to radically change the manner in which corporations buy from each other.

In the United States, price negotiations most often occur in transactions between businesses. There are many factors relating to a company's customers, competitors, and products that play major roles in the price negotiation decisions. There are compelling reasons for sellers to have a fixed price policy and to not negotiate selling price:

- Price negotiations may be time consuming.
- Price negotiations can create an adversarial relationship between the buyer and seller.
- Price negotiations can undermine the process of planning for and meeting the company's profitability goals.
- Negotiable price policies motivate sales people to use price concessions as a tool for closing the sale rather than getting a better price using the more time-consuming technique of selling product value.

A fixed price policy is not necessarily a one-price policy. The term *fixed price* means that the quoted price is non-negotiable for the specific situation for which it was given. The company may ask a different price for different market segments, order sizes, payment terms, day of the week, or time of the year. It may also be appropriate to make other allowances such as those based on the amount of other products that the customer buys. Astute companies make these allowances with solid analytical data that include an activity-based pricing analysis of each particular pricing situation. Such an analysis might examine not just the product-related economics, but the customer-related economics as well. The result of an activity-based pricing analysis might be a table of prices for each product that differentiates each situation based on the economies of scale that occur with increasingly large orders as well as a differentiation based on the cost differences in serving various categories of customers.

Rather than negotiate, most sellers would prefer to set a fair price that would allow them to capture a reasonable share of the market. This is possible in many industries where all of the competitors follow the same practice. One company is often the *price leader*, setting the prices that all competitors will follow. In other industries this is not possible, and companies must get their sales by bidding to perform unique work for their customers. Such work might include constructing a building, painting a house, preparing a tax return, or manufacturing a part that will become a component for one of the customer's products. Because each situation is different, it is impossible to know what competitors would bid without illegal collusion. As a result, each company must come up with its own quotation, which rarely will be the same as its competitors. Price competition occurs when there are differences in price.

Price competition can be cut-throat and destructive. At one time, the two major chains of appliance and electronics stores in the Detroit metropolitan area were Highland Appliance and Fretter Appliance. Both chains had a policy that they would not be undersold. This policy often allowed consumers to play one chain against the other to the detriment of both. Bryan Cody was a master at getting great deals on consumer electronics. Bryan might spend all of Saturday afternoon going back and forth from store to store, getting each store to give him a better deal. Bryan was probably not a profitable customer for either chain. To make matters worse, after he finished negotiating, he would tell all of the guys at work about how he got $200 off a $750 camcorder. They would then go to the same store and ask for the same deal. One day Bryan's co-worker Jack[1] went to Highland Appliance and told the sales person that he wanted a particular camcorder for Bryan's $550 price, and the salesperson laughed at the ridiculously low offer. The salesperson remarked that he could not sell him that product for so little, but he could give Jack $25 off of the best price that he could get elsewhere. With that offer in hand written on a scrap of paper, Jack then went to Fretter and said that Highland would sell it to him for $525. Jack walked out with the camcorder that he wanted at $525. Still not finished, he went to Highland where the incredulous sales person was forced to sell him the same model for $500. He was not done yet. Returning to Fretter with proof that he could buy the same camcorder for $500, Fretter dutifully gave him a rebate, lowering his price to $475. Now tired of the game, he returned the second unit to Highland Appliance, saving an impressive $275 off the retail price for 2 hours worth of work. Even Bryan was impressed. Both Highland Appliance and Fretter Appliance are long since out of business.

Price negotiations are both desirable and necessary in many cases. They allow the buyer and the seller to find common ground within a range of prices that is acceptable to both parties. Some negotiations have a single dimension. In these cases, the definition of the product is well understood and the buyer and seller have only to agree on the price. In other cases, the buyer and seller may make trade-offs between price, product features, delivery date, payment terms, and other factors.

The negotiation process may involve educating a buyer who has not purchased the product recently and may not be familiar with the current market price. The term *sticker shock* has been used to describe the surprise of a buyer at learning the price of a product that was priced quite a bit lower the last time it was offered. As products improve, buyers may not be aware of everything that a product will do for them; thus, buyer education also may involve communicating features and the value of those features to the buyer.

UNDERSTANDING DIFFERENCES AMONG BUYERS

All buyers are not the same. The buyers for similar products may have different needs, motivations, and internal politics within their organizations. Buyers are often classified into these four categories:

- Price buyers
- Convenience buyers
- Value buyers
- Loyal buyers

Price buyers come in all sizes. Retirees who have a limited budget but plenty of available time are often price buyers. On a much larger scale, General Motors Corporation and the U. S. government are well-known price buyers. Large organizations are often price buyers. When an organization purchases in very large quantities, scale economies make the sometimes expensive process of seeking out the best price more economically feasible.

Price shopping can be a time-consuming process. The process of obtaining a competitive bid for a product often includes the following steps:

- Developing specifications for the product to be purchased
- Identifying qualified vendors
- Meeting with vendors to explain and discuss the specifications
- Obtaining bids
- Reviewing the bids
- Deciding on which proposal to accept

Other internal requirements such as a formal process to have specifications developed, reviewed, and approved can further expand the cost of the competitive bid process.

Governments often have formal rules that require that competitive bids be sought for any purchase over a certain dollar amount. These rules may include a requirement that the bid process be advertised so that qualified bidders have equal access to the sales opportunity. Government competitive bid requirements have often been designed as a safeguard against corruption by public officials. Government corruption is an unfortunate way of life in many parts of the world.

Many books on salesmanship stress that a salesperson can get a better price by touting the quality and value of the product. However, the purchasing process used by price buyers usually places severe limitations on the ability of the salesperson to attempt to obtain a higher price based on superior product characteristics. Price buyers often limit contact within the organization to the official purchasing representative who has no control over product specifications or other terms of the sale. The role of the purchasing agents may be limited to completing a specified transaction. In such cases, considering any proposal that varies from the purchase requisition in hand may not be viewed as an efficient use of their time. Although sellers would like to overcome the price orientation of price buyers through reeducation about the value of their products, this process usually proves to be time consuming, costly, and unsuccessful for the vendor. Many price buyers will always be price buyers and will never change.

If a seller is the low-cost producer of a fairly generic product, seeking to sell to price buyers is a logical business strategy. Because the low-cost producer has an advantage in competitive bid situations, it may successfully compete for the business of price buyers. Companies with unique or differentiated products will be considerably less successful selling to price buyers and should follow a strategy of selective participation.

Selective participation is a strategy whereby the seller chooses to limit the selling opportunities that it pursues. With this strategy, sellers might tell price-buying customers that they want to participate in the bidding process in certain limited circumstances. These circumstances should be carefully selected to include only bidding opportunities where the company had a reasonable chance of making a profitable sale. Sellers may elect to participate only in opportunities that are a close fit with their expertise or opportunities that meet characteristics otherwise favorable to the company. Sellers may routinely decline to participate in a bidding where the specified product or project is not a close fit with their chosen market niche, where there is a large number of competitors, or where other bidders have a perceived edge.

Companies that use activity-based pricing are often very competitive on high-volume contracts. Accordingly, the company may choose to bid on only large contracts, avoiding those of smaller size. A small company, on the other hand, may not have the resources to manage a large contract, but may choose to target only smaller bids that are of little interest to bigger organizations.

Sellers often "low-ball" their first quotation to a large prospective customer to get their foot in the door. The theory behind this maneuver is that once the customer is familiar with what sellers can do, they will be able to get more work at a better margin, recouping the money invested in the first money-losing sale. Unfortunately, when selling to price buyers, this tactic does not usually result in a solid long-term financial return. Price buyers usually have many prospective vendors waiting for the opportunity to buy their way into their supply base. Even if the company continues to win more quotes, the dynamics of the customer's competitive bid process will continue to award sales only to companies that are willing to accept razor thin margins or none at all. Companies should feel thankful when a competitor has won a large contract at a very dear price that will preoccupy them when the opportunity arises to bid for more profitable work.

Because no two companies have identical cost structures, it is no surprise that there is often a substantial spread in price when more than two sellers bid for a contract. Much of this spread is not caused by any real difference in cost structure but by a difference in cost accounting methods and quoting methods. Any cost accounting method that is not activity based will cause major differences between real costs and the accounting cost in many situations. In addition, those companies that use traditional cost accounting methods often add "fudge factors" or "rules of thumb" to arrive at their selling price. The predictable result is that some vendors will submit bids that are mistakes due to lack of good information. The mistakes may be that the company has bid much too high or much too low. These mistakes will not "average out" because the company will win the mistakes that it underbids and lose every one of the overbid mistakes. This effect has caused some price writers to conclude that fudge factors should be added to raise the profitability of competitively bid contracts.[2] This tactic is ineffective. Although adding a fudge factor will reduce the loss on an underbid job, it makes the company less competitive on jobs that are already overpriced. Although there is a slight economic gain between these two categories of bids, the real damage from using fudge factors comes from what they do to bids for the average product. When the company is able to submit a competitive price that will earn a fair profit, adding fudge factors to the price will often put the company out of the running for the sale altogether. A better solution is to reduce the possibility for quoting error through activity-based pricing, eliminating the need for fudge factors in the first place.

One tactic that is commonly used by price buyers is to solicit competitive bids and then continue to play the low bidders off each other to obtain a still lower bid from the participants. In effect, the buyer starts with an already low competitively bid price and then turns the bidding process into an auction. The company that wins the bid under this type of bidding process is often a company that has made a mistake on its bid. There are only a few possible ways that a company can win a profitable contract when an auction process is used:

- The seller is the low-cost producer
- Other bidders make quoting mistakes, bidding too high

- The winning company understood its cost better using activity-based costing

If a price buyer responds that another company has submitted a low quote, and begins an auction process, it is a good idea for the bidder to respond something like this:

> Our quote represented our best price. If there are minor differences or if there is an error in our understanding of what we were quoting on, we could discuss changes, but we gave you our best price.

Convenience buyers are those for whom product availability is the most important concern. A buyer is most likely to make a convenience purchase when the product is relatively low in cost and the buyer has a pressing need for the product right now. Time is important to a convenience buyer. A family might ordinarily purchase their bread and lunchmeat at a supermarket, but stop in at 7-Eleven on their way home from an evening event if they are short of ingredients to make school lunches in the morning.

Convenience buyers make purchases because they are able to get the product at a particular place and time. The most important factor may be that the transaction can be executed very quickly. Many fast-food restaurant franchises fail to develop their full potential because they are slow at filling orders. Although some buyers are willing to wait in line for an *inexpensive* lunch, other buyers have chosen a fast-food lunch because it is supposed to be *fast*. A slow fast-food restaurant will lose a substantial portion of its potential business because it is not convenient.

Makers of a premium-priced product can successfully compete for convenience buyers if their product is more convenient than a product that is lower priced. Restaurants, for example, might accept pick-up or dine-in fax orders, eliminating the wait time while a meal is prepared. The restaurant also may deliver, earning a premium price for a very convenient meal.

Targeting convenience buyers makes sense for many different kinds of companies in many different situations. A company should receive a premium price for offering a convenient product, but the cost to provide convenience must be less than the premium received. The key to success with this strategy is that the convenient product must be substantially easier for the customer to buy or use than cheaper alternatives.

Value buyers analyze costs, service, and product features and seek to get the best overall value for their money. Sometimes a value buyer will purchase an inexpensive generic product while at other times a value buyer will be willing to pay more to get the extra features of a top-of-the-line model. Value buyers specifically weigh the various attributes of the product in making their purchasing decision. Value buyers represent the largest buyer category and represent an appropriate target market for companies that have a superior product and are able to communicate their product's value.

Although value buyers may purchase from one vendor for a long period of time, they do not hesitate to change their loyalties when another vendor is able to demonstrate that they have a better product at a lower cost.

Although value buyers will respond to a low price, a more profitable way of approaching this group is through communicating product value. Because value buyers are willing to pay more for a product that provides them more utility, salespeople must have a good understanding of how their product provides value to the customer. Good listening techniques are particularly helpful in selling to a value buyer. Salespeople who listen to the customer's needs are able to translate those needs into a proposal that is best tailored to each specific customer, thus creating a product package that will optimize what the customer will get from the vendor–customer relationship.

Loyal buyers value quality, consistency, and service. With loyal buyers, trust is often an important factor in the relationship, and such buyers may only change their buying relationships in instances where trust has been violated through poor quality, substandard service, or breached promises.

Price comes into play for loyal buyers, but in a very different way than with price buyers. Loyal buyers expect the price to be reasonable. It does not have to be the lowest price, but it has to be fair. A seller can violate a loyal buyer's trust by not adjusting price downward in response to changes in market rates. Vendors must be careful not to take advantage of the relationship with loyal buyers, offering price decreases when they are due and always charging a fair price.

If loyal buyers become aware that a lower price or a better product is available from another vendor, they may discuss the shortcomings of the product offering that they are currently buying and give the seller the opportunity to make corrections. Besides trust, the loyal buyer tends to understand the cost of changing vender–customer relationships.

Loyal buyers tend to be very profitable customers and may be the least costly customers to serve. Because loyal buyers tend to develop long-term relationships, fixed customer-related costs are spread over a long period of time. A company that is courting a new customer who has long-standing loyal relationships may call on the prospective customer for several years before it gets any business. During that process, any change in personnel on either side may send the relationship back to ground zero. To safeguard against this hazard, sellers may want to have several people within their organization develop relationships with several different people at the target company in order to have some continuity in the relationship should a personnel change occur on either side.

Participants in a relationship often take each other for granted after a period of time. This can all too easily happen in a vendor–customer relationship. Although there is value in having consistency in a customer relationship, a vendor may want to periodically rotate some of the people who are serving an account to bring new energy to the relationship. Such a move must be done carefully because the loss of a valued contact may prompt the buyer to consider changing vendors.

UNDERSTANDING PURCHASING DYNAMICS

Many people may be involved in a purchasing decision, each of whom may fill different roles in the buying process. The following roles are frequently identified in sales literature.

Initiators start the buying process by identifying a need to make a purchase. The initiator may be an inventory analyst or engineer, or may not be a real person at all. In many companies the majority of the purchasing transactions are initiated by a computer software package for sales, inventory management, or material requirements planning that identifies a future need for a product. When a real person initiates purchases, in many cases the initiator is also a product user.

Users are people who use the product or service to be purchased. They also may initiate the purchasing process but often do not have the authority to initiate or approve a purchase based on their own authority.

Specifiers define the standards for what is to be purchased. Engineers and other technical professionals often fulfill this role. Specifiers are important because their input often restricts the purchasing decision to specific vendors or to products that have specific features.

Influencers are people whose opinion is considered when making a purchase. Influencers may be people who are knowledgeable about a type of product but may not be users themselves. For example, a company may involve its accounting firm in the selection of accounting software.

Gatekeepers control the flow of information from the sellers to the people who make purchasing decisions. The gatekeeper's role is often to summarize the information provided by the sellers and present the information in a concise manner so that others can easily make the final decision. The gatekeeper may be one of several people who will jointly make a decision or may only have an influencer role. The gatekeeper also may be able to screen vendors but not have the authority to make a final selection. Salespeople frequently think that their customer contact has decision-making authority only to find that the contact is really a gatekeeper.

Buyers have formal purchasing authority and often have the title of purchasing agent or purchasing manager. Buyers often have no authority to initiate a purchase or to determine the specifications of the product to be purchased. In some organizations, the purchasing department may primarily handle the acquisition of the raw materials or products that are sold in the company's main line of business. Many people in the organization may have buying authority outside of the purchasing department. Other managers may routinely purchase products and services used by the organization. For example, the information systems manager may buy all computer hardware and software, while the controller may buy insurance and pension services.

Decision makers have final authority to determine whether a purchase will be made, to approve specifications, and to select vendors. The decision maker may delegate much of the purchasing process to others. In effect, other people in the organization may be making the real purchasing decision only to consult with the decision maker who "rubber stamps" someone else's decision when the final purchasing decision is made. Just as salespeople often mistake a gatekeeper for a decision maker, salespeople sometimes fail to recognize the decision maker after they have already gained their attention. Sales are sometimes lost because the salesperson has sought to use their customer contact to access the real decision maker higher up the chain of command. The decision maker may view such actions as a sign of disrespect relating to their youth or gender, effectively destroying the sales opportunity.

A single person may fulfill one or more of these roles in the purchasing process. An astute salesperson will try to understand what role each person plays early in the relationship. Many years ago a man named Paul took a job as a trucking company sales/customer service representative. One of the company's customers was just next door to his office, a small manufacturing company that leased a truck and bought maintenance services. Paul walked in one day and asked to see the person who had signed the lease on the truck. He was introduced to a responsible-looking young man in a suit and they developed a cordial relationship. Only much later when another manager in the company complained about the maintenance services did Paul find out that the person he had been calling on had almost nothing to do with trucks, but because he was the controller, he conventionally reviewed and signed all leases.

NEGOTIATION POLICY

The image that many people have of negotiation is that of threats, intimidation, and counterthreats such as those made between lawyers in a TV drama. In such negotiations, each side argues its position, using whatever tactics necessary to get the other party to budge from its position. Negotiating based on positions is a lot like war. Each side defends the position that it has staked out from attacks by the other side, getting bruised and bloodied in the process. Positional negotiating is sometimes the verbal equivalent of rugby; one party "wins" and the other party "loses."

Such methods often take a long time to conclude and damage or destroy any working relationship the parties had or could hope to have.

Positional negotiators often choose an extreme position, hoping to end up somewhere near where they really want to be when the negotiation is through. As negotiators promote and defend their positions, the ego of negotiators tends to be identified with their position, making it hard for either negotiator to give ground without losing face. All the while, the negotiator probably has been doing more talking than listening, failing to understand the interests of the other side. In positional bargaining, a hard stance wins over a soft or "nice" stance. Because the seller of a product is usually not able to take a hard stance for fear of damaging the customer relationship, the seller is at a great disadvantage if it attempts to use positional bargaining techniques. Each party may get far less than it wants, even when some concessions would cost the other side very little. The result, when a compromise is finally made, may be a solution that neither side feels very good about.

Many people consider *principled negotiation* to be the best negotiation method today. Principled negotiation is a technique whereby negotiation proceeds based on the merits of the situation and the interests of the involved parties. This method seeks an overall best result where both parties come out ahead. Therefore, this type of negotiation is often called win-win negotiation. Principled negotiation was developed by the Harvard Negotiation Project and is described in the book *Getting to Yes* by Harvard professors Roger Fisher and William Ury. They list these four basic factors that define principled negotiation[3]:

1. People: Separate the people from the problem.
2. Interests: Focus on interests, not positions.
3. Options: Generate a wide variety before deciding what to do.
4. Criteria: Insist that the result be based on some objective standard.

Win-win negotiating techniques are now almost universally accepted as the approach of choice. The price negotiation techniques discussed in this chapter follow these basic principles. Although the concept of win-win negotiation is well accepted, the techniques used to reach a win-win solution do not have universal agreement. Some negotiation authorities suggest tactics that are not so principled, but nevertheless have been shown to be very effective.

Every frequent flyer is familiar with the face of Dr. Chester L. Karrass. His picture graces the advertisements for his seminars, which have appeared in airline in-flight magazines for decades. It is perhaps not a face that a person would intuitively trust. Reserved, yet determined, it would not be hard to imagine that he is holding a poker hand out of view of the camera. Today, Karrass looks much older and mellower but he continues to preach the same mantra:

In business as in life—you don't get what you deserve, you get what you negotiate.

This slogan is the title of the fourth of Karrass' books on negotiating.[4] Karrass is a good storyteller with an entertaining style that is much easier to read than many business books that are written with an academic tone. Like Fisher and Ury, Karrass preaches win-win negotiating techniques, although he and the participants in the Harvard Negotiation Project often differ considerably on specific tactics. The tips that follow on price negotiation have been heavily influenced by these writers.

TIPS FOR SUCCESSFUL PRICE NEGOTIATIONS

Plan the Negotiation in Advance

In most negotiations, little advanced planning occurs. This is particularly true when only one person does the negotiating. There are many things that the buyer and seller should know in advance:

- Who will be involved in negotiating the deal?
- What does the other side want?
- What is the other side likely to ask for?
- How should we respond to the things that they are likely to ask for?
- What is the target price for the deal?
- Who pays for shipping?
- Is training included?
- When is the delivery date?
- What are the payment terms?

There are certain things that a negotiator should know in advance. Among the most important is what Fisher and Ury call the "best alternative to a negotiated agreement" (BATNA). The BATNA is important because it represents the worst-case scenario if the parties are unable to negotiate a deal. If buyers are not able to obtain reasonable purchase terms with their existing vendor, they may be able to obtain acceptable terms with a different vendor. Having a solid knowledge of their BATNA provides each party with a fallback position and will limit how far they can be pushed in negotiation.

Knowledge of the market for similar products can provide a powerful negotiating tool. At what price have similar deals been negotiated? Which of those deals had terms that would provide favorable evidence to support the negotiator's position? Most managers do little to prepare for salary reviews for their people. Principled negotiations work well in salaried negotiations. If both parties can agree that the employee should be at a 75th percentile wage for similar job descriptions in a particular metropolitan area, it is relatively easy to obtain salary data that pinpoint exactly how much a person should be paid. If one party is prepared for the negotiation and the other is not, the prepared person has the advantage of being able to selectively provide data that are advantageous to his or her position.

Preparation helps get the best deal in negotiation. When a deal is not planned out in advance, buyers often end up thinking of additional features that they want after the price has been agreed upon. Anyone who has contracted to have a home built knows that these "extras" become high priced when added after the fact.

The larger the deal, the more people are likely to be involved in negotiation. When the United Auto Workers Union negotiates a contract with an automobile manufacturer, there may be 10 or more people sitting on each side of the table, with more people sitting in the background supporting each side. Although negotiating teams of this size can be very unwieldy, negotiating with two or three people is a manageable size that will produce a better result than one person negotiating alone.

There are many advantages to having several people involved in negotiations. One of the major advantages is that the various people involved have to discuss the negotiation in advance so that they are informed about the negotiation. Discussion promotes thinking about the negotiation and introduces differing viewpoints that will improve the quality of the negotiation strategy.

Negotiating teams that are outnumbered are likely to feel intimidated. The seller should not want the customer to feel intimidated. By the same token, the seller does not want to be outnumbered by the buyer. A good rule of thumb is to have the same number of people on each side when negotiations are going to occur. Negotiating teams may literally take opposite sides of a table, but negotiators who are seeking to find a cooperative win-win solution often prefer to use a round table or other arrangement that allows for interspersing the members of both parties. When two people are trying to reach an agreement, it is often effective to sit side-by-side with the deal to be negotiated laid out in front of them.

The planning process should define the roles of the members of the negotiating team. One person should be assigned as lead negotiator. Other members of the negotiation team may be assigned to negotiate different issues. It is a good idea to assign one person the responsibility to observe and take notes. The negotiation team should never openly disagree with each other in front of the opposing side. If there is a disagreement, the member of the team who recognizes that there is an issue should call for a caucus and the negotiating team should recess to another room to discuss the issue.

Negotiating teams sometimes plan in advance to stage an argument during negotiations with members of their own team. This technique is often seen on television police dramas and is called "good cop/bad cop." Because this method usually involves getting mad, storming out of the room, and otherwise attempting to deceive the other party about the negotiators' true intentions, it cannot be categorized as a principled negotiation technique. Because the technique is well known, the party using it runs the risk of losing face and bargaining position if the other side recognizes it. If the other side tries "good cop/bad cop" in a negotiation, an effective response might be to say, "Hey, good cop/bad cop. I've seen that on TV. Great performance!"

The negotiating team also may wish to establish ground rules for the negotiation. Such rules may include an agreement that no point of discussion is final until there is an agreement on the entire package as a whole. The ground rules also may include how long the sessions will be and when they will occur. Weary negotiators are likely to make errors, and it is a good idea to limit the amount of time for any negotiating session.

People Considerations

Negotiators are people, and failing to recognize and deal with people issues can be disastrous to a negotiation. In a vendor–customer relationship, the long-term relationship is usually more important than the outcome of any individual negotiation. Accordingly, it is important that people be treated with dignity and respect.

Discussions should revolve around principles, facts, and the interests of both parties, leaving personalities out of the discussions. The statement, "Your facts are wrong" can easily put a person on the defensive. A statement such as "Let's try to determine the true facts in this situation" is much more likely to lead to an agreement. A person who has lost face in a negotiation becomes a difficult adversary. That person may prevent the other party from making any gains, effectively sabotaging the negotiations.

People are more likely to accept a decision that they have been involved in making. When possible, therefore, it is desirable to involve people in the buying process other than just the buyer and the decision maker when those people can influence the success of a business relationship. Users are often resistant to a change in the vendors or the products with which they are familiar. Users can sabotage a deal by refusing to use the new product. Therefore, user involvement before a purchasing decision is made can substantially strengthen the customer's commitment to using the product long term. In many cases, just asking their opinion may be enough to win user acceptance for a vendor or product change. The salesperson may be able to gain the support of the users by offering to provide samples or demonstrations to the user before the purchasing decision is made.

Different cultures have different practices for negotiating business deals. It is wise to investigate cultural differences before attempting to negotiate with people from another part of the world. Even within the United States, people from New

York, Chicago, and Los Angeles have different habits and methods of communicating that irritate people from other regions. When language and cultural differences are more extreme, arriving at an agreement becomes more difficult. Recognizing and honoring the other party's customs is a sign of cooperation and good faith.

One American company president did his homework when expecting a contingent of Japanese visitors that might want to purchase automotive parts from his company. He learned that it was customary for small gifts to be exchanged at their first meeting. He read how the gifts should be presented and wrapped. The book that he read said that the Japanese custom was to thank the gift giver but set the gift aside to be opened later in private, opposite of the American custom to open the gift right away in the giver's presence. As expected, his guests brought gifts and gifts were exchanged. His managers set them aside in keeping with their instructions, but the Japanese visitors opened theirs right away in keeping with the American tradition. This was a sign that both parties had done their homework.

Business around the world is often transacted in English. Americans are well known for lacking foreign language skills. Business people who speak another native tongue may negotiate in English but then caucus in front of their American counterparts in their native tongue. Americans may gain a negotiating advantage by including someone who speaks the other language on their negotiating team.

The goal of win-win negotiations is for both parties to come out of the negotiation feeling like a winner. No one wants to feel like the other party has taken advantage of them. Because many business relationships are recurring and involve many transactions over time, making win-win deals is important to the long-term health of the relationship. Negotiators will not feel like winners if they think that they "left money on the table." This may happen if one party accepts the other's offer too quickly. A delay in the response to do some calculations or a caucus by the other negotiators to discuss the terms of an offer may help the other party feel like it has made a very good deal. A statement by the other party such as "You have offered a fair price" also may help both parties feel good about the transaction.

Carefully Choose the Time and Place for Negotiations

In many cultures, negotiation is an art form. The buyer and seller get to know each other, break bread, and make small talk before business is even discussed. Lavish entertaining is still commonly practiced in some parts of the world. In the Far East, the buyer and seller may eat and drink until all hours of the night yet appear in their offices promptly at starting time the next morning.

In the United States, lunch is a more common time for business entertaining. Although the "three-martini lunch" has largely passed into oblivion, buyers and sellers still often get together at lunch to get to know each other better and to discuss their upcoming deal. Breaking bread together helps develop a mutual trust that will make it easier to negotiate a deal and make the vendor–customer relationship longer lasting once the deal is consummated.

Some times are better than others for negotiations. Salespeople often feel pressure to "make their numbers" near the end of a month or the end of a year. Savvy car buyers often choose the final days of the month to buy a car for this reason. Even better, buying an automobile in the last few days of December when the sales manager is feeling both month-end and year-end pressure is likely to yield a really good deal.

At one company, the author found that 50% of all sales were made during the last 3 days of the month. Sales made during the first 15 days of the month closed at an average of 92% of list price, whereas sales made during the last 3 days of the month were concluded at an average of only 85% of list price. Many companies have a lopsided sales pattern like this. Even if the compensation plan does not put pressure for end of the month sales, because buyers *think* that the sellers have this pressure, they often time their buying for month-end in order to get a better deal.

Sometimes buyers have budget constraints that motivate them to seek a certain timing on their purchases. Because many companies have a "use it or lose it" budget mentality, it may be important to a buyer to receive goods before a certain date. When budgets are very tight, a buyer may want to take delivery as soon as possible, yet in the next budget period. Accordingly, buyers often want to negotiate a deal that the vendor ships at the end of one month (to get the best deal) but the goods arrive in the next month (so that the purchase arrives and the expenditure is recognized in the next budget period).

A seller would rather deal with a buyer at a time when the company is "feeling rich" rather than a time when it is "feeling poor." It is easier to negotiate a price increase when a customer is flush with money than when there are layoffs or when the customer is scaling back.

Before a vacation, buyers may have work piled up that needs to be finished before they go out of town. After the buyer returns it may take a few weeks to get caught up again. In some cases, sellers may want to choose a time when the buyer is rushed; at other times they may want their full consideration. Knowledge of the buyer's schedule may help select the best time for an effective negotiation.

Customers often specify a deadline for submitting proposals. Some salespeople prefer to be the last company to submit their proposal. Sometimes there is merit to this tactic if sellers are able to learn about other vendors' proposals before they submit their bid. Submitting too close to the deadline can also have a negative impact on the bid. Some buyers view the deadline as the last possible time to submit a quotation and really prefer that bids be submitted long before that date. The salesperson should learn when the buyer really wants the quotation. Insurance companies are notorious for waiting until the deadline before submitting their quotes. Insurance company underwriters seem to view the expiration date of the current policy as their due date even when there is an earlier final bid submission date specified by the buyer. More than one insurance agent has called the buyer to arrange to present a package, only to find that the bid date had passed and a new insurance company had already been selected.

Cost Breakdowns

According to Chester Karrass, buyers should ask for cost breakdowns, and sellers should avoid giving them.[5] Cost breakdowns give the buyer information that may be useful in negotiating price.

Years ago, one manufacturing company controller solicited bids for his company's insurance package that included property/liability insurance, an umbrella liability policy, workers compensation insurance, and automobile policies on the company cars. One insurance agency had a substantial cost advantage on all of the coverages combined because of very favorable rates on the largest piece, the workers compensation insurance. That agency, however, was substantially higher than any of the other bidders on the automobile policy. Having this cost breakdown provided the controller with negotiating power. He called the agent and explained that although his company had a very attractive package, the cost of his automotive coverage was so high that he was considering dividing the business between two agents. The agent understood what was required to get the business and soon returned with a revised offer on the automotive policy that matched the controller's best bid.

In a principled negotiation, sharing cost data may lead to a faster and more amicable negotiation process. A vendor that provides detailed cost estimates will often be able to reach an agreement very quickly. The seller is not likely to be able to earn an above average profit but in many cases will be able to easily negotiate a fair profit. Information sharing about cost is likely to be effective with a loyal buyer or a value buyer but is much more dangerous in the hands of a price buyer.

Understanding the Interests of Both Parties

Negotiations are easier when the negotiator understands what the other side wants. Negotiators often begin discussions by stating their position, but the underlying interests that define what someone wants are often hidden. Negotiations usually go much more smoothly when both parties discuss their interests so that there is a mutual understanding of what each party is really after.

The power of understanding the other party's interest was comically illustrated in the Mel Gibson movie *What Women Want*. Gibson played Nick, a not-so-lovable cad who develops the ability to read women's minds as the result of a freak accident. Through his newfound power, Nick is able to get what he wants from women by giving them what they want. In the business world, sales and negotiations are much easier when we understand what the other party wants.

In the mid-1980s, Ford Motor Company began negotiating long-term supply contracts with key parts suppliers. Among the things that Ford asked for was a provision that the price of each part would decline by 5% a year after the first year. Understandably, most suppliers were reluctant to sign up for such an arrangement. Edgewood Tool & Manufacturing Company, one of the two companies whose merger later formed Tower Automotive, took a unique approach in solving this problem. They looked beyond Ford's stated position, to what were Ford's real interests. Edgewood realized that Ford's real objective was to reduce its costs, not necessarily to lower Edgewood's price to Ford. As a result, Edgewood proposed that it would receive credit for any cost savings that it was able to generate for Ford. Edgewood managers envisioned that most of the cost savings would come from developing cost-saving design improvements to existing products that the company sold to Ford. Many of the cost savings would come from making the parts easier to install at Ford assembly plants. As a result of this innovative solution to Ford's request, Edgewood was one of the very first companies to sign a long-term supply contract, settling on a very favorable 2.4% annual giveback formula.

It is not uncommon for a particular term in a selling agreement to be very important to the buyer but not at all important to the seller, or vice versa. For example, a small company may not be able to afford the cash flow involved in a large contract unless the buyer provides a deposit and progress payments. The cash flow considerations may be relatively unimportant to buyers as long as they receive value for the financing that they provide. Frankness about the financing need will help both the negotiators tailor selling terms to best meet the needs of both parties.

There are some interests of negotiating parties that should not be revealed. Each of the following statements is likely to substantially increase the price of the pending deal:

- "You were the only company that we could find who could do the job."
- "I absolutely love this neighborhood! We fell in love with this house the moment we saw it."
- "Work has really been slow. If we get this contract we can bring our second shift back from layoff."
- "We have shopped around and you have the best hospital information system by far."

Because sales people and purchasing people frequently negotiate as part of their jobs, they are not usually the ones who reveal too much information. More often it is the accountant, engineer, or receptionist who speaks out of turn. Individual consumers, of course, frequently have this problem as well. Negotiating teams, whether they are made up of business people trying to sell a big contract or spouses trying to buy a house, should have a signal that means "please stop talking" if they start to reveal too much.

Using Objective Criteria

Negotiation is much easier when the buyer and seller are first able to reach an agreement as to objective criteria that will be used to evaluate the deal. Introducing objective criteria into a negotiation works even if the other party does not practice principled negotiation or believe in win-win negotiating. When a prospective buyer offers a ridiculously low price for a product, the question "How did you come up with that number?" refocuses the discussion on objective ways of determining a fair price.

Offering a fair price supported by objective criteria has a way of leveling the playing field and focusing the discussion on how to come up with an amiable solution.

Imagine this real-life phone conversation between the owner of a car dealership and a customer who has waited 25 weeks for his wife's new minivan to be delivered:

Dealer:	Mr. Johnson, I got your fax today about your wife's minivan. I checked with my people. It is in and it should be ready for you to pick up tomorrow.
Johnson:	Did you read the part of my letter about the price of the vehicle?
Dealer:	Yes, it is a very unusual request that you made.
Johnson:	Yes, our van was supposed to be delivered in 6 to 7 weeks. It has now been 25 weeks, and the new models are due out soon. I have been looking through the newspapers to figure how much value a van loses just by being older and I calculate that amount to be about \$33 a week. Because the van is 18 weeks overdue, I think that you should drop the price by \$600.
Dealer:	But you are already getting a very good price for the van by paying our invoice cost.
Johnson:	That isn't the issue here. The issue is that this vehicle has dropped considerably in value because it is 18 weeks closer to the new model year than it was supposed to be when it was delivered. I think that

I used a fair methodology at coming up with my numbers. We could do a similar calculation with your "Blue Book" to see if my numbers are reasonable, but if we were going to do that, I would want you to agree that we would use whatever those numbers said before we looked at them.

(Johnson has proposed using a fair method and objective criteria for determining how much value the van has lost. It will be hard for the dealer to refute.)

Dealer: No, your estimate is actually probably a little on the low side.

(Because the Dealer knew that Johnson's estimates were conservative, he had nothing to gain by challenging his numbers. Acknowledgement that the numbers are conservative is a major concession that will leave him little bargaining room.)

Johnson: Right now if I went to another dealership I could get a similar van at year-end sales price or order the same van and get next year's model. Either way I would be better off, even if you didn't give me my deposit back.

(Johnson has revealed to the dealer two alternatives that he has that are better than the current arrangement. This will be a powerful incentive for the dealer to close the deal).

Dealer: Why don't we split the difference and make it $300?

(The Dealer has made a counter proposal. "Splitting the difference" is a common solution when there is a disputed amount and the arguments made by both sides has merit. In this case, however, the dealer has prepared no counter arguments that merit a concession from Johnson.)

Johnson: The number that I have proposed is fair. You said yourself that it might be on the low side.

Dealer: Well, we don't want to lose you as a customer and I would probably have to discount it anyhow to sell it to somebody else. Okay, I'll agree to $600.

The dealer has been out-prepared in this negotiation. Johnson won everything that he sought, but the dealer will probably not feel bad about this negotiation. He has prevented the customer from walking out on the purchase agreement and buying the vehicle from another dealership. Johnson argued based on principles and got a price adjustment that both parties recognized as fair. The dealer has kept a customer satisfied and stands a good chance of continuing to sell him cars and service for the next 30 years.

Price Setting and Concession Strategy

Writers on pricing and negotiations vary significantly in their opinions about how pricing and negotiations should proceed. Nagle and Holden at Boston University would prefer to set a fixed price, selling the customer on that price based on the value of the product and negotiating price only when absolutely necessary.[6] Fisher and Ury at Harvard University advocate avoiding taking positions, concentrating instead on interests and objective criteria for arriving at an agreement.[7] Chester Karrass notes that negotiators who start out high tend to end up with a better negotiating result[8]; however he also noted the following:

> Your knowledge of the marketplace and the supply and demand factors specifically influencing the parties in the transaction determine your opening offer or demand.[9]

There are lessons to be learned from each of these viewpoints. Beginning with a high price works well for a unique product, when prices are not easily compared or when dealing with a casual or convenience buyer. Some buyers will pay the high asking price, while the negotiator may settle on a lower price with other buyers. A risk of this approach is that the potential buyer may avoid negotiating with the high-priced seller, dealing instead with an alternate vendor.

Starting with an initial high price does not work when a well-prepared buyer has good information about pricing and alternate sources of similar products. Such a buyer is likely to have well-defined BATNA and the seller will look foolish, inefficient, ineffective, or even dishonest by proposing anything but a fair and reasonable price.

Most businesses price their product at a "fair and reasonable" price. When this price is established in reference to other companies in the industry, it is called a *market pricing strategy*. It also may be a *satisficing strategy* when it is designed to provide the seller with an adequate, but not a superior, financial return.

Even when a seller's plan is to offer a fair and reasonable fixed price, the buyer often forces the seller to negotiate a better deal. When a negotiator takes a position, any time that negotiator gives up that position to take a position nearer to the other side, that movement is called a *concession*.

The seller usually makes the first offer by establishing an asking price. Whoever makes the first major concession has a major influence on the outcome of the entire negotiation. The first major concession is usually the largest concession that will be made and the seller should avoid being the one to make it. Many salespeople get nervous when a buyer does not respond to their price right away. Salespeople anxious to get business will often react to a buyer's slow response by making a quick counteroffer. This is a tactical error. If a buyer resists the seller's initial price, the seller should leave the subject of price for a while, perhaps talking about how well the product matches the customer's needs and giving reasons why the product provides the overall best value to the customer. The seller might then resume price discussions by asking what price the buyer had in mind. This response will bracket the range in which negotiations will occur.

When a transaction is likely to be subject to negotiation, the seller should leave some room to move around. This can be tricky because the deal may have to pass a competitive bid process before negotiations finally begin. Negotiating room may come from making more than one alternate proposal as part of the bidding process. The seller might submit one bid that meets the specifications of the buyer's request for proposal, but include alternate proposals that include a lower price for contract terms that are more favorable to the buyer or a higher price for contract terms that are more favorable to the seller. These alternate proposals may increase the vendor's chance of winning the contract.

A good rule of thumb is to never give a concession without getting something in return. A price decrease may be coupled with quicker payment turns or a larger up-front deposit. Buyers may increase their counteroffer in exchange for extras like free training, quicker delivery, or extra features at no charge.

Even when the terms are acceptable, wise negotiators avoid saying "yes" too quickly. When one party agrees to the terms of a negotiation too quickly, the other party often thinks that they gave away too much and "left money on the table." Saying "no" a few times before saying yes will help the other party think that they have gotten the best deal possible. When a deal has required work, each party has a better appreciation of the final outcome.

Changing the duration or volumes specified in the contract can often bridge differences in price. Because there are fixed costs associated with every product, increasing the number of units that are sold under the contract will provide the seller with lower costs and therefore the ability to offer a lower price due to economies of scale. The seller's activity-based pricing model will identify how much an increase in volume is worth and will allow the seller to tailor a proposal that will allow for price concessions in return for more business.

Deadlines can have a major influence on negotiations. Many people get nervous as a deadline approaches. In order to meet the deadline, one party may make large concessions near the end just to get the deal completed. Large concessions made when the deadline approaches are often mistakes. Avoid being pressured by deadlines. After all, most deadlines are artificial, and when negotiations are in progress, most deadlines may be extended.

Negotiating Price Increases and Decreases

It is better to give a customer five 4% price increases over 5 years than a single price increase of 20%. This is an interesting phenomenon because 4% compounded over 5 years is actually 21.7%. Because the seller gets the benefit of the small price increase each year, the buyer is much worse off when five small price increases are given.

The reason that many small price increases is better is largely psychological. An increase of 4% does not seem like much, probably not worth the effort to get a competitive bid on the relationship. That 4% may be explained away by inflationary costs. A 20% cost increase, however, is a big percentage of the previous price. A lot of dollars may be involved with a 20% price increase. The buyer may not have had the motivation to go searching for a vendor for any of the 4% price increases, but a 20% price increase may provide that motivation to find a vendor that will be able to provide the service at the old price.

Politically, it is often advantageous to advise the customer long in advance that a price increase is coming. Although the advance notice may give the customer time to competitively shop the relationship, it also gives them the opportunity to get the increase approved in an upcoming round of budgets. This maneuver may actually forestall having the customer seek competitive bids because there is no unfavorable budget variance to motivate a reexamination of vendors.

Supply contracts sometimes provide a mechanism for price to change up and down over the life of the contract. Long-term supply contracts in the automotive industry sometimes specify that the parts supplier:

- Guarantee that once a product is awarded to a vendor, it will not be competitively bid for the life of that part except for failure to meet the customer's quality and delivery requirements.
- Will provide a price decrease each year after the first year (typically about 2.5%).
- Is entitled to price adjustments due to increases in the cost of materials.
- Is not entitled to price adjustments for any other factor other than a change in part design.

Terms such as these require that the seller maintain good records about changes in cost. Many manufacturing companies operate in environments where the understood practice is that the customer absorbs the risk of material price increases. Sellers who fail to apply for price increases when they are due may miss the opportunity for substantial rate increases in times of increasing raw material prices. Along the same line, buyers often fail to get price decreases that they deserve by failing to press the sellers for price decreases when raw material prices are declining.

Written agreements help both parties remember the terms of the deal when it was originally made. They provide the seller with protection when a large capital investment must be made to support a customer and they provide the customer with price protection in the form of relatively stable and fixed prices over the life of the contract.

Unprincipled Negotiations

Not everyone in business has high ethical standards. An unethical practice in one culture may be the everyday norm in another. Some people have a good intuitive sense of who can be trusted and make the decision to trust or not trust each individual based on their general impression. Many other people start out trusting or not trusting everyone until proven otherwise. A healthy skepticism may help each company protect its interest.

The author is familiar with two different small companies who engaged in extensive joint venture discussions with large companies before getting a formal noncompete agreement. In both cases, the smaller company had proprietary knowledge that the bigger company was trying to acquire. In one case, the joint venture actually began operations under the bigger company's roof before the small company was informed that its prospective partner had decided to go into the business without a joint venture partner. In neither case did the smaller company receive any compensation for its time or the great deal of know-how that it transferred in the process.

Do not trust the other party unless they have given you good reason to do so. The subject of unethical tactics that are used in negotiation could fill a lengthy chapter by itself. Anyone who is frequently involved with negotiations may want to read one or more of the books mentioned in this chapter to become more aware of tactics that they might encounter. Documenting conversations and agreements will help each side remember what they promised. If you make it a practice to double-check the factual assertions of the other party, it decreases the likelihood that you will be deceived.

SUMMARY

The key points discussed in this chapter are listed below:

1. There are compelling reasons not to negotiate product pricing. Negotiating price is time consuming, can create an adversarial relationship between the buyer and seller, motivates sales people to use price concessions to close sales, and undermines profit planning and meeting profitability goals.
2. Price negotiation is necessary in many instances, particularly for unique products where there is not a well-established market price.
3. All buyers are not the same. Buyers are often classified into four categories:
   - Price buyers
   - Convenience buyers

- Value buyers
- Loyal buyers

Pricing and negotiation strategies differ for each kind of buyer.

4. Attempting to sell to price buyers may be a frustrating and unprofitable experience for a company that is not the low-cost producer. Most companies should engage in selective participation when competing for sales to price buyers.
5. Activity-based pricing can give a company that is not the low-cost producer a competitive advantage in competing for sales to price buyers. Companies that do not use activity-based pricing often inadvertently overprice their products, particularly for work that is easy or high volume.
6. Sellers should avoid participating in an auction-type bidding process. In an auction-type bidding process, the company that gets the work is often a company that makes a mistake in its pricing. The winner in such a bidding process is often the company that does not get the contract.
7. Convenience buyers seek products that are easy to buy or easy to use and are willing to pay a premium price for the convenience.
8. Value buyers actively seek the best overall value for their money. Sales people can profitably sell to value buyers by listening to the customer's needs and communicating how the product will provide the customer with the best overall value.
9. Loyal buyers value consistency, quality, and service. Trust is an important factor in the vendor–customer relationship. When loyal buyers change vendors, it is usually as a result of poor quality products, substandard service, or breached promises. Loyal buyers tend to be very profitable customers.
10. Many people may be involved in the purchasing process. These are often categorized as:
    - Initiators
    - Users
    - Specifiers
    - Influencers
    - Gatekeepers
    - Buyers
    - Decision makers

    A single person may fulfill multiple roles in the purchasing process.
11. Many authorities consider principled negotiation to be today's best negotiating practice. The four basic factors of principled negotiation are as follows:
    - People: Separate the people from the problem.

- Interests: Focus on interests, not positions.
- Options: Generate a wide variety before deciding what to do.
- Criteria: Insist that the result be based on some objective standard.

12. In win-win negotiation, the objective is to make both parties as satisfied as possible with the outcome. Principled negotiation is a form of win-win negotiation.

13. Tips for successful negotiating:

- Plan the negotiation in advance.
- Identify your best alternative to a negotiated agreement (BATNA).
- Use a team approach to negotiation.
- Study the people considerations of the negotiation.
- Carefully choose the time and place for negotiations.
- Understand the interests of both parties.
- Use objective criteria.
- Avoid making the first major concession.

NOTES

1. This person's name has been changed.
2. Thomas T. Nagle and Reed K. Holden, *The Strategy and Tactics of Pricing* (Englewood Cliffs, NJ: Prentice Hall, 1995), p. 205.
3. Roger Fisher and William L. Ury, *Getting to Yes: Negotiating Agreement Without Giving In,* 2d ed. (New York: Penguin, 1991), p. 10.
4. Chester L. Karrass, *"In Business As In Life—You Don't Get What You Deserve, You Get What You Negotiate"* (Beverly Hills, CA: Stanford St. Press, 1996).
5. Ibid., p. 24.
6. Thomas T. Nagle and Reed K. Holden, *The Strategy and Tactics of Pricing* (Englewood Cliffs, NJ: Prentice Hall, 1995), pp. 190–191.
7. Roger Fisher and William L. Ury, *Getting to Yes: Negotiating Agreement Without Giving In,* 2d ed. (New York: Penguin, 1991), pp. 40–41, 81.
8. Chester L. Karrass, *"In Business As In Life—You Don't Get What You Deserve, You Get What You Negotiate"* (Beverly Hills, CA: Stanford St. Press, 1996), p. 30.
9. Ibid., p. 31.

12

CONCLUSIONS AND SUMMARY

> Activity-based pricing has changed our viewpoint on pricing. We used to think that we sold press hours. Now we know that we are also selling support services and product management time which puts our view of cost and pricing in a whole different perspective.
>
> Gary Grigowski, Vice President, Team One Plastics

PRICING FOR PROFITABILITY

In the last analysis, pricing strategy is only part of the total profitability picture. Having a good pricing strategy will not create more innovative products for a company. Pricing strategy cannot make a business run more efficiently or improve product quality. Smart pricing will not attract better people or improve the name recognition of the company's products. The benefits of activity-based pricing (ABP) are more subtle.

Activity-based pricing is the tool that links pricing to profitability. Revenue is not profit. Profit equals revenue minus expenses. Many companies have vainly pursued bottom-line profit by pursuing top-line growth, only to find that substantial increases in revenue provided no increase to the bottom line. The reason for this is simple. These companies had an inadequate understanding of their profit equation, the interrelationship of price and cost. Profit is dependent on them both.

PRICING AND ECONOMICS

As explained in Chapter 2, understanding customer demand is an important part of pricing strategy. Marketing people have various ways of estimating customer demand, which include the following:

- Expert judgment
- Customer surveys
- Price experimentation
- Analysis of historical data

Because the demand for a product generally decreases as the price increases, an analysis of customer demand should produce estimates of how many units the company will sell at different prices. When graphed, these data produce a characteristic curved line that is called a demand line by economists and a customer price response curve by marketers. Price elasticity is a measurement of the slope of the customer response curve. Elasticity is defined as follows:

$$\text{Price elasticity} = \frac{\%\ \text{change in price}}{\%\ \text{change in units sold}}$$

If a small change in price creates a big change in sales, demand is said to be elastic. When a large change in price makes little change in demand, demand is said to be inelastic. Elasticity characteristically decreases as price decreases. Revenue is maximized at the point where price elasticity equals 1.0. At this point, the product of price times unit sales volume is maximized.

In the absence of good cost information, many companies seek to maximize profit by maximizing revenue. This is a faulty strategy because revenue does not equal profit.

$$\text{Profit} = \text{Revenue} - \text{Expenses}$$

To understand how to maximize revenue, the interrelationships between price, cost, and volume must be understood.

The reason that maximizing revenue does not maximize profit is easy to understand. Revenue is maximized where the price elasticity of customer demand equals 1.0. This means that at this point a 1% increase in price will result in a 1% decrease in unit sales. At the point where revenue is maximized, raising the price from $100 to $101 will cause sales to decrease from 100 units to 99 units. Because revenue equals price times the number of units sold, a 1% increase in price will cause only a 1/10,000 decrease in revenue. This occurs because the decrease in unit volume has almost completely offset the increase in price. The calculation is:

Before:	$100 × 100 units =	$10,000 in revenue
After	$101 × 99 units =	$ 9,999
Net change		$1

How does a change in unit volume affect cost? When price is raised by 1%, total fixed costs remain the same. Fixed costs per unit increase by 1%, and total variable costs decrease by 1% as a result of the 1% decrease in the number of units sold. If fixed costs are $2,000 and variable costs are $70 per unit, the effect on costs of raising price by 1% from the revenue maximization point would be:

Before:	$2,000 + $70/unit × 100 units =	$9,000 total cost
After:	$2,000 + $70/unit × 99 units =	$8,930 total cost
Net change		($69)

Because a $69 drop in cost improves profit far more than a $1 drop in revenues, the company is better off by raising price even though doing so results in decreased sales:

	Before	*After*
Revenue	$10,000	$9,999
Costs	9,000	8,930
Profit	$1,000	$1,069

Theoretical situations can be constructed where this behavior does not occur, such as when a company has no variable costs. But in the real world, every product has some costs that are variable.

When customer demand is discussed, it is understood to describe the behavior of many customers in a market. For any individual customer, the relationship between price and sales volume is usually a "yes" or "no."

Many companies obtain their sales by competitively bidding to sell unique custom-designed products to their customers. Such contracts may be for large sums of money and may last for years. In these situations the number of units to be sold is usually specifically defined, either as a single quantity or as a range of quantities. For these companies, customer demand is an all-or-nothing proposition. In this environment, pricing for profitability hinges on understanding the costs and then quoting a price that is large enough to make a profit but small enough to make a sale.

COMPETITIVE STRATEGY AND PRICING

The sources of competitive advantage were discussed in Chapter 3. According to Michael Porter at Harvard University, the only two sources of competitive advantage are low cost and differentiation. Low cost provides a competitive advantage because buyers will purchase a lower priced product if all other factors are perceived as equal. Paying less for a product is to the buyer's advantage because it leaves them more financial resources to purchase other things. The low-cost producer in an industry can charge a lower price than other companies in the industry yet still enjoy a superior financial return.

It is generally not an effective strategy for a company to attempt to compete with the low-cost producer based on price. In the event of a price war, the low-cost producer can price its products lower than other companies and still earn a profit. For this reason, most companies avoid engaging in price competition with a low-cost producer. When more than one company attempts to compete for the same customers based on price, profitability is usually very poor for the entire industry.

Most companies compete using a differentiation strategy. Differentiators offer a product that is different from competing products in some way that is valued by some portion of the industry's customers. Many customers are willing to pay a premium to get a product that is better suited to their specific needs. In order to obtain a superior financial return, the producer of a differentiated product must be able to get a premium price for the differentiated product. The amount of the premium must exceed the cost to create the differentiation for this strategy to be successful.

If there are only two sources of competitive advantage, Porter says that there are only three generic business strategies:

1. Cost leadership
2. Differentiation
3. Focus
   a. Cost focus
   b. Differentiation focus

According to Porter's model, companies may compete using cost leadership or differentiation in a broad market or they may compete by focusing on a narrow niche. When a company's market niche is highly focused, the difference between a cost leadership strategy and a differentiation strategy becomes irrelevant if that company is the only one that does what it does. Small companies survive and often thrive by finding a small corner of a market and making it their own.

Robin Cooper of the Claremont Graduate School provides a different view of competition. Cooper's study of 20 Japanese companies found that there was a new competitive paradigm. Cooper found that competitors quickly imitated each company's innovations, leading him to conclude that there was no such thing as a sustainable competitive advantage in these industries. Porter's model, according to Cooper, applied to *mass production*, but many companies had advanced beyond mass production to *lean competition*.

Cooper observed that the quality produced by every company that he studied exceeded customer expectations. He also observed that products were priced at specific *price points* so that similar products were typically offered at the same price. Because of this, Cooper concluded that there was no real competition based on quality or price. Lean competition, Cooper concluded, was based on the features and functionality the customer received for a particular price. The company that currently had the latest and greatest features would have a temporary competitive advantage. This advantage would be fleeting, because all companies would quickly adopt the innovations of their competitors. Competitive advantage in a lean environment therefore comes from the ability to innovate quickly.

UNDERSTANDING PRICING STRATEGY

Chapter 4 discussed issues relating to pricing strategy, including pricing ethics, pricing law, and the situations in which various common pricing strategies are used.

Ethics and Pricing

Every society has different views on the ethics of pricing. Common modern pricing mores say that these factors must exist for prices to be ethical:

- Price paid is voluntary
- Price is based on equal information
- Price does not exploit the buyer's essential needs
- Price is justified by costs.

Some societies have held that it is unethical for a product to be sold at a profit. This belief, which was one of the basic tenets of communism, is no longer widely held. Today, most people believe that a profit motive is necessary for a healthy economic system.

Pricing Law

Pricing in the United States is influenced by various pieces of national legislation, including the Sherman Act, the Clayton Act, and the Robinson-Patman Act. These laws are designed to "prevent unfair competition." The Robinson-Patman Act requires that sellers charge all customers in commerce the same price, except:

- To meet a competitive price
- When there is a cost justification for differential pricing

Today the companies that are most frequently litigated for price law violations under the Robinson-Patman Act are manufacturers that supply "big-box" retailers, who have given their large customers prices far below prices given to the "mom and pop" stores with which they compete. Companies that are sued are frequently unable to cost justify the discounts that they have given their large customers. Activity-based costing (ABC) would provide a solid defense against Robinson-Patman lawsuits.

A company that sets its price irrationally low to large customers ends up overcharging smaller customers to make up for the loss. This provides more cost-savvy competitors an opportunity to profitably sell to those smaller customers, leaving the company with only its money-losing large customers.

Common Pricing Strategies

Market skimming is a pricing strategy whereby price is set at a high level to make sales only to those customers that are willing to pay a lot for the product. This strategy is common for new products where strong market demand exceeds production capacity. With a market skimming strategy, price is often reduced as production capacity increases, maintaining a balance between supply and demand.

Market penetration is a strategy whereby price is initially set low to gain market share. A new product may use market penetration to gain visibility and market acceptance. A new entrant into an existing market also may use a low-price market penetration strategy to gain market share. Setting a low penetration price creates the risk that the market leader will, in turn, lower its price, preventing the new product from making any significant market share gains.

A *loss leader* is a product whose price is set low to attract buyers for the company's other products. Retailers that sell relatively low-priced products, such as groceries, most often use this strategy. Frozen turkeys are often sold inexpensively or are given away free with a minimum purchase to attract customers into a grocery store. In order to offer a bargain price for one product, the seller must slightly elevate the price of other items. The strategy is not effective if buyers purchase only the loss leader from one company and purchase the rest of their goods elsewhere.

Complementary pricing involves planning the pricing of products that are normally sold together so as to maximize the overall profit of all complements. An example of complementary products would be parking, concessions, and tickets to an entertainment or sporting event. One product, such as a football ticket, may be priced inexpensively to attract customers who will purchase the complements at a premium price. This strategy makes sense for products that have high fixed costs but are operating below capacity, particularly when there is little competition for the complements, such as parking, souvenirs, and concessions.

Satisficing is a strategy whereby the price of a product is set at a level that will provide an adequate, but not superior, financial return. This is a common strategy that is characteristic of companies that obtain their sales through competitive bids. Because margins are usually very thin in these environments, it is important that companies using a satisficing strategy have a strong understanding of their costs. ABP is a particularly important tool in this environment.

Value pricing is a strategy whereby the seller sets its price based on the value that the buyer receives. A lawyer's contingency fees are an example. Value pricing is often advocated in articles about the pricing of professional services. However, competition limits the situations where value pricing can be used. Few companies use value pricing to set high prices, although many businesses will reduce their price if their normal charge is more than the value that their customers receive.

Competition based on price is a strategy that may be effectively used by a company that is the low-cost producer of a product. However it is common for the low-cost producer to set its price at the same price points as other competitors to avoid a "cheap" image. The low-cost producer is often the market leader, setting the price standards for the rest of the industry. Wise competitors avoid competing with the low-cost producer based on price.

There is one situation where a company that is not the low-cost producer may successfully compete with the low-cost producer based on price. If the low-cost producer is not using ABP, a company using ABP may "cherry pick" profitable jobs where the low-cost producer has mistakenly overpriced certain products due to a lack of good costing information. The low-cost producer may be unaware of why it is losing sales, particularly in a competitive bid environment.

COSTS

Costs are an important element in the pricing process because price cannot be established at a profitable level without knowledge of cost. Chapter 5 noted that cost accounting techniques have substantially improved since the introduction of the personal computer in the late 1970s. Traditional cost accounting generally broke costs into three categories:

- Materials (including purchased parts and services)
- Direct labor (including benefits on direct labor)
- Overhead (everything else)

Traditional methods applied average costs to products. As a result, traditional cost accounting was able to determine the cost of an average product sold at average sales volumes, but did a poor job at identifying the specific costs relating to any product in particular. This problem could be particularly serious for any product that was not average, leading to large differences between real costs and "accounting costs."

Traditional allocation methods normally assign overhead costs to products as a function of direct labor hours. Therefore, the three major categories of costs used by traditional cost accounting were all treated as variable costs that were directly dependent on the number of units of the product that were produced. Because traditional cost accounting treats all costs as variable, it is unable to distinguish the major cost differences that may exist for similar products that are sold in radically different sales volumes.

Today businesses need a more sophisticated understanding of their costs than the averaging methods of traditional cost accounting provided. Many companies have poor costing information because their financial reporting systems were not set up to meaningfully collect and categorize costs. Particularly in smaller companies, financial information is often organized using techniques that were required by the limitations of manual ledger books.

Today a company's chart of accounts should reflect the company's organizational structure, recognizing the divisions, location, and departments that exist for the business. Using a *structured chart of accounts* will improve the company's ability to do cost accounting, budgeting, responsibility reporting, and other financial functions. By using a structured account segment format, the company will be better able to handle the information requirements of twenty-first century competition.

Because businesses are usually organized functionally, a structured chart of accounts mirrors this organizational structure. The best practice for structuring a business today is believed to be a process-oriented organization. Structured financial reporting methods are able to adapt to however the organization is structured. ABC recognizes activities as the right level of detail of cost accumulation. Most business functions and business processes are made up of several to many activities. Operating data or other estimates may be used to apportion functional or process-oriented costs among activities.

ACTIVITY-BASED COSTING

Traditional cost accounting has severe limitations when looking at individual products because it uses averaging techniques to lump large pools of cost together. Such averaging has serious consequences in product pricing because the sales of overpriced products and underpriced products do not average out. When a company overprices a product, it loses the sale. When it underprices a product, the sale is made but the company loses money. Only when a product is priced appropriately does the company both make a sale and earn a profit.

Chapter 6 discussed ABC, a technique that has substantially improved the quality of the cost information that is available to managers making pricing decisions. ABC is a discipline that uses common-sense techniques to assign costs according to the factors that caused the cost to be incurred.

Traditional allocation methods assign costs to units of output. Overhead costs are usually assigned to a pool of overhead costs and then are allocated to units of output based on an arbitrary measure of cost consumption, most often direct labor. As a result, expensive automated processes may be assigned little overhead, while inexpensive manual processes may be assigned considerably more overhead costs. Traditional allocation methods treat all costs as variable; thus, traditional cost accounting techniques arrive at a single cost that is supposed to be valid over some undefined "relevant range." This feature causes traditional costs to be valid only when an "average" product is produced in "average" volumes. All other products are either overcosted or undercosted depending on how far these products vary from average. These distortions can lead management into making poor pricing decisions.

Most companies have a wide spectrum of products, customers, and processes. Understanding the differences in costs to produce various products, serve various customers, or perform various processes is vital to identifying those sales opportunities that will be profitable.

Activity-based costing assigns costs according to the causes of cost. Unlike traditional cost accounting, ABC costs are situation specific. ABC uses a multistep cost assignment network to assign the costs of resources to activities and the costs of activities to products based on the factors that caused each cost. ABC may assign some costs to products, some to customers, some to product launch, some to batch setup, and some to each unit of production. Costs from one activity may be assigned to other activities then others until they are finally assigned to products or customers.

The method used in ABC for assigning costs mimics the causes of costs in the real world. Because fixed costs, variable costs, and step-variable costs usually exist for every product, ABC shows a characteristic relationship between unit cost and sales volume where unit cost decreases constantly as volume increases. When production volumes are very low, the fixed cost per unit is very large. As production volumes increase from very small numbers, unit costs drop dramatically. The drop in unit volume is less dramatic when moving from average production volumes to high production volumes, but knowing the amount of the cost drop is still enough to provide a significant competitive advantage to any company that understands how these costs behave.

ACTIVITY-BASED PRICING

Activity-based pricing was discussed in Chapter 7. ABP is a pricing method that uses knowledge about customer demand and knowledge about the costs of a particular selling situation to establish a price that will result in a specific planned profit. ABP marries marketing data about the relationship of price and sales volume with information about cost at each of those volumes to allow the company to maximize profitability.

The goals of ABP are as follows:

- Establish price based on a solid knowledge of customer demand and product cost.
- Never unintentionally price a product at a loss.
- Know how much of price is profit.
- Generate a superior financial return through superior financial knowledge.

The four commandments of ABP are:

1. Know thy product.
2. Know thy processes.
3. Know thy customers.
4. Know thy competitors.

The relationship between price and cost is important because most companies in most industries are working with thin profit margins that are measured in terms of a single-digit percentage of revenue. Because competitors will rarely allow a company to make a sale at a large profit, the company must prevent losing the modest profits that it has been able to earn. Small profits on many profitable products are often wiped out as a result of a single sale that results in substantial losses.

Activity-based pricing also can be used in competitive bid situations for a single customer when a price response curve cannot be developed. In this situation, ABP can identify costs in a volume-sensitive format, allowing the company to set price profitably for any specified volume.

Understanding the relationships between price, cost, and volume is vital to motivating salespeople to make profitable sales. Salespeople should never simultaneously have control over price and be paid a commission based on sales dollars. Such a plan will motivate salespeople to maximize revenue at the expense of profit. If salespeople are to have authority to negotiate price, sales compensation plans should provide rewards based on some measure of profitability. Value-added is a better commission base than revenue, gross margin is a better commission base than value-added, and an activity-based measure of profit is better still.

ACTIVITY-BASED PRICING MODELS

Activity-based pricing is often the first and only use that a company will have for ABC data. Chapter 8 provided examples of ABP models used by several different companies. Companies that use computerized ABC software often do not use the pricing features of that software but extract cost information from their ABC system and do their price analysis using computer spreadsheet models in packages such as Lotus, Quattro Pro, or Excel.

A key characteristic of an ABP model is that the price is volume sensitive. Pricing models for service businesses and manufacturing businesses are usually very different. Service business pricing models often use a work program format. The model itself may have no volume-sensitive features, but because the model is organized according to fixed, variable, and step-variable costs, the end result is that the scale economies are recognized. In service business models, the hierarchy of fixed, variable, and step-variable costs is usually identifiable on the face of the quotation worksheet.

In manufacturing company quotation models, the hierarchy of cost is usually built into the model itself. The volume-sensitive features of the model may operate behind the scenes in a subtler fashion. Manufacturing company product launch costs may be dependent on the type of product and are usually quantified based on factors from a rate table. A manufacturing quotation model also may calculate step-variable costs behind the scenes. A common method is to take the number of units to be produced, the amount of time required to make the product, the amount of material to be purchased, and batch setup costs, and determine the number of batches to be produced each year based on an economic order quantity algorithm. Variable costs are usually explicitly identifiable in an ABP model and are often handled in a manner identical to more conventional costing methods.

Activity-based pricing models allow management to control the pricing process without being involved in the preparation of every quote. ABP models allow the company to develop and modify quotations very quickly. Unlike traditional cost calculations that are valid for only a narrow relevant range, a well-designed ABP model will be valid for any quantity from a single unit to millions.

INFLUENCE OF CAPACITY UTILIZATION

Capacity utilization is an important consideration in pricing. A company that is inefficient or is operating well below normal capacity for its industry cannot expect to recoup all of its cost and enjoy a normal profit. Chapter 9 discussed the pricing strategy considerations related to capacity. ABC normally excludes the cost of excess capacity from product costs. In ABP, however, the costs of excess capacity should be carefully evaluated so that they may be recouped through price where appropriate.

Pricing theory suggests that in general, the costs of all fixed investments should be recovered over their useful lives using a method that matches costs with revenue. Companies may choose to vary how costs are recovered from quote to quote according to the competitive considerations relating to each situation. Some long-lived assets such as buildings or metal stamping presses may actually appreciate rather than depreciate. Companies will usually want to consider the costs of their fixed assets based on the economic reality of the situation rather than based on some historical accounting measure of costs.

TARGET PRICING

Many categories of product have a well-established market price. In retailing, the prices of products are commonly set at price points that are at or near "nice round numbers" such as $99, $99.95, $99.99, or $100. A product could not expect to sell well at $129 if similar products sold for $30 less.

Chapter 10 discussed the considerations related to target pricing. *Target pricing* describes an environment in which the selling price is established up front as a given. When a target price is established, the target profit also can be calculated; thus, whatever remains is the target (or allowable) cost. Therefore:

$$\text{Target cost} = \text{target price} - \text{target profit}$$

The most basic rule of target pricing is that the target cost must never be exceeded.

In a target-pricing environment, the task becomes designing a product and processes to produce that product at a cost that is no greater than the target costs. This philosophy, which has its roots in Japan, has interesting implications for organizations. Unlike Western design engineering methods that seek to minimize costs, target pricing allows the product and process design to be completed and stabilized once the target cost has been met. Because some 90% of the cost to produce a product is established at the time of product and process design, most costs cannot be influenced after the design has been completed. Once the design has been completed, all that operations personnel can control are the variances.

Value engineering is the term used to describe a structured examination of the cost of product features compared with the value that customers ascribe to those features. This term is most commonly used with multifeatured products such as an automobile. This analysis is important for complicated products in order to prevent the seller from expending resources on product features that the customer does not value.

For complicated products, the target cost of the final product is normally subdivided among the various components that comprise that product. For example, the cost of an automobile may be broken down into major subsystems such as the engine, wheels, exterior sheet metal, and other components. In turn, the target cost for the engine may then be broken up into smaller segments.

When the target cost of a product is subdivided into the cost of its components, some of the target costs will apply to components that are purchased from outside vendors. Purchasing personnel are not always honest with their vendors about their real target cost for an item to be purchased. The engineering and cost accounting personnel who develop target costs may not always be well informed about what costs should be. The inevitable result of these factors is that sometimes the target costs given to a vendor by a buyer may be unreasonably low or generously high.

When the target cost for a product cannot be met, the company may go back and examine the product features, the processes that will be used to make the product, or in some cases cancel the product or increase the allowable target costs.

Activity-based costing is an important tool that should be used in a target pricing effort. ABC provides a relatively accurate measurement of "true" or "real" costs for a product, considering such factors as sales volume, product complexity, customer or distribution chain peculiarities, and the many other factors that can cause a product to be different from the average sale that the company makes.

PRICE NEGOTIATIONS

Chapter 11 discussed various aspects of negotiating price. There are many arguments for not negotiating with customers:

- Price negotiations may be time consuming.
- Price negotiations can create an adversarial relationship between the buyer and seller.
- Price negotiations can undermine the process of planning for and meeting the company's profitability goals.
- Negotiable price policies motivate sales people to use price concessions as a tool for closing the sale rather than getting a better price using the more time-consuming technique of selling product value.

The chapter discussed various pricing considerations relating to the four basic kinds of buyers: price buyers, convenience buyers, value buyers, and loyal buyers. Each of these types of buyers has different motivations for buying, and the techniques for negotiating with each group varies. The chapter also discussed the various roles that people may play in the buying process and provides insights into how the people playing the various roles may interact.

The best negotiation practice today is *win-win negotiating*, where the goal is to make both parties as happy as possible with the outcome of the negotiation. One method of win-win negotiation is *principled negotiation*, which was developed as a result of the Harvard Negotiation Project.

The following are important considerations when negotiating:

- Plan the negotiation in advance.
- Know your best alternative to a negotiated agreement (BATNA).
- Separate the people from the problem.
- Spend time to understand the people considerations of the negotiation.
- Carefully choose the time and place for negotiations.
- Understand the interests of both parties.
- Develop a strategy for setting price and making concessions where necessary.
- Avoid making a concession without getting something in return.

Negotiating price increases and decreases requires forethought and planning. It is usually better to seek several small price increases over time than a single big increase. Getting price increases will be easier if an objective method was discussed up front for identifying when price will be adjusted.

CONCLUSION

There are three things that can happen in pricing, and two of them are bad. No pricing method can guarantee a sales completion every time, much less a touchdown. This book has had the modest hope of reducing the frequency of the unfavorable outcomes that businesses experience when establishing price. By marrying marketing, cost accounting, economics, business strategy, and engineering considerations together, the methods presented here attempt to provide better outcomes than can be achieved by any single discipline alone. There is a better way to evaluate those complicated interrelationships of price, cost, and profit. That method is activity-based pricing.

GLOSSARY

Absorption A process of attaching manufacturing overhead costs to inventory, usually through arbitrary methods such as allocating costs according to direct labor hours.

Account A categorization of financial information. In a general ledger system, the term *account* may refer to an account base or a specific combination of account number segments.

Account base In financial accounting, the account base is the segment of a general ledger account number that describes the type of account, such as overtime pay, medical benefits or travel expenses. Other account segments define the organizational structure of the entity, dividing the organization into locations, departments, or other organizational segments.

Accounting Equation Financial accounting uses a closed system where individual transactions and the accounting system as a whole must balance. This system is represented by the equation: Assets = Liabilities + Equity.

Account number In financial accounting, a specific combination of account segments in the chart of accounts describes the type of account for a specific portion of the business. The term also may be used to refer to a general type of expense represented by the account base.

Account segment A portion of a general ledger account number that describes the type of account (an account base) or the part of the organization to which an account belongs. An account number might be structured in three segments such as CC-AAAA-DD, where CC represents the company, AAAA represents the account base, and DD represents the department.

Activity A set of work steps that converts inputs into outputs, consuming resources such as labor, materials, floor space, or equipment time.

Activity-based budgeting The development of budgets by calculating the costs that will need to be incurred to support a particular level of business activity using activity-based costing data regarding what activities cost to perform.

Activity-based costing A method of cost accounting that attempts to identify the activities that generate cost, assigning costs to those activities, and then assigning activity costs to products, customers, product lines, or other cost objects according to their consumption of those activities.

Activity-based management The planning and control of an organization through a study of its business processes using activity-based costing information.

Activity-based pricing A method of establishing price that considers both customer demand response to price and the full cost of the product at the corresponding sales volume using activity-based costing. Activity-based pricing examines the interactions of price, volume, and cost in an interdependent manner.

Activity dictionary A list of activities that a business performs, including the attributes that describe that activity. Attributes would include inputs, outputs, cost drivers, and methods of measuring the activity.

Allocation The process of assigning cost to a cost object. The term usually infers that the assignment of cost has been performed in an arbitrary manner that does not reflect the factors that actually generated the cost.

Allowable cost The amount of cost that will be allowed based on the target price and target profit for a product. *Allowable cost* is another term for target cost.

Barriers to entry Any competitive situation that limits the ability of other sellers to enter the market for a product. Barriers to entry may include high capital costs, government regulation, patent protection, and other factors.

BATNA Best alternative to a negotiated agreement, from *Getting to Yes* by Roger Fisher and William Ury.

Bill of activities A list of activities relating to a business, product, service, or customer or other cost object.

Bill of materials The list of materials necessary to produce a product.

Bottleneck The constraining operation in a process. The operation in a process that has the least throughput capacity is the bottleneck operation.

Burden rate A concept of traditional cost accounting where overhead costs are assigned to a direct cost such as labor and are then assigned to a product. Burden rates are often stated in terms of percentage of direct labor or in dollars per labor hour.

Capacity Productive ability or a measure of productive ability.

Chart of accounts A list of account numbers and account names for a company. See also *structured chart of accounts*.

Commodity A product that is undifferentiated from those of competitors.

Competition To seek anything (such as a sale) for which another is also striving.

Complementary pricing A pricing strategy that considers the interactive nature of prices for a group of related items. For example, the sales of food, souvenirs, and parking at an entertainment venue would be influenced by the ticket sales of the event itself.

Cost The amount of resources required to acquire a product or service through purchase, fabrication, or a combination of the two.

Cost driver A factor that generates cost.

Cost object Anything to which costs have been assigned, such as an activity, customer, product, product line, or product family.

Cost plus A pricing method where price is established based on a markup of cost.

Demand A measurement of how many buyers are willing to purchase a product at various prices.

Die A tool used to impart a particular shape or form to materials in a manufacturing process.

Direct costs A cost that is easily identifiable as related to a specific cost object.

Downspout The place where hot material is introduced into a mold.

Elastic demand Demand is elastic when a small change in price results in a large change in the number of units that buyers are willing to purchase. The opposite is inelastic demand.

Electronic spreadsheet A computer software product organized into rows and columns that allows free-form calculations to be performed. VisiCalc was the first electronic spreadsheet designed for personal computers. Examples are Microsoft Excel, Lotus 1-2-3, and Quattro Pro.

Fixed costs Costs that do not change for a business activity over a relevant range of volume.

Function Groups of related activities. Functions often correspond to the departments defined by a company's organization chart.

General journal The place where financial transactions are accumulated for posting (originally a book where transactions were recorded, today the computer file where accounting transactions from every software module are collected for posting).

General ledger Originally a book with a list of all of the company's accounts and the transactions that made up the balance for each account, today a computer software package for recording financial account balances and transactions.

Hierarchy (of cost) In activity-based costing, costs are assigned at different levels of business activity. Costs may be assigned at the unit level, batch level, product level, or customer level, or they may be based on various other levels of activity, thus creating a hierarchy of costs.

Inelastic demand Demand is inelastic when a large change in price results in little change in the number of units that buyers are willing to purchase. This is the opposite of elastic demand.

Journal entry An accounting transaction posted to a general ledger system.

Loss leader A product that is sold at a favorable price to the buyer in order to attract the buyer to purchase other goods from the seller. See also *profit leader*.

Macroactivity Two or more activities that are caused by the same cost driver that are aggregated together.

Market The interaction of buyers and sellers to exchange goods and services or the place where business transactions occur.

Market niche The market for a narrowly defined product or group of customers.

Market penetration A pricing strategy whereby price is set relatively low in order to gain market share. This strategy is often used when a company is competing in a well-established market. This strategy also may be used to get new users to try an unfamiliar product.

Market price The prevailing price charged for a product.

Market segment A group of buyers and sellers for a category of goods or services. A market segment normally refers to buyers and sellers for a category of goods that is more narrowly defined than the market for all the products of an industry but more broadly defined than a market niche.

Market skimming A pricing strategy whereby the seller establishes a relatively high price in order to sell to those buyers that value the product the most. This strategy is often used with a new product because the seller has limited production capacity or it may be used for a product that is positioned in a high-end market niche.

Matching principle A financial accounting principle that says that costs should be expensed in the same period as the corresponding revenues are recognized.

Mold A hollow form that gives shape to material that is in a plastic or molten state.

Monopoly Exclusive control over a product or service in a given market that makes it possible to fix prices.

Natural price A cost-based price that represents the lowest price for a product that will exist for more than a short period of time. The natural price is based on the cost of the inputs and the profits required by the capital used in the business. From Adam Smith's *An Inquiry into the Nature and Causes of the Wealth of Nations*.

Offal Unusable excess material generated by a manufacturing process that does not become part of the product. For example, the slugs punched from holes made in a product.

Oligopoly Control over a product or service in a given market by a small number of companies.

Overhead Any costs that are not directly associated with the cost of a product, for example, rent, utilities, supervision, and administrative costs.

Predation When a company sets an unprofitably low price to discipline a competitor or to eliminate a competitor from a market.

Price The amount of money asked or given for something.

Price competition A process whereby sellers attempt to attract buyers for their product using a strategy of having a lower price than the competition.

Price elasticity A quantification of the elasticity of demand measured by the percentage change in price divided by the percentage change in sales volume.

Price fixing Where two or more companies that are in competition with each other make an agreement about how they will price their products. This practice is illegal in much of the modern world.

Price point A price at which a particular product is normally sold. Price points are often set at or just under a nice round number such as $100, $99.99, $99.95, or $99.

Pricing model A representation of how price should be derived. Price models usually consist of computer programs or electronic spreadsheets that contain rate tables and formulas that allow the user to make decisions about price based on information about the product to be sold and the knowledge about competition and customer demand.

Pricing strategy A plan that specifies how the company will price its product in various competitive situations.

Principled negotiation Developed by the Harvard Negotiation Project, principled negotiation is a form of win-win negotiation that attempts to use objective criteria to reach an agreement that is in the best interests of both parties.

Process A group of activities that are linked together by the outputs that they exchange.

Product The output of an activity, such as a business, whether the product is a service or tangible object.

Profit The amount of money left over when the selling price for a product exceeds the cost of the resources required to produce that product. See also the *Profit Equation*.

Profit equation Profit = Revenue – Expenses.

Profit leader A product that is sold at a favorable price to the buyer in order to attract the buyer to purchase other goods from the seller. See also *loss leader*.

Profit motive The inherent tendency for people to engage in activities that make them better off financially.

Progressive die In metal stamping, a die that has multiple stations. A coil or bar of steel is fed through the die in fixed progressions, allowing a different manufacturing operation to occur at each station as the material is advanced.

Rated capacity A measurement of the ability to do work based on a theoretical measurement that equates to 100% of the available time.

Rate table Part of a quoting model that defines how much will be charged or other factors to be considered when determining the price for a product.

Regrind In plastic injection molding, material that is ground up to be melted again. Regrind is often mixed with virgin material to limit the portion of used material that goes into a product.

Return on investment Any one of a number of similar financial calculations that measures the financial return on a business activity compared with the investment required to engage in that activity. Return on investment is often measured as profit divided by stockholders' equity.

Routing A list of processes that are used to make a manufactured product.

Runners The part of a mold that connects the downspout to the parts.

Satisficing A pricing strategy whereby price is set at a level that provides an adequate but not superior financial return.

Scrap Material that does not end up as part of a finished product. Scrap may consist of offal or products that are not of saleable quality.

Selective participation A strategy whereby a company limits the sales opportunities that it pursues. Companies pursuing a differentiation strategy most often use this practice.

Sequential skimming A pricing strategy whereby a price is set initially high, but is reduced as a product matures or is produced in higher volume.

Service Any intangible output of a business activity.

Spreadsheet A paper or electronic page organized into rows and columns that facilitates performance of calculations. See also *electronic spreadsheet*.

Sprue The runners and downspout in a molding process.

Stamping A product made by cutting, punching, or forming metal in a die.

Step-down analysis A method of allocating or assigning costs that successively apportions costs from one cost object to other cost objects. This technique produces a spreadsheet whose columns get progressively shorter from left to right, giving it a stair-step look. A step-down analysis may use arbitrary traditional cost accounting methods or objective measures of activity drivers. The technique can be used in either traditional cost accounting or activity-based costing. Its development was an important step in the evolution of activity-based costing.

Strategy The positioning of a business in terms of customers, competitors, products, product features, markets pursued, technology used, policies, procedures, and other facets of running the business.

Structured chart of accounts A chart of accounts that has been organized in a manner that facilitates extraction of data by computer. A structured chart of accounts is usually organized hierarchically using combinations of account segments. In a structured chart of accounts, similar accounts are ordinarily grouped together, and like expenses for different parts of the organization have the same account base.

Sunk cost A cost that has already been committed. Contrast with *fixed cost.*

Survival triplet According to Robin Cooper, the survival triplet describes the three factors—price, quality, and functionality—that must be in an acceptable range for a product to survive. Cooper notes that functionality may have many dimensions.

Tactics Operational considerations in implementing strategy. In military strategy, tactics are the maneuvering of troops after the battle begins.

Target cost The amount of cost that is allowable given a desired target price and target profit. Target cost =target price – target profit.

Target price The price at which management seeks to sell a product or the price at which a purchaser seeks to buy a product.

Target profit The amount of profit that a company seeks to earn on a sale, given a particular target price.

Trust A form of business combination where the stockholders of the major companies in an industry turn over their stock to an entity that issues them ownership certificates and pays them dividends. The Sherman Antitrust Act of 1890 made this form of business combination illegal.

Value engineering A structured examination of the product features that generate cost in order to be able to produce a product within the constraints of a target cost.

Value pricing A method of pricing whereby price is established based on the value that the customer receives from the product or service.

Variable cost A cost that changes in proportion to changes in the volume of the cost object to which it is related.

Win-win A method of negotiation that strives to make each party as satisfied as possible with the outcome of the negotiation.

Work center A machine, group of machines, or work station where inputs are converted into outputs.

INDEX

Wiley: ch
spelling fo
Proctor &
Gamble?
Procter?

T

U

V

W

X

Y

Lightning Source UK Ltd.
Milton Keynes UK
03 February 2010

149467UK00001B/37/A

9 780471 415350